D0424530

LIVING AS
A RIVER

BODHIPAKSA

LIVING AS A RIVER

Finding Fearlessness in the Face of Change

SOUNDS TRUE

Boulder, Colorado 80306

Sounds True, Inc.
Boulder, CO 80306

Copyright © 2010 Bodhipaksa

Sounds True is a trademark of Sounds True, Inc.
All rights reserved. No part of this book may be used or reproduced in any
manner without written permission from the author and publisher.

Published 2010
Photo credit, page 137 © NASA

Jacket design and book design by Jennifer Miles
Printed in Canada
Permission to reprint "Intermezzo," by Janina Degutytė, tr. M. G. Slavėnas,
by Lithuanian Writers' Union.
Excerpt from "Saint Francis and the Sow" from *Mortal Acts, Mortal Words*
by Galway Kinnell. Copyright © 1980, renewed 2008 by Galway Kinnell.
Used by permission of Houghton Mifflin Harcourt Publishing Company.
All rights reserved.

ISBN 978-1-59179-910-8

*"Go into yourself and see how deep the place is
from which your life flows."*
— RAINER MARIA RILKE

CONTENTS

Acknowledgments

When I consider the degree to which we're interconnected, I realize I could end up thanking the entire universe for helping make *Living as a River* possible. Well, why not? Thank you, universe! I couldn't have done it without you.

But to get more specific . . .

I'm deeply grateful to Tami Simon, founder and owner of Sounds True, who shared my enthusiasm for the premise of this book and encouraged me to get started. I'll never forget the "happy dance" we did as we first discussed this project. I'm indebted also to Kelly Notaras, my first liaison with Sounds True, who was unfailingly helpful and encouraging as I began writing this book. She has since moved on, and I wish her well in her new career as a freelance writer. My editor, Haven Iverson, has been a delight to work with. As a result of her many constructive suggestions, this is a far better book than I could ever have produced on my own. Thank you, Haven.

I extend my deep gratitude to Urgyen Sangharakshita. By introducing me to the Buddha's teachings and practices, he helped change the course of my life and thus saved me from a great deal of suffering. Dharmachari Suvajra, who ordained me in 1993, was the first person to formally teach me the Six Element Practice. Such a gift, and from such an extraordinarily wise and kind man! From the bottom of my heart, thank you.

Thanks also to my family. My wife, Shrijnana, went out of her way to make it possible for me to write. She also looked over portions of the manuscript at various stages of its development and was a source of invaluable feedback. My daughter, Maia, and my son, Malkias, have been my most potent, loving, and challenging teachers. If you want to find out who you really are, live with young children.

Lastly, key portions of this book were written in Horizon House, an orphanage in Addis Ababa, Ethiopia. I'd like to thank all the staff there for their hospitality. I'd like to thank them also for the wonderful work they do in giving love and care to homeless and orphaned children, helping these children find their way to new families, including my own.

Introduction: Fear and Clinging in the River of Life

"I spent the afternoon musing on Life. If you come to think of it, what a queer thing Life is! So unlike anything else, don't you know, if you see what I mean."
— P. G. Wodehouse[1]

Here's a very "queer thing" about life: sometimes the things we think will make us miserable actually make us happier. When Professor Eric D. Miller of Kent State University's Department of Psychology asked people to imagine the death of their partner, they reported feeling more positive about their relationships and less troubled by their significant others' annoying quirks.[2] We live in a world marked by constant change and impermanence. The things we love decay and perish. The people we love will pass away, or we ourselves will pass away, leaving them behind. Wary that thinking about impermanence will be too much of a "downer," we try not to think about these things too much. And yet, ironically, when we do happen to experience the fragility of existence, we often find our appreciation of life enhanced rather than diminished.

Often the things we *think* will make us happier—like impressing the boss or getting that raise—ultimately deprive us of happiness. As a well-known saying goes, "Few people on their deathbed think, 'I wish I'd spent more time in the office.'" And yet that's so often how we live our lives. Life has the potential to be glorious. There's the joy of witnessing birth and growth. The joy of loving. The joy of learning. The joy of deepening relationships. Sometimes there's the sheer joy of simply being alive. But those moments can be rare and, again rather ironically, we're often too focused on things that don't give us lasting joy to pay attention to those that do.

Our existential situation is such that it's hard to have anything but a sporadic experience of security and well-being. After all, the world is inherently insecure. There's nothing in the world upon which we can absolutely rely. True, it's pretty certain the sun will rise tomorrow morning, but then again, there's no guarantee we'll be around to enjoy it. Sometimes we forget this, and it's been argued that in fact we try very hard to forget it. An entire movement in psychology is predicated on the hypothesis that we have strategies for dealing with the painful reality of uncertainty and loss. Studies have shown that we frequently try to find something unchanging and reliable with which to identify, something that acts like a secure island amidst a river of change. Often what we cling to is an ideology, or a religious identity, or a sense of belonging to a group or nation. This response is one of fear and clinging. We see change around us and we're afraid. And so we try to find something to cling to—something more permanent and stable than ourselves.

Another strategy we all employ is to imagine that we *ourselves* are small islands of stability in the river of life. We cling to the idea that we have this "thing" called a self. And we imagine this self to be separate and permanent. We become the thing we cling to. But as Sylvia Plath once wrote, although with a rather different intent, "I am myself. That is not enough." Our selves are not enough. We find ourselves incomplete, lacking happiness and—despite all our cling-ing—security. And so we grasp for those things we think will bring us happiness and security, while trying to keep at bay those things we think threaten our happiness and security.

Fundamentally, we all just want to be happy, secure, and at peace. The problem is that as strategies for finding happiness, clinging and aversion just don't work very well. They don't deliver the goods. It turns out that thoughts of impermanence often enrich our lives and make us happier. We cling to status, material possessions, approval, and pleasure, and yet the pursuit of these things often turns out to have been a misuse of our time. We think that focusing on our own needs will maximize our happiness and well-being, but this often merely impoverishes us, while including others in our sphere of con-cern brings us greater satisfaction.

We can swap our ineffective strategies for others that work bet-ter, but this requires that we change the way we see ourselves. We imagine the self to be separate and unchanging, but it is not that way at all. The self is, in a simile I'll return to frequently, like an eddy in a stream. It has the appearance of being a separate thing and of hav-ing permanence, but in what sense can an eddy be separate? There's no borderline we can say for sure marks where the eddy stops and the river begins. The eddy cannot exist without the stream, and the stream itself is nothing more than a mass of eddies and other currents. I suggest that the self is like that too. We are not separate from the world around us; we instead exist as the sum total of our relationships with a vast web of interconnected processes. We are not physically separate, and we are not mentally separate, and realizing these facts is infinitely enriching.

I'll be suggesting that we embrace the fact that nothing permanent constitutes us. Each of us is an ever-moving flow of matter and consciousness. Just as an eddy can exist only because it's continually changing, so too do our selves exist only because they are a process, and hence impermanent and contingent upon things that we take to be non-self. For example, we think of our bodies as being an important part of our identity, but 90 percent of the body's cells are bacterial rather than human. Ninety percent of you is not you. In fact, when you look more closely you can see that your entire physical being is made of material that was, sometimes not long ago, not you. Every atom comprising your body is borrowed, and will be returned to the outside world. Some of it is returning this very moment. Physically, in fact, much of the external world around us is actually "us"—plants, animals, and even soil and rocks made from material that was formerly part of our bodies. Mentally, we are each "networked" to other minds through the action of mirror neurons, which allow us to share other people's experiences. You could not in fact have a conscious self, in the sense that you have one now, without having encountered other conscious selves. Consciousness is something "caught." In fact, there's no such "thing" as consciousness. Consciousness is not an entity that sits within us, awaiting contact with the outside world; rather it's a series of activities that arise in dependence upon contact with the world. The ultimate act of letting go is to abandon the delusion that consciousness and the world are separate things. The more we reflect, the more we can recognize that there is nothing permanent or separate in the body or mind that can constitute the very limited and limiting kind of self we commonly assume we have.

But is it possible to live without clinging to the idea of a self? Yes, it is.

Over the course of our explorations, we'll peel away, layer after layer, the assumptions that we exist separately and that there is some kind of permanence to our existence. I will not be suggesting that you do not have a self. I will simply try to demonstrate that the self is not what you take it to be, and that it's *our idea of having a definable self* we must let go of. I'll suggest that we need to stop clinging to an idea of who and what we are, in order to start living more spontaneously and unselfconsciously. I'll suggest that we let go of our self-definitions— of thinking of ourselves as being essentially static—so that we can become freer of the constraints that limited self-definitions impose. By doing so, our experience can become increasingly vibrant, rich, compassionate, and free from anxiety.

I'll suggest that we cease clinging to the idea of having a self so we can embrace a life that is spontaneous and flowing, like an athlete in "the zone," with a mind clear, focused, and non-grasping. I'll suggest that, rather than managing our terror through clinging, we do just the opposite: that we learn to let go and move beyond our fear of change. I'll suggest that the best kind of life is a joyful and fearless life—one in which we have looked impermanence in the face and seen it not as an enemy or even simply as how things are, but as an opportunity for growth. I'll suggest, mainly, that we let go of the idea of our own specialness—our separateness and permanence. This does not mean we diminish ourselves. In fact, paradoxically, in letting go of the idea of our specialness we open ourselves up to recognizing we're more special than we ever could have imagined.

This is very much a book exploring the overlap of science and spirituality—two fields of exploration that fascinate me. I became fascinated by science in my early teens, and by philosophy and religion a few years later. It was in fact science that led me to explore spirituality, because the biology of perception led me to reflect on how we construct our experience. In this book, lots of compelling science will help keep us grounded and will help us understand how it is that nothing that constitutes us is static or separate. We'll look at what we're made of, physically and mentally, and how our bodies and minds connect us to the wider world, and how an awareness of this connectedness can lead to a more expansive sense of our selves. We'll look at the ways that the bodies and minds constituting our selves are not static things but are ever-changing processes. We'll look at how those same bodies and minds (and the selves they constitute) are not in any way separate from the world or from other selves. We'll use science to help us let go of the counterproductive strategy of trying to grasp the ungraspable, of trying to find permanence in a world of change.

On the spiritual side, I'll borrow heavily from a reflective meditation practice from the Buddhist tradition: the Six Element Practice. In this practice, we reflect on what constitutes the body and the mind. We call to mind the solid matter (Earth), liquid (Water), energy (Fire), and gases (Air) that make up the body—as well as the form they comprise (Space), and notice how none of these is a static thing onto which we can hold, but instead is a process. We also notice that each element is "borrowed" from the outside world. With the sixth element, Consciousness, we note how our experiences—our sensations, feelings, emotions, and thoughts—continually arise and pass away, once again leaving us nothing we can identify as the basis of a permanent and separate self.

The Six Element Practice is a reflection specifically designed to undermine our delusions of separateness and of having an unchanging self. It's a practice of letting go. This book isn't a meditation manual, and I won't be giving you a step-by-step guide on how to sit down and meditate. Instead I'll be borrowing from the analytical method of the practice; the book itself is intended to be a meditation practice. Although one would normally do the Six Element Practice seated and with closed eyes, I hope that your reading will be an extended form of the practice—perhaps less intense than if you were in fact meditating, but perhaps more far-reaching given that we have plenty of time and space for exploration.

Most of the spirituality in this book draws from the Buddhist tradition, which is the one I practice within and with which I'm most familiar. I've tried, however, not to make this a "Buddhist book." I'm not assuming you're a Buddhist. I'm not trying to convert you. It's my intention to engage you and to encourage you to reflect, not to get you to adopt a particular religious identity (which would be a peculiar aim, anyway, in a book that purports to be examining and deconstructing identity).

I consider myself a skeptical Buddhist, even an agnostic one. While I believe that the Buddha's core teachings are admirably free from superstition, I do see in Buddhist scripture a considerable amount of legendary material and "popular" teachings that I believe were meant to be helpful for uneducated people rather than taken as serious philosophy. I'm also aware of the difficulties that arise when we pick and choose from canonical scriptures, as I do. After all, where do we draw the line? Are we at risk of paying attention only to those teachings that are compatible with our prejudices? In doing so might we perhaps ignore teachings that challenge us more deeply? There are also teachings I just have to set to one side: scientifically, I can't see any way rebirth could work, for example, but since it's a teaching I can neither verify nor disprove (and that doesn't affect my day-to-day life), I simply don't devote much thought to it.

I hope that you'll get to know and appreciate the Buddha as a philosopher and as a teacher through our explorations of his thought and the practices he recommended. I think he was a remarkable person for his time, and would have been held as a remarkable individual in any era, including our own. I want to share my enthusiasm for his insightful perspectives on life. He pointed to an alternative way of living, which is that we radically embrace impermanence. In his path of training, we systematically notice all acts of holding on, all acts of trying to resist impermanence, and learn to let go. In doing so repeatedly, we start to see the disadvantages of clinging and the advantages of non-clinging. Training the mind in this way, we cling less, we experience more freedom and expansiveness, and we find we can face impermanence with less fear.

Managing Terror in a World of Change

The movement in psychology that I referred to earlier—the one based on the premise that we employ strategies to defend ourselves from the fear of death—is called terror management theory (TMT).[3] It's an outlook that has a lot to teach us about the relationship between fear and clinging. In an intriguing experiment in Magdeburg, Germany, TMT researchers investigated how reminders of impermanence affected people's attitudes toward their own nation. Posing as marketers, the researchers said they were investigating behaviors related to consumption and television. In addition to filler questions meant to obscure the real purpose of the experiment, the researchers posed questions such as these:

Imagine you've won a contest and can buy a car. How likely is it that you would buy an Audi, Toyota, Volkswagen, or Renault?

How much do you like traveling within Germany?
How much do you like traveling to foreign countries?

How likely is it that Germany will win the soccer World Cup and become the world champion?

The study's unwitting participants were questioned in two different locations—outside a shopping mall or within sight of the gates of a cemetery. Those subjects questioned near the graveyard, rather than at the more prosaic location, were far more likely to have a favorable attitude toward things German. They were more likely to want to vacation in Germany and to eat German foods. They preferred German television. They were more optimistic about Germany's chances in the World Cup. In short, they were more nationalistic. The mere sight of a cemetery gate is enough to cause people to cling to something—in this case nationality—that offers a sense of immortality or a sense of belonging to something greater than oneself.[4]

A reminder of death is something we used to call a *memento mori*—a Latin phrase meaning "remember you will die." Old gravestones commonly bore memento mori in the form of winged skulls, hourglasses, or grim reapers to remind us of our mortality—as if the gravestone itself were not reminder enough. Modern-day psychologists use the more colorless term, "mortality salience condition" for something that reminds us of death. In a U.S. study involving mortality salience, judges were asked to estimate what bail they'd set in cases of alleged prostitution. But before being presented with the fictional (although realistic) cases, they were given questionnaires to complete. For half the judges, there was a mortality salience condition—a question that directly prompted thoughts of their own deaths by asking about their belief in the afterlife—while the remainder completed questionnaires lacking that question. Judges who'd been reminded of their own impermanence went on to set bail at levels *eight times* that of the other jurists. The judges' sense of morality tightened up considerably as a result of the mere reminder of death. One researcher noted, "Moral principles are part of the cultural anxiety-buffer that protects individuals from anxiety concerning their vulnerability and mortality."[5] Here, merely mentioning death in a questionnaire can cause people to cling to what they perceive as God's will, or to what they see as timeless moral values, or to the notion of preserving a stable and moral society.[6]

It's not just TMT psychologists who remind us of death. Real life provides its own mortality salience conditions. The attacks on September 11, 2001, functioned as a mortality salience condition on a massive scale. Any one of us could have been on those planes. Any of us could have been in Manhattan that day. We inevitably found ourselves thinking, What would I do if I were on a hijacked plane or in a burning building? Perhaps the most unsettling scenes were those of people jumping to certain death from the Twin Towers. To jump or not to jump? There's no good answer to a question like that, and we all live with the deeply troubling feelings it evokes.

One person's response is described in a much-cited article on fear and political affiliation, published in *Psychology Today*. The article, "The Ideological Animal," opens with the case of Cinnamon Stillwell, a lifelong liberal whose political views were flipped 180 degrees by the tragedies of 9/11.[7] Convinced that the victims were getting less sympathy than the terrorists, she started to feel that liberals sided with the attackers and were consumed with hatred for the United States. She started a group called "9/11 Neocons"—soon inundated with members—for former liberals who found themselves catapulted into the conservative camp by the tragedy. As the article recounts,

> "At first, she felt resonance with the right [only] about the war on terror. But soon she found herself concurring about 'smaller government, traditional societal structures, respect and reverence for life, the importance of family, personal responsibility, national unity over identity politics.' She embraced gun rights for the first time, drawn to 'the idea of self-preservation in perilous times.' Her marriage broke up due in part to political differences. In the lead-up to the invasion of Iraq, she began going to pro-war rallies."

This desire for stability and social coherence is all too understandable as a response to a fearful situation. Researcher Tom Pyszczynski, one of the originators of TMT, suggests that the cultural worldviews people cling to when confronted by a reminder of their own impermanence represent a "conception of reality that imbues life with order, permanence, and stability . . . through which individuals can attain a sense of personal value."[8]

There are "liberal" forms of clinging as well, incidentally. A paper in the *Personal and Social Psychology Bulletin*[9] reported that the notion of "progress" could play the same role as religion or nationalism in providing a buffer against our fear of impermanence. People asked to think about their own deaths were subsequently less likely to agree with an essay claiming that progress is a myth. Thinking about death promotes faith in the idea of progress—a concept that gives people a sense their lives have a meaning beyond their own fleeting existence. As further confirmation of this pattern, people who read an essay claiming that progress is a myth were subsequently more likely to think about their own deaths. Take away the comforting notion that we're part of a larger plan, and we're made aware of the brevity and fragility of our lives.

Stillwell may have had a point in thinking that at least some liberals were sympathetic to the terrorists. Studies have found that liberals who embrace tolerance tend to become more tolerant when reminded of mortality. They even become more tolerant when they evaluate a person who criticizes his or her own country.[10] Tolerance may strike many as self-evidently a good thing, but of course whether tolerance is good or not depends on what it is you tolerate; should we tolerate racism or sexism, for example? Some liberals, as a result of 9/11, were indeed busy trying to understand and sympathize with the motivations of those antagonistic to the United States at a time when the wounds of the attacks were still wide open. In effect, these liberals clung to their notions of tolerance as a supreme value and gave the *impression* that they were unconcerned about the victims of the attacks, even if that wasn't actually the case.

But such is how we deal with fear: we cling, sometimes blindly. Clinging to cultural worldviews, in the way that these examples suggest, illustrates the way in which we create an *identity* in order to shelter ourselves from the fear of change and the inherent insecurity of life. We take something larger than ourselves—nation, religion, race, politics, the idea of progress—and to make life seem more secure than it actually is, we identify with that larger something, making ourselves in effect a part of it, and it a part of us. By aligning the self—the ephemeral, relatively inconsequential self—with forces greater than ourselves, we ride on the coat-tails of the immortal, at least insofar as we believe such things as nations and religions and progress to be permanent.

There are of course more subtle and omnipresent reminders of impermanence than terrorists who fly airplanes into buildings. We look in the mirror and see signs of aging. We're surprised by how quickly our children grow up. We're saddened and disoriented to see the obituaries of the icons of our youth appearing at an ever-increasing rate. Our possessions wear out. Our livelihoods are often insecure. The policemen start to look impossibly young. On some level, the fact of our lives' impermanence is visible in every moment, even if we choose not to dwell upon it. Clinging is our defense mechanism against the fear of death.

The Vicious Cycle of Fear and Clinging

Clinging is a strategy for dealing with change, but it's also a strategy that is woven through with denial, and that isn't very effective. Even though we may think of religion, nation, and progress as immortal, they're of course not immortal at all. While the world we live on is 4.5 billion years old, few nations have endured for more than a few centuries. Entire civilizations flourish, then collapse into barbarism. The gods we presently worship are, on cosmological timescales, newborns, and the majority of gods from the past are as dead as their erstwhile followers. The religions practiced by the vast majority of humankind did not exist three or four millennia ago. Our political philosophies are even younger.

We may deny the impermanence of the things we cling to in order to avoid thoughts of our own mortality, but such denial never provides a watertight barrier against reality. Many people who see a religion as an important part of their identity do indeed get reassurance from those affiliations, but they're also aware that not all share their convictions, and they may in fact feel besieged by heretical or secular values. It's as if all religions seem to think they live in especially degenerate times, and that the world is going to hell in a handbasket, their faith under threat. It's simply not possible to escape fear by clinging to religious or nationalistic viewpoints—and in fact they may worsen things. In a controversial study, John Hibbing of the Department of Political Science, University of Nebraska-Lincoln, along with a number of colleagues, identified individuals who took either conservative or liberal positions on issues such as gun control, defense spending, immigration, and patriotism. When these people were taken into the lab and exposed to unpleasant imagery (such as maggots in a wound or a large spider crawling over a terrified face) or to loud and unexpected sounds, the conservatives were found to exhibit much stronger startle responses than the liberals.[11] There's no value judgment placed on this, incidentally. Fear may be a good thing, alerting us to dangers that are very real, and a lack of fear may be a sign of recklessness or naiveté. The lesson I'd like to draw from this study is not essentially a political one. It is simply that if clinging to nationalism and other protective responses is meant to guard against fear, it evidently doesn't work very well.

There are no ultimate refuges in a temporal world. All attempts to use impermanent phenomena to shelter from change are doomed to fail. Clinging may *seem* to imbue life with a sense of stability and permanence, but those feelings are based on illusions and lead ultimately to more fear. Fear leads us to clinging through identification, and identification leads back to fear as we observe the objects of our identification under threat. It's a vicious circle.

We cling to many things as ways of finding security. We cling to sources of pleasure and try to avoid sources of pain. We cling to material goods and fear their loss. We cling to familiar habits that reinforce our sense of who we are, and feel strangely disordered when forced out of habitual patterns of action, even if it's just that our preferred blend of coffee isn't available or a favorite website's layout has changed. We cling to beliefs and views, and we can become irate with people who are inconsiderate enough to disagree with us. We cling to emotional states. We cling to status. Sometimes we'll defend almost to the death a belief we know to be wrong, simply because we don't want to concede an argument. Sometimes we cling to a negative status, comfortable in seeing ourselves as the victim and having someone to blame. We cling to approval, sometimes assenting to absurdities in order to fit in with a peer group. All these forms of clinging become parts of our identity. Clinging can even become compounded. Clinging is a habit we find hard to give up, and so we cling to clinging itself.

At the core of our sense of identity is our sense of self. That we have a sense of self is so obvious it almost seems absurd to point out. It seems, well, *self*-evident that we have a self—a source of separateness, permanence, and autonomy. You probably have a sense that something about you is distinct and separate from the world around you. You may well feel that something permanent and unchanging defines you. You may think that you, in some sense, existed before your conception and will continue to exist in some form after the death of your body. (Even committed atheists often fall into this kind of thinking, as we'll see later.) You probably think of yourself as an agent endowed with free will, freely and consciously making choices that steer you through life. That's how we like to think of ourselves. Our ultimate layer of security comes from holding on to a view of ourselves: separate, enduring, self-owning.

This sense of a permanent self is deeply paradoxical. After all, if we truly believe our selves are permanent, why should we fear death? Why should the mere sight of a cemetery gate have us running for the foxhole of national identity, or a question about the afterlife make us more moralistic and judgmental? The paradox is precisely this: because we fear our own eventual extinction, we construct the idea of a permanent self. (There are other reasons too, I believe, but we'll go into those later.) We are uncertain about our own nature. We're not sure how to think of our selves.

This book is about our selves and how we think of them. It's about the identities we construct and the problems caused by clinging to a sense of a fixed and separate self in a world marked by constant change. And it's about how living with a sense of self may not be the ideal way to approach life. I'm going to argue that our sense of separateness is an illusion; that our sense of having a permanent identity is an illusion; and even that the sense of the conscious mind—the conscious "I"—being in charge of ourselves, owning our selves, and directing operations, is flawed. This all may sound rather abstract and even like a bit of a downer, but we've already seen that the things we think will bring us down can often be uplifting. It's my aim to uplift. Denial's not a good basis for a life, and as a famous teacher once said, "The truth will set you free."

The very idea of abandoning our belief in a fixed and separate self may well strike you as quixotic. In fact, I'm often struck by the passionate intensity with which people cling to the idea that they have a separate self, usually with an unchanging core, with conscious decision-making at the helm of their actions. For most people, it's simply inconceivable that there could be any other way of seeing things. I obviously have my work cut out for me if I'm to make a dent in such strong convictions, and I ask you to bear with me as I lead you through a traditional method for deconstructing our sense of self, using illustrations from science to highlight what the Buddha was trying to get us to recognize.

Do I think that, having read this book, you'll have lost your sense of self? No, I'm not that naive. I lost my own sense of having a self some time ago, and while I may be a slow learner (or perhaps unlearner, since I was learning to let go of a belief in a self that I now see as false), it took many years of reflection, observation, discussion, and meditation to make a breakthrough into a more self-less way of seeing myself and the world.

Can we face the truth of impermanence and the terror it brings without the self tightening up around an ideology, without submerging ourselves in a group, or without naively clinging to vague promises such as progress? Can we fully embrace the flow of our being and accept the flow of the river of life? Is it possible to find security in the midst of life's torrent? Is it possible to *be* the river rather than fight its flow?

I hope that as a result of engaging with this book you *will* start to see yourself differently—start to see yourself, even if just for brief periods, as more fluid and dynamic than you normally think you are. I hope you will start to appreciate yourself as more expansive—as part of an interconnected whole. I hope you will start to see yourself as being both *less* than you normally do (less static, less separate) and as *more* than you normally do (more connected, more significant). And although the glimpses you may have of a different way of being may be fleeting, something once glimpsed may be remembered for a long time and, perhaps, dwelt upon as the basis for future insights.

We'll be opening the door to a different way of seeing and being. With that door opened, perhaps even only momentarily, I hope you're tempted to explore further what you've glimpsed on the other side.

CHAPTER ONE

The Self I Don't Believe In

"I do not know myself and God forbid that I should."
—GÖETHE[1]

Hen Yossarian, the protagonist of Joseph Heller's novel *Catch 22,* speaks of God in an insulting way, the atheist wife of Lieutenant Scheisskopf springs to His defense: "But the God I don't believe in is a *good* God, a *just* God, a *merciful* God,"[2] she protests. Perhaps it's time for me to describe, if not actually defend, the kind of self in which I don't believe.

Throughout recorded history, and presumably for a considerable period of time before, philosophers and mystics have debated the kinds of selves that they do or don't believe in. The self has been seen as purely material and as immaterial. It has been seen as mortal and immortal. It's been seen as primary and as something derived from the world. It's been seen as a unitary phenomenon and as a "bundle" of perceptions. It's been seen as something aloof from the world and as an activity inseparable from the world. It's been seen as illusory and as ultimately real. It's been seen as a problem to be solved and as the ultimate solution to all our problems. More recently, scientists—and particularly, neuroscientists—have added their voices to the discussion. They often use different terms from the philosophers, but they inevitably recapitulate the same positions. I could not even attempt to summarize all the competing theories, let alone evaluate them. But I do want to clarify what kind of self the Buddhist tradition doesn't believe in and in which I don't believe.

It bears repeating, because it's a point so often mangled, that the Buddha never denied the existence of the self. He did point out repeatedly that it is impossible to define the self in any way by saying that *this* is the self or *that* is the self. But saying you can't define the self is not the same thing as saying there is no self. He of course used the term "self" often, in a conventional sense, by saying things such as, "One truly is the protector of oneself," and, "Difficult, indeed, is self-control." This is an unproblematic use of the word "self," used simply because language requires that we talk about reflexive actions—that is, those actions where we are both the subject and the object. When we're talking about a conventional self, then, we mean one where the individual recognizes him or herself as an individual and acts in accordance with that recognition. In other words, there is some degree of reflexive recognition and reflexive action.

The recognition of a conventional self is found even in some animals. A common test for self-awareness is to surreptitiously place a mark (a splash of paint, for example) on an animal's face and then put the animal in front of a mirror—a test devised by Gordon G. Gallup Jr. in 1970. Elephants, magpies, dolphins, chimpanzees, and many other primates recognize that they have selves, according to the mirror test. When they see themselves in a mirror they try to touch or remove the mark. Human babies, it turns out, are unable to recognize themselves in a mirror until they are several months old and will treat the mirror image as if it were a separate individual. Young babies do not have conventional selves. Dogs too, for all their intelligence, will either ignore the "other dog" in the mirror or will bark at it. (These tests, by the way, strike me as being rather chauvinistically fixated on the sense of vision. Perhaps an intelligent race of dogs would conclude that humans are not self-aware if the latter failed to recognize their own scent.) The conventional self revealed in the mirror test is simply a function of reflexive recognition and action. The animal can visually recognize itself as an individual, and it can act upon knowledge gained through that visual recognition. There's no metaphysical or philosophical statement being made about the nature of that self beyond the fact of self-recognition.

Our assumptions about our selves, however, transcend mere self-recognition. The understanding of the self against which the Buddha argued vigorously, and which many contemporary scientists and philosophers also dispute, is the notion of a self that is unchanging and separate. We assume these qualities belong to the self, not so much as part of a thought-out philosophical standpoint arrived at after careful deliberation, but as an instinctual response. This response is at least partly based on the fear of acknowledging our existential situation as fragile and transitory creatures, but also based on a number of perceptual distortions that we'll examine shortly.

In psychology, the term "self" can refer to those personal attributes we can't imagine ourselves without—those things that represent, for us, the core of our being, or our identity. What is considered to constitute that core will vary from person to person. Gender or sexual preferences or ethnicity may often be seen as intrinsic to the self—we can't imagine being ourselves if one of those things were to be magically changed. Other qualities, such as our occupation or our food preferences, may be seen as more peripheral. You can no doubt think of examples that you consider either core or peripheral to your own sense of self. If we identify certain attributes of the self as "essential," then it stands to reason that the core self must be something unchanging. After all, if something is essential, it must be permanent. Although this kind of thinking predominated at the time of the Buddha, he disagreed that there was an unchanging core to the self. Instead he saw the self as composed of a number of ever-changing processes.

Once we see the self as static, it then becomes a kind of *thing* separated from other things—the various inanimate objects, plants, animals, and of course other selves that exist in the world. And we tend to see *things* as being separate. You have your self. I have my self. My self perceives this thing called the world, and sees itself as being separate from the world. How could it not, since it considers itself to have an unchanging core? If the self has an immutable core, then the self must be in some way untouched by and independent of the world. But the self, the Buddha explained, is a process that arises entirely in dependence upon things that are non-self. The physical self arises in dependence upon things that are not-self, and our inner experience also arises in dependence upon things that are not-self.

Often this perspective is talked about in terms of interconnectedness or interdependence—terms the Buddha never used but that are useful nonetheless. In the Six Element Practice, we're reminded that each Element is not divided into a "me" element and an "other" element. There is, for example, no "me" Earth Element as opposed to an "other" Earth Element. There is just one element, which is in a certain sense "borrowed" from the outside world in order to constitute a self. The self, however, mistakenly taking itself to be something substantive and separate, confuses borrowing with ownership, much like the person who keeps a borrowed book for so long that he regards it as his own possession and resents having to return it to its true owner. A large part of the effect of the Six Element Practice hinges upon cultivating the recognition that we cannot truly own anything. We observe the elements flowing from the outside, non-self, world, through our selves and back into the outside world again. The entire self is made, then, of stuff that is non-self. What composes our self is not some separate collection of "stuff" owned in any way by the self—we can't hold onto any of the matter that flows through us. In fact, we can't even hold onto any of the experiences that flow through our minds. So in effect we own nothing, and therefore nothing that constitutes us can be seen as constituting a self.

So this is the kind of self I do not believe in. I do believe I have a conventional self, which right now is busy typing words on a keyboard. I see my body and recognize it as me rather than you. I experience a flow of experience that is unique to me. But what of anything beyond that? I do not believe that I—or you, for that matter—have a self that is permanent and separate. And when I talk about belief and non-belief I am not talking about "blind faith." I mean to say that my *experience* is that I do not have a self of this sort.

The Kind of Self I Do Believe In

So what kind of self *do* I believe I have, or what kind of self do I *experience* myself as having? Whenever I turn my attention to my sense of self, what I find is nothing but an ever-changing stream of experiences. This stream changes so rapidly that I fear it would be misleading to call it a self, so loaded is the word "self" with notions of permanence. When I observe my experience, for moments it appears that I do indeed have a (static) self—much as when you glance at a clock with a second hand you may momentarily be convinced that the clock has stopped until that hand takes another tick around the dial. But the moment passes and so does the sense of having a self. I can see my experience as being an endless succession of selves, each of which exists for a few moments, but frankly it seems more like there is no "real" self there. It's hard to describe the quality of this experience, but it's generally delightful to notice the ever-changing constellation of experiences that never quite seem to constitute a self. There's a sense of freedom that accompanies this perspective.

I should point out that I didn't realize the extent to which I used to believe I had a static, separate, self-owning self until finally my sense of having such a self evaporated. In fact, I think that it's often the case that we don't fully realize how limiting a view is until we abandon it. I don't in any way mourn the loss of my belief in a self—in fact it had the delightful quality of the laying down of some kind of burden and an expansive feeling of liberation. The notion of a self that is static and separate is a source of stress and even misery.

Blind to Change

There are several reasons, I believe, why it seems natural for us to assume the self is static and permanent when in fact it is not. The first of these is that we're simply not very good at detecting change. Imagine this: you walk into a university building to be interviewed as part of a psychology experiment. At the reception desk, a young man takes the consent form you hand to him and tells you you'll need to receive an information packet and then go to another room to be questioned. He ducks behind the counter, picks up the packet, hands it to you, and gives you directions. It's just an ordinary encounter. Nothing unusual. You glance at the information you've been handed and go on your way. The bizarre thing is that the person who ducked beneath the counter and the person who stood up to hand you the form were two different people! They looked completely unlike each other. They were different heights, had different hairstyles, and wore different clothing of different colors. They spoke in different voices. And you didn't notice—or at least the vast majority of people don't notice. This was a psychology experiment carried out by Dan Simons and Christopher Chabris at Harvard University.[3]

In an earlier experiment, Simons had another experimenter stop passersby on a university campus to ask for directions.[4] Mid-exchange, two men carrying a door would rudely walk between the two people. Afterward, the passersby were asked if they'd noticed anything unusual. Half did not notice that the person they'd been talking to had been switched for another person who had a different appearance, build, and voice, and who was wearing different clothes. That's a lot of change not to see. But these experiments, which illustrate what's called "change blindness," have been repeated in many different forms, and change blindness is our default method of perception, or of non-perception.

There are websites that give you the opportunity to test your ability to notice change.[5] Typically, two photographs alternate, with a brief moment of blankness between them. The two photographs have what you might expect to be obvious differences—in a scene of an aircraft at an airport, for example, a building has been Photoshopped out of one version of the image—but it can take many, many attempts to note the change. Once you see the change, it seems obvious. But until that point when the difference comes to your attention, you'd swear the two photographs were identical. And remember, unlike in the college-campus studies mentioned above, you *know* that changes are taking place and you're actively looking for them. The change is there, and it almost seems as if our brains resist seeing it.

A large part of the explanation for change blindness stems from the fact that the brain can only deal with so much information at one time. In the reception area where the participants largely failed to notice one receptionist being replaced by another, a lot was going on. There was furniture. There were signs, the sound of the air conditioning, the exchange of pieces of paper, verbal instructions to process, textures and colors on every surface, smells—and of course part of your brain is already taken up with thinking about things like, "Am I on time? Will I enjoy this interview? When will I get paid? Did he say the waiting room was the second door on the left or on the right? I wish I'd been listening more closely. I never pay attention." The average person can only keep about seven things in conscious awareness at one time, and only about four things in visual short-term memory. We're so busy selecting the few things absolutely crucial to the task we're involved in that there's not much attention left for other things—like noticing that the person staffing the reception desk is now taller, dressed in different clothes, and has different facial features.

The most famous change-blindness experiment involved showing a video of a basketball game. Participants were asked to count how many times one team's members passed the ball to each other. The participants were so busily involved in this task that they failed to notice someone in a gorilla costume walk slowly across the basketball court, right between the players![6] More than any other, this experiment highlights the limited processing capability of the human brain.

Self, Interrupted

Have you ever experienced going upstairs to get something, but having forgotten the purpose of the trip by the time you arrived? I'm sure you have. Another reason for failing to notice change, and one that is related to change blindness, is that our consciousness is inherently discontinuous. Think again of the change-blindness experiment where the person behind the desk is switched. Each time there's an interruption to our stream of consciousness—having to answer a question, checking that you have the invitation letter in your pocket, the disappearance and reappearance of the desk clerk—your mind has to regroup. The mind focuses on the same subject—the desk clerk, for example—that it was perceiving a few seconds earlier, but you find that you're no longer paying attention with exactly the same mind. The new mind—the one that's recovering from the disappearance of the desk clerk and that has probably dealt with several stray thoughts in the moments before his replacement appeared—is not the same one that saw the first desk clerk. When you find yourself upstairs, wondering what on earth brought you there, you've almost certainly brought about this peculiar form of amnesia by interrupting yourself with a train of thought about another matter entirely. To remember why you went upstairs, you may have to return to the place where you originally had the thought to fetch something. In effect you're reconstructing the self that existed before the interruption—the self that knew why going upstairs was necessary. Interruption is an important factor in many change-blindness experiments. In the experiments that involve switching between images, the brief flash of a blank screen seems to be an important component of our inability to detect even quite major changes in the photographs—in a sense, a different consciousness looks at each picture.

The point here is that if we don't even notice that a person we've been talking to has been replaced by someone else, or if we can't notice a missing building as we repeatedly flip between two photographs, how are we going to notice that our selves are changing? Just as we look at two different receptionists, one after another, and assume they are the same person because we detect no change, so too we see different "selves" emerging one after another within ourselves, and assume that this is the same person. Even though there has been change, we assume that the self is unchanging. Moment by moment, our perceptions, thoughts, moods, and emotions are changing, reconfiguring, and creating a new self. Continue the process of change—accompanied by change blindness—for years or decades, and we start to assume that there has in fact been no change, or that the change has been purely superficial.

Wired for Belief

A further reason for tending to assume that the self is unchanging hinges on our inability to "think outside the ontological box," for want of a better term. Since we experience something that we call a self right now, we tend to assume that this entity will continue to exist in the future and has always existed in the past. Jesse Bering, director of the Institute of Cognition and Culture, at Queen's University Belfast, in Northern Ireland, suggests that humans suffer "the unshakable illusion that their minds [are] immortal," something he terms a "hiccup of gross irrationality."[7] We have trouble imagining our own non-existence, whether that's imagining never having existed or our own demise. When I was conceived, for example, one sperm out of hundreds of millions happened to meet the ovum my mother had produced shortly before. When I speculate what would have happened had a different sperm met that ovum, I find myself wondering whether I would have grown up as a radically different person. Note that I assume *I* would be a different person, as if I would (inevitably) have existed. I have at times wondered what *I* would have been like had a sperm carrying an X chromosome made that fateful encounter in 1960, so that *I* had started life as a female. But of course, had a different sperm—carrying either an X or a Y chromosome—met the egg, then *I* would not exist. But it's hard to conceive, if you'll pardon the phrase, of not having been conceived. Knowing that I exist, it's hard for me to imagine never having existed, and so in my own mind there's a certain inevitability about my existence.

To consider the sheer contingency of our existence is to leave the safe ground of our assumed selfhood, and so a kind of existential vertigo can arise. The basis of my being is undermined, right at the very beginning. Spiritually, this feeling of disorientation is a helpful thing. It is the felt response of the mind as it lets go of false certainties and opens up to a view of the self as an impermanent, changing, conditioned phenomenon. We can learn to love this sense of mystery, this sense of ourselves being an open question rather than a fixed and known quantity. As Rilke said, in giving advice to a fledgling poet, "Have patience with everything that remains unsolved in your heart. Try to love the questions themselves, like locked rooms and like books written in a foreign language."[8] We can learn to be comfortable with uncertainty. We can learn to let go of the need for instant answers, joyfully living in the midst of the unknown. We can learn to have a sense of wonder and awe regarding who and what we are.

The situation is similar when we try to imagine what it would be like to cease existing. When we try to imagine death, what comes to mind is imagining an *experience* of nothingness, as if we'd still be around to have a non-experience.[9] We see non-existence as involving what we could call a positive experience of the negative. Death is imagined as dark, silent, cold, and static—as the experience of numerous absences. The experiencing individual, now deceased, is imagined to be surrounded by (and experiencing) these states. And so death is "eternal night" or "an empty black abyss." We simply cannot imagine not being able to experience anything at all, because experience is all we know, and so we're forced to imagine experiencing non-experience. We assume that an experiencing individual is in essence immortal.

So powerful is the assumption of our selves being essentially immortal that even avowed rationalists, who disdain the notion of the continuity of consciousness after death, can fall into the trap of imagining that the self continues to function after life ends. Jesse Bering quizzed a group of undergraduate students on the post-mortem experiences of a hypothetical individual, Richard, who dies in a car crash.[10] Not surprisingly, students who professed a belief in the immortality of the self thought that Richard would still experience mental states after death. But around a third of the answers given by those who held "extinctionist" views—those who believed that consciousness terminates at death—indicated a belief in some kind of residual consciousness. Perhaps the ultimate irony was one student pointing out that Richard would know, after death, that there was no afterlife!

Bering points out that when we try to imagine our own non-existence, we do what we usually do when imagining the future—we run an internal simulation in our imaginations. But this of necessity means that we have to imagine experiencing *something*. And so we imagine that our selves will continue to function even after death. All in all, we imagine something approaching immortality for ourselves. We have an intuitive sense of our own inevitability, as if we in some sense existed before our conception and birth, and we imagine some kind of experience continuing after death—even, in many cases, if we are ideologically committed to the belief that there is no afterlife. Since we assume that the self existed before conception and will exist after death, we'll inevitably imagine that it persists—unchanged—throughout our life.

Virtual Selves

Perhaps another factor in imagining the immortality of the self is what developmental psychologists call "person permanence." I haven't talked to my Aunt Margaret in Dundee, Scotland, for several months, but I can imagine her tut-tutting at the latest television news or pushing a shopping cart around a supermarket. I naturally assume that her being continues in my absence. This assumption trips us up at times. A longtime friend of mine was killed in a climbing accident, and for several years after I'd find myself thinking of him—"I wonder if Clive would enjoy this book?"—and then experience the sinking realization that he was in fact dead. I knew his favorite books and music. I knew Clive's opinions on many subjects. I could predict how he'd respond in various situations. Of course I still remember what he looked and sounded like. I can imagine his laugh. More than ten years after his demise, a virtual Clive still exists in my mind, to the point where I can have a conversation with him any time I choose. Sometimes he appears in my dreams. I have in effect a mental program that runs a simulation of Clive.

The mind, having devoted a considerable amount of resources to accumulating a rich database of memories and knowledge about a person, doesn't simply jettison it when the person dies, as one might delete from a computer a program one no longer uses. Instead, the *experience* we have of another person lives on after their death. It's therefore not surprising that we tend to believe in the continued existence of the self after death. In fact it is easier to imagine that a dead person continues to exist in some way than it is to accept the possibility of their non-existence. The mind's default option is to assume a permanence of the self, even after death. And what applies for others may well apply to ourselves as well. If imagining the continuity of deceased friends is the mind's default assumption, then why should things be any different for ourselves? If we believe that selves in general have some kind of immortality, then our own particular selves would presumably have the same attribute of surviving death. We end up once again assuming that we have a self that is unchanging.

The Language Trap

I consider the most profound reason that we believe in the permanence of the self to be connected with the way the mind simultaneously identifies and reifies phenomena. This reification arises because of the nature of the two most basic verbs we use: "to have" and "to be."

It's hard to speak even a sentence or two without using some form of "to be" or "to have." They are absolutely fundamental to our language. And both of these verbs encapsulate assumptions about the nature of the universe we inhabit. Both mislead us into thinking that things are different from how they actually are.

Take the verb "to be." It's the most irregular—and common—verb in the English language. You say "I am," but "he is." You can say "they were," "we are," or "I have been." One reason that "to be" has so many forms is that it wasn't originally one verb at all. What's happened is that three different verbs have been torn apart, mixed up, and recombined over the millennia. "To be" is a Frankenstein verb, cobbled together from the remains of three verbs that were originally independent and complete.

1. One of the verbs that was cannibalized to give us "to be" was from a root, *as,* that is often referred to as "the substantive verb," meaning "to have independent existence," or "to be self-existent." This root gave us the forms "is" and "am." To say "I am" (as in Descartes' famous "I think, therefore I am") is essentially the same as saying "I exist."

2. Another of the verbs was from a root *wes,* meaning "to remain." This root *wes* lives on in the modern forms "was" and "were." This root suggests that things don't just exist independently, but that they also endure as separate and unchanging. First things just "are" (they have substantive existence) and then they "remain," or continue to have substantive existence. This suggests a kind of permanence.

3. The third root, *beu,* is rather different. It was a verb that originally meant "to become" or "to grow." This root gave us forms such as "be" and "been." This third root is one that, when you think about it, conveys a sense entirely opposite that of the first two. "Becoming" and "growing" are dynamic ways of describing reality. When something is becoming, it's in the process of changing into something else. It never *is;* it's evolving. It never *remains;* it's moving on to become something else. The idea of something having a "substantive" nature—it just *is*—or a nature that "remains" couldn't be more different from the idea of something "becoming."

So the verb "to be" contains two essentially contradictory senses. One is contained in the substantive root and in the root meaning "to remain," and the other is found in the idea of "becoming." To say that the self *is* and that it *remains* suggests permanence and separateness. On the other hand, to say that the self *becomes* suggests that there is nothing static or separate about it; the self is a process, something produced, something in the process of changing, something that is ultimately impermanent.

The verb "to have"—the other most common verb in the English language—is also problematic. It comes originally from a root that meant "to grasp" or "to seize." And this concept depends very heavily on the "substantive" and "remaining" senses of "to be." We can only grasp or seize "things" that are substantive, that have separate, independent existence, and that have a degree of permanence. You can't reach into a river and grasp an eddy.

The Sapir-Whorf hypothesis—an axiom developed by the linguist and anthropologist Edward Sapir and his colleague and student

Benjamin Whorf—is that the nature of a particular language influences the thought and perceptions of that language's speakers. The idea that such a fundamental unit of language as the verb "to be" can result in distortions of the way we see things would be an example of this hypothesis. By the time we've named something and considered it "to be," we have the mental conception that it *is,* and that it *remains*—we've seen it as being fixed and unchanging. The tertiary sense of "to be" as *becoming* is then overwhelmed and ignored, because it contradicts the verb's primary and secondary meanings. Our language, unless we are very careful, traps us.

But we can't entirely blame language for distorting the way we see things. Who created language? And why did we create it in the form it currently takes? All human languages are the products of human minds interacting with other human minds and with the world. Our minds have a tendency to try to fix things, to assume that things are separate and static when they are in fact "becoming," interdependent, and ever-changing. This tendency to see processes as static things appears to be much deeper than language, and in fact it gives rise to how we use language. But once we start naming things, our language reinforces our underlying tendency to see them as fixed.

We name things, and then we assume that because the name is static, so too is the thing named. The mind takes the language it uses to label reality as if it *were* reality. We confuse the map with the landscape, the recipe with the meal. Having labelled, we cease to pay attention to the process to which we've attached the label. This labeling isn't even necessarily verbal. We just have to recognize a thing as a thing, to have a wordless concept of it, and that seems to be enough for the mind to start taking shortcuts, to start ignoring the reality it encounters in favor of its own categorizations.

Referring back to our change-blindness experiments, we wordlessly label the person behind the counter as "the person behind the counter" and we ignore the fact that everything that constituted that person—their appearance and personality—has been switched. We label the photograph, wordlessly, as "a photograph of an airplane" and we see two versions of it, totally failing to notice the absence, in one version, of a building in the background.

The Six Element Practice, we'll see, has the effect of taking the self—the body and mind—and exploring its dynamic nature. We probe beneath the surface labels to see what is actually happening, and inevitably we end up seeing the self as a process (becoming) rather than a thing (being).

The More Things Change . . .

Often, for good or bad, people don't seem to change much, which is another reason why we tend to view the self as permanent. We may not have seen a friend for years, but then on a chance meeting we instantly recognize him, feel we still have a lot in common, and experience the familiarity of his voice, sense of humor, storytelling style, personality traits, and so on. The friend may be fatter or fitter and have more or less hair (and, especially for men, some combination thereof). He may have more wrinkles or may be frailer than we remember. He may have more wisdom and perhaps more battle scars, depending on how much time has passed. But John is still John, and Janet is still Janet. Does this relative stability suggest that there is some core self that is unchanging?

I don't think it does. Here's why. Think again of an eddy in a stream—preferably one formed by the way the flowing water interacts with the shape of the riverbank. You can watch the eddy over time and see that it's constantly changing. The water that constitutes the eddy constantly self-replenishes, so there's no question of there being an actual substance that forms the eddy's essence or core. Yet there's a certain degree of stability. The eddy occupies roughly the same spot each time we look at it. It's roughly the same size. It's spinning in the same direction. But what this indicates is that the same conditioning factors—the rate of flow of the water, the conformation of the bank—are, in each moment, re-creating an approximately similar eddy. The eddy changes in such a way that it remains more or less the same. The similarity doesn't have anything to do with any kind of essence or core; it is due to the same conditions giving rise to the same flow pattern. Add change blindness, plus the tendency to see something as unchanging because we've applied a static term to it— such as "the eddy"—and the illusion of ongoing sameness become even stronger.

In certain respects we are like eddies. We change all the time, but most often we change in ways that keep us more or less the same. We are not as passively produced as eddies in rivers, because unlike eddies we choose and shape our environments. We are like eddies that create their own riverbanks. And we tend to choose and shape our life circumstances in such a way that they reinforce our sense of who we are.

Imagine being suddenly transplanted to a new and unknown city. Suddenly everything in your environment is different. There is uncertainty and openness: the possibility of a new way of living. But you are used to certain ways of being. There are certain kinds of supermarkets you like, and others you don't like (the one with the wide selection of organic vegetables versus the low-end grocery store with the bruised bananas). You have certain leisure pursuits you'll seek out (the coffee shop that's good for people-watching, the bar with the lively crowd, the cinema with the foreign movies). You'll tend to gravitate toward the kind of people you're most comfortable with (the sports fans, the arty crowd, or the political activists). You'll likely decorate your new dwelling in much the same style as your old one. You'll read similar (perhaps even the same) news sources and watch the same (or similar) television programs. In other words, you'll have much the same kinds of experiences that you had before. There's a moment of freedom and openness when you're first transplanted, but then your life starts to crystallize around you in a way that resembles what you're familiar with and that keeps you much as the same person you were. Maintaining the same kinds of relationships with the same kinds of people and places and activities maintains our sense of self, and keeps our habits (speech patterns, general outlook, political views, and so on) looking remarkably similar over a long period of time.

Now we may not move from city to city very often, but every day we make choices that maintain our sense of self. In all likelihood we probably take much the same route to work, read the same papers, watch the same news, have the same kinds of conversations with the same kinds of people, and think (with some inevitable variations) the same kinds of thoughts. In choosing to live the same life over and over again, we end up maintaining a self that's as stable as the eddy. We *can* choose a different part of the river in which to manifest, but we generally don't. We put so much effort into not changing that it's no wonder we have a sense that there's an enduring self.

None of this is to deny the possibility of our exercising our freedom and creativity to choose different circumstances. None of this denies that we can choose new ways to respond to our circumstances. We have that freedom, and some people use it. Nor is it to deny the possibility of radical change happening suddenly. Sometimes due to accidents, illness, bereavement, or an insightful experience, people have radical shifts in character. I mentioned how Cinnamon Stillwell was propelled from liberal to conservative views as a result of 9/11. Stanford Addison, a small-time Navajo drug dealer and robber, dedicated himself to healing after an accident rendered him quadriplegic. Scott Harrison was a hedonistic, drug-using, BMW-driving nightclub promoter in Manhattan until he took a vacation in Africa; then, realizing that his life was shallow and self-involved, he started a charity that has raised tens of millions of dollars and provided clean water to nearly a million people in Africa and Asia. Tererai Trent was a battered, illiterate cattle herder in Zimbabwe until she heard an aid worker say that women should have goals. Instantly Trent reoriented her entire life around studying abroad and working toward a PhD, which she recently earned at Western Michigan University. Sometimes the change is sudden, as in these examples, but other times the changes accumulate gradually, the result of learning new skills and of changing our perspectives as we accumulate life experience. Gandhi, as a young lawyer, was so nervous he could barely speak in court. Over time he developed more confidence. Many other people, through meditation, therapy, or self-examination, have changed themselves radically over the course of their lives. The very fact that such changes can come about, whether suddenly or gradually, is an indication that what we call the self is in fact not something fixed and unchanging. The self is not as fluid as water, but neither is it carved in stone. And yet many people cling to the notion of an unchanging self as if life itself depended on it.

The Three Fetters

From the point of view of Buddhist practice, the idea of a fixed self is something to overcome. On this path of personal and spiritual development, three "fetters" must be broken in order to fully accept the impermanent nature of reality. The breaking of these fetters represents abandoning the failed and counterproductive strategy of trying to deny and resist change. The first fetter is the belief in a fixed self, and it's accompanied by the second fetter of doubt (including the doubt that we are able to change and to find a more fulfilling way of being.) The third fetter is dependence upon rules and observances, which is not so much a "Protestant" rejection of ritual as it is a rejection of the idea that external change can in itself bring about lasting inner change. These three fetters are seen to coexist and to mutually support each other. All three are broken simultaneously.

Fetters imprison and limit us. We unfetter and free ourselves by directly experiencing that the self is not something fixed. Most people take many years of practice before they realize the self is something forever in flux. I should emphasize that realizing the impermanent nature of the self is not an intellectual act—a relabeling, if you will, of what we are. Instead it's an emotional act of ceasing to cling and of letting go of the fear that drives our clinging. It's a massive "Aha!" moment in which we realize that we've been mistaken our entire lives about who and what we are.

These three fetters point to some of the sources of suffering that arise from viewing the self as fixed. Firstly, with the notion of the fixed self, there is the consequence of seeing ourselves as "stuck." We become convinced that change is not possible. We find that we have character traits and exhibit behaviors that cause suffering for ourselves and others, but we think, "That's just how I am." The possibility of change isn't open to us, because we are unable to accept it. We're therefore doomed to repeating the same mistakes over and over.

The fetter of doubt manifests in a number of ways. Not accepting that the self is something created and re-created time and again—that it lacks any kind of unchanging essence—we fear that some hidden baggage holds us back from change—inimical, Freudian, *id*-like "stuff" that will fetter us indefinitely. This results in a lack of confidence in ourselves, an undermining doubt that amounts to a self-sabotaging lack of belief in our own power. Also, the inability to accept that the self is characterized by change makes us believe that there is something fundamentally different between how we are now and how we would like to live. We imagine ourselves being, for example, more patient, compassionate, or perceptive, but it seems as if there's an unbridgeable gulf between our present self and our imagined ideal, as if we're being asked to change base metal into gold. We see people who are wiser and kinder than us, and we think that they have something we don't, that they're "made of better stuff." Again, there is an undermining sense of disempowerment.

Lastly, the third fetter of dependence on rules and observances leads to our perpetuating our suffering by not addressing it in an appropriate way. There's an old joke about seeing someone searching under a streetlight at night. You ask him what he's doing, and he says he's looking for his keys. You help him look but the keys are obviously not there. "Are you sure you dropped them here?" you ask. "No," he replies, "I dropped them over in that dark alley." You ask him why, then, is he looking here? "Because the light's better," he says. The third fetter is the habit of looking for answers in the wrong place, or of asking the wrong questions, or of asking the right questions in the wrong way. We may, for example, find ourselves endlessly roaming from one personal-development workshop to another, skimming the surface of personal change without ever diving in. We see personal transformation as something that will happen from the outside in. We hope some new technique (the more expensive the better) will free us from our suffering.

In reality, we become liberated from the inside out, by developing greater mindfulness of our experience and by directly observing the impermanent nature of the self. If we use techniques to analyze our experience (and we inevitably do), we need to stick with them and explore them deeply. The third fetter has been called the fetter of superficiality, because rather than seeing spiritual practices as ways of transforming ourselves, we see them as ways to bolster a fixed sense of self. We treat spiritual activities as status symbols with which to impress others, or we treat them as ways to feel good about ourselves. We may even turn spiritual practices into distractions so that we don't have to look seriously at our experience.

Breaking the first fetter allows a sense of freedom. Breaking the second fetter leads to a sense of confidence. Breaking the third fetter leads to a deeper sense of integrity and commitment. I cannot, of course, guarantee that the reflections in this book will lead to your breaking any of these fetters, but I entertain the hope that you'll experience the fetters as ever-more malleable as your sense of self begins to shift, as you begin to have a greater sense of wonder and connectedness, and as you begin to engage with your assumptions and challenge the way you habitually see yourself and the world around you. I hope that the kind of self I don't believe in becomes the kind of self you don't believe in, and that the lack of a fixed self that I see becomes the way you see things too.

CHAPTER TWO

An Encounter in the Workshop

*"The beautiful souls are they that are universal,
open, and ready for all things."*
—Michel de Montaigne[1]

S ome 2,500 years ago, in a country called Magadha in the fertile
plains of northeast India, an itinerant philosopher was wandering. The dusk gathered as he reached a fortified town called Rajagaha, which sat in a valley surrounded by five hills. Rajagaha means
King's House, the town having been the former seat of the Magadhan
rulers. The philosopher, looking for a place to rest for the night, went
to the house of a potter named Bhaggava—the name simply means
"potter"—and asked if he could sleep in his workshop.

So begins the historical background to the Six Element Practice.
This teaching, which will provide the method for our deconstruction
of the self, is set in a narrative that is satisfyingly earthy and credible.
The practice is found in a text called the "Discourse on the Elements,"
or *Dhatu-vibhanga,* which I'll henceforth refer to as "the Discourse."

This teaching was probably first written down about 2,200 years ago, having been passed on by word of mouth for two to three centuries before that. In the Discourse we meet the Buddha—the itinerant philosopher mentioned above. The Buddha wasn't a god, or a prophet, but an introspective philosopher who attempted to live a life of ethics and intellectual integrity, based as much as possible on truths discoverable by the unaided (although not untrained) mind. Because the title "Buddha," which means "awakened one," can be a bit offputting for some people, for the purposes of this chapter I won't refer to him as "the Buddha," but by his family name, Gautama. Perhaps this may bring him down to earth and make him seem less of a "religious" figure.

The Discourse describes what is, from some points of view, a very down-to-earth encounter. Gautama had no entourage, human or divine, and he didn't appear to be a person of any special status. Bhaggava apparently didn't even recognize his guest, who appeared to be just an ordinary wanderer. The potter pointed out that there was already a mendicant camping in his shed, but that Gautama was welcome to stay if he didn't mind being a little cramped. Apparently Gautama was perfectly happy to share a hut with another spiritual seeker, and perhaps he even looked forward to discussing matters of practical philosophy with his new roommate. In this way Gautama met Pukkusati.[2]

The tradition of homeless wandering was an important part of the culture in those days, but it was also a relatively new development.[3] Until not long before, the religious and philosophical role in society had been monopolized by the priestly Brahmin class, who made their living interpreting the ancient Vedic scriptures. The Brahmins charged for the sacrifices that would bring a plentiful supply of sons and keep the rains coming at the right time, guaranteeing fruitful crops, and they would have conducted all kinds of religious and social rituals. The Brahmins were also the guardians of the ancient religious and social laws, and it was their duty to keep the other social classes in line. Indian society in that region was divided strictly into four classes: the Brahmins, the warriors, the merchant and farmer class, and the serfs. Strict rules governed how people within each class should behave. Following the rules of your social class and respecting the social and religious preeminence of the Brahmins was not just a social but also a religious duty, for the division of society into different classes was not seen as a socioeconomic phenomenon, but an essentially religious one. Spiritually and morally, the various classes of people were seen as having different essential characteristics, going right back to the creation of humankind, which was a fourfold creation. The gods had ordained how society was to be structured and who was in charge—the Brahmins, naturally—and if the divine ordinance of the gods was tampered with, who knew what might happen? The entire cosmos—the turning of the heavens, the procession of the seasons, and the order of the social classes—was united as one system. To tamper with the machinery of the cosmos was to invite disaster.

But at this point in history, society had in fact been changing for some time. Iron Age technology had arrived, allowing for improved forest clearance and plowing. This in turn led to the creation of surpluses, with an explosion of wealth and the rise of a powerful trading class. Money had been invented. Cities had sprung up. The iron-rimmed wheel allowed transport, trading, and the evolution of a mercantile, rather than a subsistence, economy. Society had been turned upside down, with the supposedly lowly traders and farmers having immense worldly power. Kings (who identified with the warrior class and who weren't Brahmins) were asserting their authority, establishing control over all this new wealth and the power base it could support. The kings came into competition, seeking to consolidate their control over natural and human resources. Wars became more prevalent as a result, resulting in further social upheaval and unease.

The gods had decreed a social structure with the Brahmins at the top, but now the warriors and lowly merchants were reaping the greatest material rewards. Something was clearly wrong. The gods weren't doing their job. Where were they? What were they up to? Did they even exist? The Brahmins had lost some of their credibility, and people began to look elsewhere for spiritual guidance. As was happening in Greece at almost the same moment, there was a general sense that the old religious ways no longer had as much relevance. And as was also the case in the Hellenic world, there was a new leisured class with the time to think about how life is best lived. Discontented with the religious status quo advocated by the Brahmins, the merchant class demanded new philosophical and religious outlooks. Philosophy and religious innovation were being born.

In parallel with and actually as one part of this development, many people had decided, like the hippies of the 1960s and 1970s, to drop out and seek the truth. They took to living in the forests or on the outskirts of society. Many begged for a living in order that their time not be taken up with the distracting task of working. They spent their time meditating, reflecting, debating, teaching, and engaging in a bewildering variety of spiritual practices. Gautama was one of these homeless wanderers, as was Pukkusati. For wanderers like them, the agriculturally rich area of Magadha would have been especially popular given its many outbuildings to sleep in and an ample surplus of food for begging.

Prior to his visit with Bhaggava, and after following a number of spiritual traditions in the forest but being satisfied with none of them, Gautama had an insight experience in which he experienced a profound letting go. This insight experience involved seeing through the mind's trick of interpreting reality in terms of *being*. Observing nothing but change in his experience, Gautama came to understand the mental processes that give rise to the sense of a separate and static self. He came to experience in a direct and non-conceptual way the world as it was, devoid of being and consisting only of becoming. This experience, he found, brought freedom from the suffering that arises from clinging. It also brought freedom from the fear of change. This was the liberation he had sought but never found in previous explorations. Having had this insight, Gautama went on to establish a loose-knit community of disciples and taught a variety of techniques to help them recapitulate his own spiritual journey. According to tradition, many thousands of people attained the same insight Gautama had originally discovered.

Pukkusati, as it turned out, was a follower of Gautama's teachings, although the two men had never met and Pukkusati had no idea with whom he was to share accommodations. A later tradition has it that Pukkusati was a minor king who had received a golden plate inscribed with some verses of Buddhist teaching from a neighboring monarch, and that he had been moved to retire from his kingdom in order to seek instruction from Gautama himself. Whether or not that's true, at this point in the story he was a novice monk en route to seeking full ordination.

There's a nice moment of decorum in the story where Gautama asks, "If it is not inconvenient for you ... I will stay one night in the workshop." It's obvious from Pukkusati's response—he addresses Gautama in a friendly but informal way—that he has no idea he's inviting one of the most important teachers of the time, and one who happens to be the very teacher he's been seeking, to spend the night with him. Having made their introductions, Gautama and Pukkusati begin to talk philosophy. Clearly the senior in terms of spiritual experience, Gautama takes the opportunity to outline some of his key spiritual teachings, including an exposition on the Six Elements. By the end, of course, Pukkusati comes to realize that the person he shares a dirt floor with is none other than the teacher whose discipline he's followed.

Unweaving the Self

The Six Element Practice, as taught to Pukkusati by Gautama, is a systematic analysis of the self. The reflection looks at the self in terms of:

The Earth Element, or everything solid within the body,

The Water Element, or all that is liquid within the body,

The Fire Element, or the energy that allows for metabolism,

The Air Element, or everything internal that is gaseous,

The Space Element, or the form constituted by the physical elements (you can think of this as your appearance), and

The Consciousness Element, or the emergent property that arises from the other elements, by which they become conscious of themselves.

You'll recognize the first four elements as the classical elements, which were used as an organizing principle from Ancient Greece to the European Renaissance. Aristotle modified the Greek four-element system by adding a fifth element called *aether*, which roughly corresponds to space. Aether is the "substance" comprising the heavens and heavenly bodies; incidentally, it was the last of the classical elements to go to its conceptual grave, being widely accepted in science until proven not to exist by an elegant experiment carried out by Albert Michelson and Edward Morley in 1887. The classical element model was modified by Arabic and European philosophers and scientists, but of course it turned out to be inadequate and was later replaced by the more elegant and flexible model of the chemical elements that we know today.

One might wonder, what can be the purpose of reflecting on a primitive scientific model long since superseded? The answer is simply that Gautama was not making scientific claims about the nature of the world. He was not interested in investigating the chemical structure of the body or of the world. The Six Elements merely provided a handy way of analyzing the mind and body in order to appreciate the essential truth of impermanence. By seeing how each of the elements flowed, and how each has its origin in that which is "not self," we can begin to undermine our notions of separateness and permanence. In essence, we could do that just as well by substituting Earth, Water, Fire, and Air with the contemporary chemical elements (plus energy), appreciating how each flows through the body. However, since there are about ninety naturally occurring elements, the meditation practice would be rather long.

While the later Buddhist tradition tended to see the classical elements not as physical realities but as qualities of experience (Earth is resistance, Water is fluidity, Fire is temperature, and Air is mobility), there's no hint of this in the Discourse or elsewhere in Gautama's teachings that I know of. The examples chosen to illustrate the Elements in the earliest stratum of Buddhist teachings describe them in terms of simple physical realities, with Earth being that which is solid, Water being anything liquid, etc. The Elements were seen as being interpenetrating, so that a solid log, for example, contained not just Earth but also the other three classical elements: it can emit Air and Water if heated, for example, and when it becomes very hot it can release its latent Fire.

With each of the five physical elements Earth through Space (Consciousness takes a different approach), we go through a pattern of investigation. This pattern helps us understand how nothing that constitutes the self belongs to us in any real way, and thus can't constitute a static and separate entity. After all, how can "I" be made entirely of stuff that is "not me"?

Here's a brief example of how I approach the Earth Element within the traditional form of the reflection: first we bring the Earth Element within the body—everything solid—to mind. We then reflect on everything solid in the outside world. We consider that whatever is solid within the body comes from the outside world and will return (and is presently returning) there. We visualize this, and thus see the Earth Element as flowing relentlessly through the body. We realize that there is in reality no "me" Earth Element and no "other" Earth Element; there's just one Earth Element. We come to see the Earth Element as "borrowed" from the outside world. We don't own it. We simply *identify* with it as being "me" and "mine" during the brief time it passes through this human form. Lastly, having connected with the flowing nature of the Earth Element, seeing it as being more like a river than a static thing—something that can't be owned or held onto—we reflect, "This is not me. This is not mine. I am not this." We begin to let go of the act of identifying with the element.

We repeat this pattern of reflections with each of the subsequent elements in turn, with the exception of the Consciousness Element, where the emphasis is rather different. Traditionally, the emphasis with the reflection on Consciousness is not on the element coming from and returning to the external world, but simply on realizing how our experience is a flow of events—such as sensations, feelings, and thoughts—arising and passing away. It is this flow of events that constitutes what we call consciousness. Consciousness is not seen as being something separate that "has" experiences. Consciousness is the *activity* of experiencing.

The Six Element Reflection is designed to challenge the notion of the self as separate and static. The Reflection encourages us to see:

That everything we identify with as being ourselves in fact comes from outside of ourselves, so that the "self" is made up of stuff that was originally "not self,"

That everything we identify with as being ourselves will eventually no longer be part of ourselves,

That everything we identify with as being ourselves isn't really a part of ourselves even when we think it is,

And that in fact there's no physical support for the separate or permanent self we like to believe we have.

This, I freely admit, is a lot to get out of one reflection. In fact it's not really "a" reflection at all, but an extended series of reflections, with six elements to be considered and a number of sequential reflections for each of those elements. In essence, however, it's a simple practice, although it can have profound effects on how we see ourselves.

I must point out the assumption in this reflection that there is a specific goal to be attained—a loosening and eventual abandonment of clinging to our sense of self—and that the practice will lead us there. The practice is an exploration, but it's not a freeform exploration where there are no assumptions about what we'll find. In this I see a parallel with the dual role of science first as an exploration of the unknown and second as a body of knowledge and skills to be cultivated. Many a scientist has set up an experiment with only a tentative hypothesis of what will be found. Some experiments involve going beyond the bounds of the known to see what we'll find. We collide particles together at high speed, for example, and see what happens. But once a particular experiment has been performed, it's common for other researchers to then follow instructions step-by-step in order to verify those results. Gautama's spiritual exploration and the insight it led to are like the first of those scenarios; the Six Element Practice is more like the second. Gautama's method is to state what he has found and to outline the steps by which you can verify his discovery. So the Six Element Practice is a kind of lab manual for recreating his experiment and verifying his findings.

The reflection is meant to be engaged with repeatedly, rather than just once or twice. The practice is, like all meditations, a form of training. We can't simply do the practice one time and reap a true sense of what it's about, any more than physical training can consists of one or two trips to the gym. In these reflections we challenge some very deeply held views that hinder our ability to appreciate impermanence, and those views are generally let go of a little at a time, over a long period. Doing the practice is similar to reading a favorite novel, where repeated exposure leads to deeper insights as we see connections and plot subtleties we'd previously missed. The practice has to be repeated in order for it to do its work. The reflections reveal layer upon layer of implications that unfold as the practice collides over and over again with our assumptions about how things are.

Traditionally the Six Element Practice is said to be the antidote to conceit. However, we're not tackling conceit in the sense of excessive pride, but rather the act of "conceiving" of oneself as separate and permanent. Conceit is the notion "I am." It's the notion that we have a permanent and separate self, with all that follows from that: our attachments and clinging to whatever "props" reinforce our sense of self and provide a bulwark against our fear of impermanence. The practice strips away our attachments by making us realize that not only is there nothing to cling to, but that no "thing" exists to do any clinging in the first place. The practice allows us to experience the full freedom that comes from a thoroughgoing appreciation of our own impermanence. Having let go of the sense that we are essentially fixed and separate, we are free to appreciate ourselves—and all things—as dynamic, ever-changing, full of potential, and part of an infinite number of interconnected processes. Rather than look for some illusory refuge of permanence in the ever-flowing river of life, we're able to let go and realize we're the river itself.

The experience people typically have while doing the practice is that their sense of self changes in some way. Sometimes these changes can be hard to verbalize. Often there's a sense of spaciousness and expansiveness, or a sense of attenuation of the self, as if the body is becoming lighter. Sometimes there's a deeper sense of connectedness, gratitude, and even of awe and wonder as we realize the extent of our connectedness with the world. There can be a sense of calm and freedom, as if a burden has been laid down. There can be a powerful sense of compassion as we realize the extent to which beings create unhappiness for themselves through clinging. These are all pleasant and enriching experiences. Sometimes, however, the practice can be disorienting and even frightening. If our clinging to a sense of self is a way of avoiding the fact of our own impermanence, then stripping away our protective buffer can leave us feeling exposed and raw. For this reason it's highly recommended that the Six Element Reflection be done in a state of lovingkindness—a warm and appreciative state that gives us the inner resources to cope with the potentially threatening perception of change and not-self. With lovingkindness well developed, we're able to be fearless in the face of change.

But we've left Gautama and Pukkusati hanging. Gautama has explained the Six Element Practice. Having done that, he outlines the state of insight that the practice leads to, and spells out the benefits of experiencing that insight. Having abandoned conceiving, the person penetrating the truth of impermanence is free from fear and becomes a "sage at peace." The sage at peace recognizes that aging and dying are simply stories we weave for ourselves. No change in life can shake or agitate him, not even death itself. As Renaissance philosopher Michel de Montaigne's rather lovely phrase quoted on page 25 puts it, the sage has a soul that is "universal, open, and ready for all things," even the most challenging.

Upon hearing all this, Pukkusati realizes that he is talking to someone who has a high degree of insight. He apologizes for his overly familiar introduction and is duly forgiven. Asking to have his status changed from a novice to a full monk, he requests admission to the community, but learns that he must first present the correct requisites—the robe and bowl he will need for his new life. And then comes what strikes me as note of literary artifice introduced a little jarringly into what has until now largely been framed as a realistic exchange between two historical figures. Pukkusati, on going out to procure his requisite robe and bowl, is gored by a stray cow and is killed. Gautama confirms to a number of disciples, who have shown up at his temporary residence to give news of his student's demise, that Pukkusati had obtained a deep degree of letting go of attachment to the notion of self and had obtained a deep level of insight into impermanence.

Even though the abrupt ending smacks of a literary device designed to show the power of the Six Element Practice (Pukkusati hears it described only once and becomes awakened!) and to provide a neat ending (Gautama is able to say exactly what level of awakening Pukkusati has achieved), this story remains one of my favorite encounters from the Buddhist tradition. In it we see a simple and honest exchange between two human beings, a philosopher and his student, and the sharing of a spiritual perspective that profoundly changes the latter. Whether or not Pukkusati did die immediately after learning the Six Element Practice, he certainly died at some point, and I like to think that in any case he died fearlessly, accepting death as just another change to be experienced with equanimity.

CHAPTER THREE

Self Is a Verb

"We are like violins.
We can be used for doorstops, or we can make music."
—Barbara Sher[1]

Through investigating the nature of the mind, Gautama discovered a way of experiencing deep peace in a world where everything is impermanent. Rather than battling the forces of change, trying to find something stable and reliable in an attempt to find happiness, security, and peace, his method was to practice radical letting go. The goal was to completely accept impermanence, fearlessly, and without attempting to create illusory refuges. In later texts, this attitude is described as "stand[ing] nowhere, like infinite space,"[2] and as living "not bewildered and in no way anxious"[3] without the need to pin down and define reality. This is far from being an uncaring state of quiescence. Although one in this state of realization is "peaceful among the restless," has "released his burden," and has "transcended disputation,"[4] the mind is also full of compassion: "Just as a mother would protect her only child at the risk of her own life, even so, let him cultivate a boundless heart toward all beings"[5] is said to be the attitude of one who is realized. It's in fact only because of non-clinging and non-fear that a completely compassionate life is said to be possible. When avoiding fear and consolidating a fragile self are our main drives in life, little energy remains for empathizing with others. And until we've seen through the existential fear that is the root cause of all suffering, we can't fully appreciate the pain that other beings experience.

The "peace" that comes from a full acceptance of impermanence is a positive peace, something that goes beyond even mere happiness. "Pleasure" is a shallow response that arises in dependence upon the temporary presence of what we like and the absence of what we dislike; it's no refuge. "Happiness" sounds too self-centered; happy people often want to do nothing more than tell you how happy they are. "Contentment" sounds too static, as though we passively kick back in our own little worlds, not much bothered with what's going on around us. "Equanimity" is accurate but is an emotionally cold word, and one that doesn't often find its way into our everyday speech. "Peace" may be the most suitable word; it implies that on some deep level we are able to accept life's ups and downs, although we are still touched by them. We can be peaceful and engaged, peaceful and compassionate. Oddly, the opposite of suffering turns out not to be simple happiness, but something indefinable.

Suffering, the Buddha had found, was the result of trying to grasp—ironically enough—after sources of happiness. We may seek wealth or approval or love. We may try to shelter ourselves from an awareness of impermanence by identifying with a nation or a religion or with an abstract principle such as progress. We may simply immerse ourselves in the forgetfulness of busyness or hedonism. Ultimately these are all attempts to screen out an awareness of impermanence, and to deny the fragile nature of our life on Earth. To cling is to seek a stable refuge in the midst of a torrent of impermanence. These refuges are not necessarily bad in themselves, but they can only ever be temporary. Inherent in each of those refuges is the possibility of change. Anything we cling to, seeking permanence, is itself impermanent, and the more our sense of well-being is dependent upon something impermanent, the more there is an undercurrent of fear. We fear we will lose what we value. We fear we won't get what we want. We fear we'll end up with what we don't want. Fear leads to clinging, which leads to fear. The only true refuge is to let go of clinging, so that we can accept impermanence fully.

Ethics, Meditation, and the Cultivation of Insight

The Buddha taught a classic path of ethics that's strikingly similar to the writings of the Greek and Roman Stoics of the third century BCE to the sixth century CE. Epictetus, for example, said that the Stoic would be "sick and yet happy, in peril and yet happy, dying and yet happy, in exile and happy, in disgrace and happy."[6] The Stoics advised us to avoid making our happiness dependent upon impermanent things, and to observe life's ups and downs with equanimity. They, like Gautama, advised the practice of meditation (Marcus Aurelius: "Allow yourself a space of quiet . . . and learn to curb your restlessness"[7]), and reflection ("Reflect often upon the rapidity with which all existing things . . . sweep past us and are carried away"[8]). Where Gautama went further than the Stoics was in saying that the archetype of all grasping was identifying *something* as being the self—something that *is* and that *remains*. What we seem to do, as we've seen earlier, is to assume we have a self that is separate and unchanging. We inevitably start to identify what exactly constitutes that self (for example: the mind, the body). Finally, while clinging to a sense of self, we begin to grasp after things we think will bolster that sense of self and try to keep at bay those things we think threaten it.

Gautama's path of training involves working with all levels of this process in order to cease clinging to the idea of having a self. The three aspects to this training are ethics, meditation, and the cultivation of insight. As an ethical teaching, Buddhism encourages us to notice and let go of craving and aversion as they manifest in our day-to-day existence. And so we're encouraged to live virtuously, cultivating kindness instead of hatred, and generosity and contentment in place of craving material goods or sensual pleasures. These are not seen as commandments, the breaking of which will lead to punishment, but as training principles. If we let go of craving and aversion, we're told, we'll experience greater well-being. This is not a reward, but a natural consequence.

In meditation we're encouraged to develop greater mindfulness so that we may observe the workings of the mind. In effect this is the same practice as with ethics, but directed toward our inner experience rather than toward our external actions. Through meditating, we become more adept at spotting the thought patterns that lead to grasping and to hurting others. We also cultivate positive mental states such as lovingkindness and compassion, which undermine our clinging to self by widening our sphere of concern to include other people.

Lastly, in cultivating insight we're encouraged to recognize impermanence and to see through the delusion of a fixed and separate self.

In doing so we have to let go of even very subtle forms of clinging. The Six Element Practice is a form of insight meditation and
therefore comes under this category. Insight is not the same as intellectual understanding but is a direct recognition of impermanence
in our experience.

Deconstructing the Self

In the Six Element Practice, we challenge our assumptions about the
body and the mind—the two things we take to be the locus of the
core self. We observe how everything that we identify with as being
ourselves in fact comes from outside of ourselves. We note that everything we identify with as being ourselves will eventually no longer
be part of ourselves. Because everything that constitutes us is in fact
a *process,* rather than a thing or object, we realize that there is in fact
nothing to grasp onto, any more than we could hold onto water flowing through our fingers. We realize that the act of grasping is futile,
since nothing can be owned or clung to. Eventually we come to the
realization that there's no "thing" there to do any grasping, anyway.
When we let go of grasping after identifying any particular thing as
the locus of the self, we abandon the very need to define the self.

Once again, I don't say that there's no self. It's often said that
Buddhism teaches a "no-self" doctrine, but actually what it teaches is
a "not-self" doctrine. We look at each of the elements in turn, realize
that each element cannot be the basis of an unchanging and separate
self, and come to learn, more and more deeply, that each of the elements is "not mine, not me," and that "I am not this." We're still left
with what we've called the "conventional self"—a recognition that
there is a body and a consciousness functioning in the world—but

there's no clinging to those things, no sense that the body or mind are separate from the world, and no sense that the body or mind are unchanging. We don't identify the body, the mind, or the combination of the two as being a self. Instead, we're left with something that's essentially indefinable.

Buddhist texts often use analogies to help us see the nature of the self. Interestingly, the most common analogy is one the Buddha, as far as I'm aware, never used. It's the analogy of the self as a chariot. A Buddhist teacher, Nagasena, is famous for having answered questions put to him by the Indo-Greek king Milinda,[9] who reigned in Bactria in the second century BCE. One of that dialogue's most famous parts is the one in which Nagasena illustrates his understanding of not-self by discussing the chariot in which the king arrived.[10] Nagasena asks Milinda whether any of the components of the chariot—the axle, wheels, pole, banner, etc.—constitute the chariot. The answer of course is no. The chariot's "chariotness" isn't contained in any one part.

Nagasena goes on to extend this analogy to himself:

> "In exactly the same way, your majesty, in respect of me, Nagasena is but a way of counting, term, appellation, convenient designation, mere name for the hair of my head, hair of my body . . . brain of the head, form, sensation, perception, the psychic constructions, and consciousness. But in the absolute sense there is no self here to be found."

Here's where, from a Buddhist point of view, we hit a potential snag. Gautama explicitly rejected the idea that there is no self. Believing that there is no self, Gautama said, is still a belief about the self, and this is just another limiting view—as limiting as the belief in a fixed self but perhaps even more so, since a person believing he has no self would be inclined to nihilism. It's not clear that Nagasena is saying that there is in fact no self. He says that it is in "the absolute sense" that there is no self, and he does leave us with the conventional self—the "convenient designation" of "Nagasena." But the impression we're left with is that there is no self, and that this can be demonstrated by deconstructing the chariot or self into its component parts. Nagasena seems to be treating the self as a noun (a static, separate object) and says that it doesn't really exist because it can be broken down into other nouns (static, separate objects that are the component parts of the chariot). The chariot is just an appearance. The components are real.

Although the Buddha doesn't seem to have used the chariot analogy, he did use a superficially similar one: the analogy of a lute. In this analogy, a king hears the sound of a lute for the first time and asks to see what made such sweet music. A lute is produced, but the king is not satisfied. He wants to see the music. His ministers say,

> "This lute, sire, is made of numerous components, a great many components. It's through the activity of numerous components that it sounds: that is, in dependence on the body, the skin, the neck, the frame, the strings, the bridge, and the appropriate human effort. Thus it is that this lute—made of numerous components, a great many components—sounds through the activity of numerous components."[11]

Similarly, Gautama points out, a practitioner investigates the body and mind and finds that "thoughts of 'me' or 'mine' or 'I am' do not occur."[12] There's no suggestion in Gautama's analogy that the self doesn't exist. Instead we simply let go of any identification with the body or mind as being the self. We stop clinging to any sense of the self being static, separate, or definable in any way. We cease thinking about "me" or "mine" or "I am," and this thinking has ceased because we have ceased emotionally clinging to any idea of ourselves.

In this analogy, the "self" is the *functioning* of the body and mind, and is therefore not a "thing." The self is a process arising out of the functioning of both body and mind. Of course we can't locate the self in any component of the body. Nor is the self identified with the mind or any component of the mind. The self cannot be reduced to any component or collection of components, any more than the sound of the lute can be found in any one component of the lute or even in the entire, assembled lute. The self is an activity. It's a process. It's a verb. As such, it's not a noun or a "thing" because a process by definition is not a thing we can grasp onto. A self that is a process is not the kind of self that can be static and unchanging. A self that is a process is not the kind of self that exists separately.

Also, one of the components that makes the sound of the lute possible is "appropriate human effort." The lute in itself is not an instrument unless it's in human hands. Without interaction with a human being it is simply a collection of glue, catgut, and various pieces of wood. Without interaction the lute is close to being an assemblage of nouns. The lute has to be in relation to something else before the sound can happen. Thus the idea of a separate self is challenged. If the self, in the analogy, is the sound of the lute, then the self can only exist in relation to something else. In this case the self only exists in interaction with the world and with other selves. There is no such thing as a self in isolation. The self is therefore something inherently dynamic, interactive, and relational.

The provocative philosopher and neuroscientist Alva Noë, in his book *Out of Our Heads,*[13] makes essentially the same points as I have above. Nowadays, many scientists and philosophers continue the millennia-long struggle to define the nature of the self. Many take a reductionist approach, identifying the self with the body by saying the mind is merely a byproduct of the brain. Our consciousness is seen as being located in the brain, so that our brains represent the essence of our selves. Experience, in this view, is reduced to the status of electrical and chemical activity in the gray matter between our ears. It's like saying the sound of a lute is simply catgut and wood vibrating, without reference to the qualitative experience of hearing the sweetness of the instrument's music.

Noë highlights this reductivism by quoting a statement by the Nobel Prize-winning co-discoverer of DNA, Francis Crick. In a book called *The Astonishing Hypothesis,* Crick says: "You, your joys and your sorrows, your memories and your ambitions, your sense of personal identity and free will, are in fact no more than the behavior of a vast assembly of nerve cells and their associated molecules."[14] Noë terms this the "gastric juices" conception of philosophy, in that consciousness is seen as taking place in the head in much the same way digestion takes place in the gut. So what's the alternative? Noë posits that you are not your brain, although the brain is part of what you are. Noë suggests that consciousness is akin to a dance: "You can no more explain mind in terms of the [brain] cell than you can explain dance in terms of the muscle."[15] Consciousness, he suggests, "is not something the brain achieves on its own. Consciousness requires the joint operation of brain, body, and world . . . [and] is an achievement of the whole animal in its environmental context."[16] Noë talks about *consciousness* rather than the self, but in the context of his book, where he regards consciousness not as being an event in the head but the joint operation of brain, body, and the world, the distinction doesn't make much difference. In Noë's thinking, as with the Buddha's, we have a vision of the self as an *activity*. That is, the self is not a "thing" but a process that arises in a complex interaction between the mind, the body, and the environment (an environment that contains other selves).

This is the main thesis of this book. What we call a self is not a thing. It is a process. It is an activity. It is the sum total of what we do. It is not static. The self does not exist as a separate entity that interacts with the world, but is the sum total of the interactions of a living being and its environment. Living with the notion that the self is separate and static leads to suffering, because such a notion flies in the face of reality.

If analogies of lutes leave you unsatisfied, and you hunger for a more "human" analogy that conveys what it would be like to live with no thought of a self, think of an expert basketball player weaving through the opposing team's defense toward the basket. If he's in the "zone," if he's experiencing what's called "flow," there's no thought of "Here *I* am, and there *they* are, and *I* have to get past *them* and *they're* going to stop *me,* and there's the basket in front of me and somehow *I* have to make it over there." That kind of thinking leads to tension, fear, and paralysis. Instead there's a wordless, focused mind, intent on a goal with laser-like clarity. The mind isn't wandering; it's not conceptualizing. It's not thinking in terms of self and other. It's perfectly in the moment, attentive, responsive, and aware. The body and mind are one. Adjustments are being made all the time in response to challenges from the other team, too quickly for the discursive mind—the one that tells us stories about who we are, what we're doing, and all the things that might happen—to be able to act. Grace manifests effortlessly, and creativity emerges spontaneously from the wordless depths of the mind. At their best, moments like this can be pure and free from any conception of a self. There's no clinging. There's instead inner calm, clarity, and joy.

These qualities can manifest in our lives too. We can let the surface clutter of the mind die away. We can still the constant chatter that tells us stories and reinforces our thoughts of who we are, what's wrong with us, what we need to have in order to be happy, and so on. And when the mind does clear in this way, we do not find a blankness. Instead we find ourselves living attentively, spontaneously, and joyfully. Creativity wells up without conscious intervention. We know what to do and what to say without even knowing how we know. And we weave around life's obstacles joyfully, with, in the words of Montaigne, minds that are "universal, open, and ready for all things."

This book is a practice. In order to change the way we see more deeply into the nature of the self, we will explore each of the six elements—Earth, Water, Fire, Air, Space, and Consciousness—in order to understand what these elements are and how they reveal our impermanent and interconnected nature. We have one task to complete before we do that, however, and that is to examine, briefly, the nature and role of the imagination.

CHAPTER FOUR

On Reflection

*"You take the blue pill—the story ends, you wake up
in your bed and believe whatever you want
to believe. You take the red pill—you stay in Wonderland and
I show you how deep the rabbit-hole goes."*
— MORPHEUS IN *THE MATRIX*[1]

The Six Element Practice is an insight meditation involving reflection, but there are potentially confusing preconceptions
about both insight meditation and reflection that we need to address.

Both the term "insight meditation" and its near-synonym, *vipassana,*
have two meanings. Each has a wider, traditional sense, and a narrower, more contemporary sense. Vipassana is a Pali word, Pali being
the language in which the earliest preserved Buddhist teachings are
found. *Passana* means "seeing," and the *vi-* prefix indicates intensifi-
cation, so that vipassana means "truly seeing" or "insight." Vipassana
refers to directly perceiving the reality of impermanence; it also refers
to the kind of meditation leading to that direct perception. The term
"insight meditation" is also used to denote the kind of meditation that
leads to a perception of impermanence.

Traditionally, vipassana and insight meditation cover a wide variety of practices. There are practices that involve the contemplation of conditionality, which is the whole process by which we create and perpetuate our experience. There are insight-meditation practices based on the contemplation of the qualities of the spiritually awakened mind. Some of these practices involve visualization, while others are more conceptual and involve the recitation of verses. There are insight-meditation practices where one bears a scriptural verse in mind as a reminder of impermanence. There are practices that involve sitting in a charnel ground, witnessing the decay of a corpse. There is of course the Six Element Practice. And, most famously, there is a form of insight meditation taught by the Buddha, and popularized in the present day by the Burmese meditation master S. N. Goenka and by various western teachers including Sharon Salzberg, Joseph Goldstein, and Jack Kornfield. Variations of this style of meditation have been applied in medicine and psychiatry, in the form of Mindfulness-Based Stress Reduction and Mindfulness-Based Cognitive Therapy, to name but two, thanks to the pioneering work of Jon Kabat-Zinn.

In this particular breath-based form of insight meditation we note the sensations of the breath arising, existing, and passing away. When distracting sensations, thoughts, and emotions arise, we bring a kindly awareness to them, similarly observing their arising, their existing, and their disappearance. In doing so we become aware that these experiences are impermanent and are not part of the self, and we see how clinging to these experiences is a cause of suffering. In other words we gain insight by breaking through our delusion of having a separate and permanent self. Incidentally, this practice is essentially the same as the reflection on the Consciousness Element found in the Six Element Practice.

The problem is that this popular form of vipassana practice is so well-known compared to the other forms of insight meditation I've mentioned, that the terms vipassana and insight meditation have become virtually synonymous with this one technique. When most people think of insight meditation, they tend to think of the kind of meditation taught by Goenka, Goldstein, et al., as well as in various therapeutic settings. Often they simply aren't aware of the other approaches to vipassana meditation that I've mentioned. Just to be clear, I have no quibble at all with this form of meditation. It's a traditional and very effective practice. It's just not the *only* form of vipassana/insight meditation.

So vipassana, or insight meditation, has two senses—a traditional sense covering a wide range of practices designed to cultivate insight, and a more narrow contemporary sense where it stands for one particular style of meditation. This leads to some confusion, because having practiced insight meditation in the more contemporary sense of the term, some practitioners come to think that the form of insight meditation they know *is* insight meditation. Not being aware of other styles, they can sometimes be confused, perhaps even critical, when other forms of insight meditation (in the wider, traditional sense) are brought to their attention.

For some practitioners of the more widely known style of insight meditation, the notion of reflecting on our experience in the way we do in the Six Element Practice can seem odd, and even contradictory to what they understand of meditation and of mindfulness. For their benefit we should briefly explore the differences. In contemporary insight meditation, when thoughts and images come up, they are to be observed without interference and allowed to pass. The impermanence of thoughts and images is noted, but thoughts and images themselves are not actively cultivated. S. N. Goenka states in one of his books, "Vipassana uses no imagination,"[2] and variations of the phrase "no imagination is involved" are scattered throughout his teachings. Clearly he's talking about vipassana in a narrower and more contemporary sense—where what he says is accurate—rather than to the wider and more traditional sense. In the Six Element Practice, in contrast to Goenka-style vipassana, we do in fact consciously cultivate the arising of thoughts and images. In other words, we reflect and imagine.

In the Earth Element reflection, for example, we call to mind everything solid within the body. This includes *some* aspects of the body that we can directly sense, such as the mass of the muscles, the hardness of the teeth, and the resistance offered by some of the bones. But being aware of what is solid in the body goes far beyond what we can directly sense, and takes us into an awareness, for example, of the internal organs, the bone marrow, and even the contents of the stomach and the bowels—all things of which the Discourse asks us to become aware. These are things we can't perceive directly, and so we have to imagine them.

Similarly, in the Earth Element reflection we call to mind the solid matter in the outside world. When I'm leading others through the practice I usually draw attention to some examples: the solid floor that supports us and the building covering us, the ground below, rocks and boulders, the distant mountains, the trees and other plants in our environment, buildings, vehicles, the bodies of people and animals, etc. As I say these things out loud for the benefit of the students, I find that images spring into my mind, evoked by the words I'm speaking. Sometimes, in order to cultivate a sense of the solidity of the external Earth Element, I'll recall or imagine grasping a handful of soil, or feeling the weight of a stone in my hand, or pushing against the rough bark of a tree trunk.

Imagination allows us to see aspects of reality that aren't immediately obvious to the unaided senses. Our senses end up fooling us because they're unable to directly perceive process. When I become mindful of my body, aware only of what is available to my raw senses, I can be fooled into thinking that my body is more static and separate than it is in reality. Einstein once referred to our sense of separateness as a kind of "optical delusion of consciousness." He was using the term "optical delusion" as a metaphor, but the metaphor is actually very accurate. When I look at my body I see a boundary separating self from other. I also see something that is relatively unchanging. This is what my senses present to me—the body as a "thing." And yet in my imagination I can recall the way in which my body has come into being by ingesting nourishment, so that other becomes self, and I can recall how the constituents of my body are constantly changing from being self to being other. By recollecting in my mind's eye the various ways in which the elements flow through my body, I can have a truer perception of what the body is: something neither separate nor static.

All this, however, rather goes against a certain idea of mindfulness, which is that mindfulness involves being aware only of what arises in our present-moment experience, such as the sensations presented to our bodies and any thoughts and feelings that arise naturally. In the Buddhist tradition, however, the mind is considered to be a sixth sense, so that when we reflect on our internal organs or on the solidity of the earth we are simply paying attention to the present-moment experience of our visual and tactile imagination. Mindfulness can include these things.

Thinking, Not Thinking, and Reflecting

Many people identify thinking, and even experience itself, with *verbal* thinking—a scrolling tickertape of more-or-less connected words that streams endlessly through the mind. Incidentally, in meditation the mind can slow down considerably, to the point that verbal thoughts become fewer. Sometimes in meditation, for a while at least, verbal thought may cease altogether. When people learn about this possibility they sometimes assume that the aim of meditation is a state of blankness. They may even assume that a reduction in verbal thoughts is a nihilistic state of near-nonexistence. Just recently someone expressed to me his concern that he might not be able to learn to meditate: "I'm a never-ending thinker. [Having] no thoughts would be like death to me," he wrote.

I take all this to be a reflection of the extent to which we are "in our heads." We are so caught up in thinking, and so identify our thinking with ourselves, that we imagine not having verbal thoughts to be equivalent to not existing. Not thinking is pictured as a kind of non-experience, akin to the way we imagine death. In fact there are many different kinds of thought, not all of them verbal. We often think symbolically and visually. Give a chimpanzee a stick, a box, and a bunch of bananas suspended from the ceiling, as the psychologist Wolfgang Köhler did in the 1920s, and the chimp may well figure out that standing on the box allows it to reach the bananas and bring them crashing to the ground. The chimp may even, as one of Köhler's did, short-circuit the experiment and leap onto the experimenter's shoulders to grab the fruit![3] Now, I don't know exactly how a chimp thinks, but I'm quite sure it doesn't have a train of thought that goes "Hey, this stick's too short to reach the bananas, but if I stand on this box I might just reach them." Presumably the chimp is thinking visually, or spatially, or kinesthetically, or in some combination of these modalities. But it's certainly not thinking verbally. Similarly, most of our thinking is not verbal, and it's a mistake to confuse thinking as such with *verbal* thinking, which is only one modality of thought.

The corollary of the misconception that verbal thinking is the only form of thinking is the notion that meditative reflection involves the tickertape thought I've described. In fact, although we may use an element of internal verbalization in reflective thinking, visualization and kinesthetic thinking are even more important. To give just one example, in the form of insight meditation that involves turning a verse over in the mind, we do indeed start with verbal thought. As part of the Six Element Practice, for example, we may repeat the phrase, "This is not me; this is not mine; I am not this." A verse such as this is, as it were, dropped into the mind. Often when teaching students a technique like this I'll suggest that they imagine they're dropping a stone into a deep well. The verse is released into the depths of the mind, plunging into the waters of the subconscious. Then we simply "listen" for a response. For several breaths, and perhaps longer, we simply attend to our experience, noting any physical responses, such as sensations that arise in certain parts of the body, or emotional responses, or images that may appear in the mind. After the period of attentive "listening," the verse is dropped in once more, and the cycle continues. The verbal thought is simply the first step in a process of reflection that begins in conscious awareness, affects our unconscious mind, and then returns to consciousness in the form of sensations, images, etc.

When we reflect, much (and perhaps even most) of the process goes on outside conscious awareness. Even with relatively mundane information processing, parts of the mind to which we have no conscious access crunch away at problems and then present the answers to us. We've all had the experience of not being able to remember someone's name, only for the answer to arrive suddenly in our consciousness minutes or hours later, when we're focused on some other task. Or an answer may come to us after we've taken a nap—the memory having been retrieved during sleep. The retrieval of the name has gone on at an unconscious level, and although the end result is verbal and conscious—"Susie! That's her name!"—there's simply no conscious awareness of how we reached that result.

Even more so than in mundane problem-solving, nonverbal processing is extremely important in creative thinking. The German chemist August Kekulé's discovery of the ability of carbon atoms to form chains came to him in a dream when he dozed off on the Clapham omnibus in London, after his conscious processing had failed to resolve just how organic molecules are structured. Both the conscious and unconscious forms of processing were necessary, but evidently his unconscious "thinking," in which atoms of different kinds danced and linked up, Disney-cartoon-style, was what solved the problem.[4] Kekulé's subconscious repeated this trick a decade later as he struggled to understand the structure of benzene. As he dozed by the fire, dancing atoms formed themselves into a snake that bit its own tail, revealing benzene's annular structure.

Einstein was another nonverbal thinker. Regarding himself a poor mathematician, he would first employ his visual and kinesthetic senses to approach a problem, such as what would happen as a particle approached the speed of light. Fortunately, Einstein described for us how his mind worked:

"The words of the language, as they are written or spoken, do not seem to play any role in my mechanism of thought. The psychical entities which seem to serve as elements in thought are certain signs and more or less clear images . . . The above mentioned elements are, in any case, of visual and some of a muscular type."[5]

Einstein confided to a reporter, Dimitri Marianoff, that he had struggled with the general theory of relativity without success for years, and that the answer had finally come to him in a vision. Having gone to bed in a state of deep depression, convinced that a coherent theory was forever beyond his grasp, Einstein suddenly had the solution appear "with infinite precision, and with its underlying unity of size, structure, distance, time, space, slowly falling into place piece by piece . . . [until] like a giant die making an indelible impress, a huge map of the universe outlined itself in one clear vision."[6] His insights were subsequently expressed in mathematical and verbal form, but they began on a more visceral level. Again, the conscious mind struggles, and the subconscious delivers. Both parts of the process are crucial to the final insight that arises.

Without the conscious struggle to define and clarify the problem, the subconscious would have nothing to work with. Creativity does not operate in a vacuum—it needs information to work with. Similarly, with reflective practice in the Buddhist tradition, processing goes on at a subconscious level, but this is based on knowledge gained consciously. In reflecting on a verse such as "This is not me; this is not mine; I am not this," it's necessary to have thought about the issues involved and it's even more necessary to have worked with them in real-life situations. The conscious mind makes a certain amount of progress with understanding the verse, but the final insight will come like a lightning bolt from another dimension of thought.

In reflecting on the Six Elements, we tap into our life-knowledge and sensory experience in the form of the imagery and tactile sensations we conjure up. We tap into images of the body and of the outside world, and a tactile awareness of their solidity. We tap into our knowledge of the world, recollecting the processes by which the external element enters the body and then leaves again. We see and feel the flow of the element. We remind ourselves, using inner dialogue, "This is not me; this is not mine; I am not this." At every stage the images and verbalizations are stones dropped into the well of the mind. The verses plunge into the depths, and echoes reverberate in the form of gut feelings, emotions, images, or as new understandings. These understandings are fundamentally nonverbal, but they can be expressed in words. The next time someone asks you a question about some certain area of your expertise, note that your own sense of understanding precedes anything you might say, so that you are able to express what you know in many different ways. That is, understanding is not like an encyclopedia entry that you consult and read off, but more like a complete tactile, visual, and auditory map of a realm of experience that is familiar to you.

It's best not to be confused by the word "thinking," which may convey the idea that the kind of insight we're trying to evoke in meditation is similar to the logical problems Kekulé faced in understanding the arrangement of chemical bonds in organic molecules, or even Einstein's mind-boggling attempt to understand general relativity. These are problems with definite answers that can be understood on a rational level. It's a fairly simple thing to understand the basics of organic chemistry, and although it requires more training to understand relativity, the effort is one principally involving the intellect. The kind of insight we seek in a reflection such as the Six Element Practice, however, is not one that can arise purely intellectually. Instead this kind of insight requires the reorientation of our emotional drives and the deconstruction of our deep-rooted assumptions about the nature of the self and of the world. The Six Element Practice is to be "understood," ultimately, by our entire being, and we know the degree to which it has been understood by the degree to which we can see that our entire outlook, our emotions, and our behaviors have changed.

As you read this book, I suggest that you treat the material as a reflection in the sense I've discussed above. I intend to give you plenty to think about. But I'd suggest we treat all that as stones to be dropped into the well of the mind. You need to allow time and space to listen to the returning echoes. When the conscious mind excitedly grasps an idea and goes hurtling off on a train of thought, quiet echoes from the depths may go unheard, and you will have missed the opportunity to find "how deep the place is from which your life flows."[7] So I'd suggest pausing occasionally as you read, giving your subconscious time to process the words and images evoked. I'd suggest that as I present metaphors, you visualize them in the mind's eye so that they become *your* metaphors and therefore *your* experience. Where I don't provide images, or where my images don't work for you, I suggest you find your own. The subconscious thrives on images.

Some of the images I'll present to you are from mythology. I do this not because I believe that myths are literally true, but because they are metaphorically true. The elements have often been personified as deities, for example, and the myths that bear these stories can provide rich fodder for the imagination.

Traditionally we would not undertake the Six Element Meditation without two essential supporting conditions. First, we'd have calmed the mind using mindfulness meditation, for example focusing on the sensations of the breath in order to allow any mental agitation to settle down. This state of calmness allows us to focus undistractedly, and gives us the attentiveness with which we can listen to the echoing communications of the unconscious. Any time spent stilling the mind—even just sitting quietly, looking out a window, or going for a mindful walk in the park—will help you get more out of our reflections together. Second, and perhaps most importantly, we'd ensure that we were in a positive state of mind by cultivating lovingkindness. Deconstructing our sense of the self should not be undertaken on the basis of self-hatred, which unfortunately is common in the West. I'd suggest that throughout the remainder of this book you spend as much time as possible appreciating yourself and others. Life is short, and as the Buddha once pointed out, those who truly understand that fact find it easy to set aside conflict in favor of love and appreciation.

CHAPTER FIVE

The Body as Mirage

"All that is born, all that is created, all the elements
of nature are interwoven and united with each other.
All that is composed shall be decomposed; everything returns
to its roots; matter returns to the origins of matter."
—Gospel of Mary Magdalene[1]

In 1911, a thirty-two-year-old sportsman and daredevil called Calbraith Perry Rodgers, with a scant sixty hours of airtime in his logbook, set off to cross the United States from coast to coast in his specially modified Wright airplane—the first in private ownership.[2] His dream was to win the $50,000 that tycoon publisher William Randolph Hearst had offered to the first person to fly across the continent within thirty days. But Rodgers, as much a canny businessman as an adventurous pioneer, had a financial backup plan in case the trip took longer than the allotted month. He'd persuaded J. Ogden Armour, a Chicago entrepreneur, to underwrite the costs of the mission in exchange for the words "Vin Fiz"—Armour's brand of grape-flavored soda—being emblazoned on the craft's tail fin and wings. And so, *The Vin Fiz Flyer* became the name of Rodgers's airplane.

The *Vin Fiz* took to the air from a field in Sheepshead Bay, near New York City, late on the afternoon of September 17, its pilot swaddled in layers of sweaters and sheepskin to provide warmth in the unheated cockpit. Seven weeks and almost seventy landings later, the craft touched down at a racetrack in Pasadena, California. Sadly, Rodgers failed to win Hearst's prize. For all his courage and persistence, his flight had taken far longer than the thirty days allowed, and as a further blow to Rodgers's hopes, the year-long window for participating in the competition had expired before the *Vin Fiz* reached Pasadena. But a week later, buoyed by the glory of having made aviation history with his epic voyage, Rodgers set off to cover the remaining twenty miles to Long Beach and the Pacific Ocean. In retrospect, this was not such a good idea. The last leg alone took almost a month, with two crashes, one of which was serious enough to cause a broken ankle. All for a distance that could be comfortably cycled in two hours.

Although Rodgers didn't win Hearst's $50,000, his having crossed the country in such a primitive aircraft was an astonishing achievement. The *Vin Fiz* was a fragile thing made from a spruce frame covered with linen, its body looking more like a box kite than a modern plane. It was powered by a tiny 35 horsepower engine: no more powerful than some modern lawnmowers. Rodgers had no navigational instruments, and he found his way across the country by the simple expedient of following a train, which also pulled a white boxcar packed with spare parts for the journey. And Rodgers was to need a lot of spares. The doughty *Vin Fiz* malfunctioned, crashed, or was damaged in rough landings so many times during the eighty-four-day crossing that by the end of the journey only one wing-strut and a rudder remained from the original machine that had left New York.

Without in any way undermining the magnificence of Rodgers's achievement, when I first heard this tale many years ago, I found myself wondering in what sense the *Vin Fiz* had actually completed the journey. Only two components survived the trip, and given a few more miles it's possible that even those remaining original parts would have been replaced from the dwindling supply of spares in the white railroad car, in which case nothing would have remained of the original craft. In a sense, one plane took off from Sheepshead Bay and another landed in California. With each repair, the machine had become in some sense a new aircraft. The *Vin Fiz* struck me as being a perfect example of the Buddhist teaching of *anatta,* or the non-permanence and insubstantiality of the self.

Flight of Imagination

Compressing time and space in the theater of the imagination, let's visualize the cross-country flight of the *Vin Fiz*. Let's see the frail craft at the midpoint of each of its hops, suspended midair, the images strung together to form a brief movie. Squeezing the entire journey into the space of a minute, notice that the craft is continually changing. In a sudden jump of perception, a tattered wing becomes whole again. A rattling bolt falls to earth and at that same moment is replaced. A propeller, a wing-strut, a stretch of linen, a wheel, an entire engine—each vanishes and is instantaneously regenerated. As we watch the *Vin Fiz* in this way, it is a plane forever in the process of becoming another plane. And when at last we visualize the final touchdown, only that stubborn wing-strut and hardy rudder remain unchanged. And we can, if we wish, imagine one more frame of this imaginary movie and see even those components being replaced.

So what was it that flew across the United States? What was the *Vin Fiz?* The craft that arrived in Pasadena was not physically the same one that had departed New York. The form was the same, the name was the same, but almost everything constituting the aircraft had changed. No one component was the *Vin Fiz.* No single component contained the essence of the aircraft: certainly not the wing-strut and rudder that happened to survive the journey, and which were merely accidental survivors. The *Vin Fiz* was also not the entirety of its components, since they were forever changing. When we try to look for the *Vin Fiz,* it becomes mirage-like, its "thingness" vanishing under scrutiny.

The *Vin Fiz* clearly existed. But it was a process rather than a thing, an ever-changing assemblage of parts functioning in a particular way, not a static object. It was a process that had continuity rather than identity. It had no essence, but consisted of a series of ever-changing components brought together in a manner that allowed an ever-changing form to cross a continent. What arrived in Pasadena was not identical to what left Sheepshead Bay, but there was a continuous process connecting the craft's various iterations as it evolved over the course of its journey. The continuity of the *Vin Fiz* is also maintained in the mind. Had the *Vin Fiz* suffered only one devastating crash halfway between coasts, and had a new craft been assembled from the parts in the railroad car (including only one wing-strut and a rudder from the original aircraft) and continued the journey, would Rodgers be credited with the first continental crossing by air? Naturally not. We would not have believed that one craft made the crossing. It would seem like a stunt had been pulled. And yet an assemblage of replacement parts (including one wing-strut and a rudder from the original aircraft) was precisely what did arrive on the West Coast.

What held together the *Vin Fiz*, just as much as the rivets and bolts, was the sense of continuity that the mind sees, which allows us to say that a process had continually functioned as an aircraft, despite modifications. When we look for a "thing" called the *Vin Fiz*, it now seems mirage-like and undefinable.

The same is true of the human body. As the body makes a journey across the continent of life, from the coast of conception to the far shore we call death, it too is continually changing, the physical and mental components forever being replaced. What arrives at the final touchdown is a far cry from what originally departed at the beginning of life. The body you're born with is not the one you'll die with. Looking at the body the same way we did the *Vin Fiz*, we can see there is similarly no essence within it. There is no locus within the body where a self can be found. Our physical selves seem mirage-like, held together not so much by chemical bonds but by a physical process of continuity and an idea of selfhood.

Our ideas of what constituted the boundaries of the *Vin Fiz* are also limited. At some point after its historic flight, the *Vin Fiz* was broken up, its parts dispersed to rot or burn. We no longer have the sense that there is a thing or process we can label *"Vin Fiz,"* and yet the continuity has simply taken a different form. Parts of the aircraft—the ash from burned wood and linen, metal parts that long ago turned to rust—have become soil, supporting manifold forms of life. The carbon dioxide from its burning has become plants, which have since been eaten and transformed into uncountable living things. Just a few years before it crossed the continental United States, the *Vin Fiz* had not yet come into being; it was trees, flax, soil, and ores buried deep underground. We could look at these things and never dream they would one day fly across a vast continent. When we look in this way we can see there was no beginning to the *Vin Fiz*. Nor was there an end to it. But the mind tries to impose boundaries on processes that in essence are boundless. We think of the *Vin Fiz* beginning and ending. We see the craft in the air as being the *Vin Fiz* but the components on the train as not being the *Vin Fiz*. We impute to the *Vin Fiz* a false sense of separateness.

We also impute the same false sense of separateness to ourselves, and the purpose of reflecting on the elements is to dispel the mistaken assumption that the self is a thing—static, separate, and enduring. The purpose of reflecting on the elements is to see the truth of flow, of impermanence, of insubstantiality, and of interconnectedness. And on the way to seeing this truth we have to let go of the idea that the body is a thing—that it is separate and has some kind of permanent essence. When we do that, we start to realize that we can't "own" the body. The body is not ours in any real sense, nor is the body "us" in any real sense. The self cannot be found within it. This, as we'll see, isn't to diminish ourselves. Rather, it's to free ourselves from a limited way of seeing the self so that we can appreciate that we're much, much more than we habitually assume.

The Problem of Change and Identity

The story of the *Vin Fiz* is in fact a modern version of an ancient tale called "The Ship of Theseus." The legend has it that Theseus's ship set sail to ply the seas, but over the years various parts began to rot or otherwise wear out and were replaced. Eventually every nail, timber, and rope had been replaced, bringing up the question: Is Theseus's vessel still the same ship? Does replacing every part mean it's a different vessel? Does, perhaps, replacing even one part make it a new ship? And what, as the seventeenth-century philosopher Hobbes suggested, if we were to take all the rotted timbers and reassemble them according to the original plan?[3] We would now have two ships. Which ship, if either, is the "real" Ship of Theseus? What if we were to disassemble the ship, to put the components into two equal piles, and then to use entitely new parts brought in from elsewhere to build *two* new ships. Would either of those be the real Ship of Theseus? Would both? Would neither?

The problem of change and identity is one philosophers have grappled with for millennia. For philosophers, the issue is not to find the "correct answer" to the Ship of Theseus problem, but to use it as a way of examining and questioning our assumptions, including what it means to say that something is the same, or different, or that something has an identity, or what it means for some "thing" to change. These questions are not merely theoretical. In 2005, Boyd Leon Coddington, a respected hot-rod builder and TV presenter, pled guilty to a "Ship of Theseus Fraud." In order to ease the financial problems his business faced, he had mixed parts from antique automobiles with new parts to make complete cars. That in itself is no problem, since it's doubtful there's a single antique car on the road that has all—and nothing but—its original parts. But Coddington went too far, creating new "antique" cars in order to sidestep emissions restrictions and tax liabilities.[4] In essence, the charge was that he took one antique car and turned it into many. The problems of change and identity can be very practical ones.

The Buddha was just one of many thinkers who wrestled with the problem of change and identity. The prevailing orthodoxy in his day held that each person and thing had an unchanging essence that defined it. Although there was the appearance of change on the surface, the underlying essence of each thing remained unaltered. Most of the Buddha's contemporaries seem to have believed that a person had an *atta* (in Sanskrit it's *atman*) or "real self" that was a kind of unchanging soul. ("Atta" was the ordinary word for "self," but it also came to have a more important philosophical connotation.) But this approach was deeply unsatisfying to the Buddha. It depended upon positing an essence that could never be directly experienced— and was therefore an untestable hypothesis—while the Buddha was someone who liked to verify important matters by his own experience. And, philosophically, the question arose of how an unchanging essence could in any way affect or be affected by the impermanent "shell" of matter in which it was incarnated; if the atta interacts with the body or mind then it is not unchanging.

There were moral implications of this view of the "essence" being the "true self." The problem with essentializing human beings is that in so doing we limit them. In ancient India it was believed that if you were rich and attractive, this must reveal that you had a particularly "holy" kind of atta. There was a correspondence between the invisible "real self" inside and the body within which this essence had incarnated. Conversely, if you were born into a poor family, had a menial job, or were in some way unattractive, this revealed that your inner self was spiritually flawed. These views resulted in a rigid stratification of society: a caste system in which it was believed that some people (the upper classes and their descendants) were inherently pure and spiritual, while the lower classes were to varying degrees inherently polluted, to the extent that the mere physical touch of the most polluting individuals was thought to confer a kind of spiritual "cooties" that would have to be eliminated by ritual action.

To the Buddha, all this was unacceptable, morally and intellectually. He witnessed, in his day-to-day life, high-caste individuals who acted badly, and he encountered supposedly outcast individual, at the other end of the scale who demonstrated dignity, kindness, and wisdom. And people from every stratum of society had, he believed, the potential to lead lives of moral and spiritual excellence. Because he recognized the potential for spiritual awakening in all beings, the Buddha allowed people from all walks of life—hereditary priests, warriors, workers, serfs, outcasts, men, and women—to join his monastic community, violating many of the norms of the society in which he lived. Employing a water metaphor, he said that the four social classes were like rivers flowing into the same sea; upon entering his spiritual community, individuals lost their caste identity. There was, he believed, no defining essence to a human being, and he judged individuals by their actions rather than by their gender, family, or caste. A human being had existence but no essence. A human being is a river.

If you think the beliefs in personal essences are outmoded, you might in a sense be correct, but the idea still has potency in our society. One in three organ transplant recipients believes he has taken on some of the personality traits, memories, and experiences of his organ donors.[5] Professor Bruce Hood, a cognitive neuroscientist at the University of Bristol, asked students to imagine they were in need of a heart transplant, and then showed them pictures of potential donors. Initially the students were asked how happy they would be to accept an organ from each person, but then the photographs were shown again, with each potential donor being labeled good or bad. Although there was only a small increase in interest in receiving an organ from a supposedly good person, there was a dramatic decrease in interest in accepting a donation from a supposedly bad person. The largest effect was seen when a heart offered for donation was said to have come from a murderer. In one real-life case, a British teenager had to be forcibly given a new heart because she feared she would no longer be the same person with someone else's heart beating inside her.[6] It seems we instinctively believe in essences.

At roughly the same time the Buddha was exploring the nature of the self, how to reconcile change and being was being thrashed out in the Hellenic world. Heraclitus (who lived circa 540–480 BCE in what is now Turkey) said that no man can step into the same river twice. He recognized that both the person and the river are forever changing. The man, having stepped into the river, can never at a later moment step back in. He is a new person, and the river is a new river. For Heraclitus, change was the only reality.

Heraclitus would presumably have said that there is in fact no *Vin Fiz*. Or that at least there is no thing (in the sense of a permanent, static entity) called the *Vin Fiz*. What we call the *Vin Fiz* would merely be a label imposed on a process of change. There was also, in reality, no airfield from which it took off, and no California in which it made its final touchdown, for those as well are merely ever-changing processes, lacking in any fixed essence. For Heraclitus, "All things flow, and nothing stands." For Heraclitus, all things resemble rivers, in that they are eternally changing. For Heraclitus, as for the Buddha, there is no being, only becoming. There is no identity, only change.

Parmenides, who lived in southern Italy (also about 540–480 BCE), thought that if a thing exists it must always have existed and always will exist. Change didn't really happen. For Parmenides, there was no coming into existence or ceasing to exist. Change was an illusion, and in reality things were static and permanent. Of course he saw the world around him changing, but he came to the conclusion—strictly logically—that this must be an illusion, otherwise we're left with Heraclitus's position that there is no essence to things or people, and when, for example, a single nail is replaced on Theseus's ship, the vessel is in the absurd position of being a new vessel, and therefore different from itself.

Parmenides's view isn't very far from the belief that the real part of a human being is the atta, or the essence of the self. The shell of the body—the part of a human being that changes—exists in the unreal world of the senses. The true self does not change and is eternal. From the fragments of his teachings that remain, it's not entirely clear what Parmenides's views were in detail, but they may have been similar to those held by his Indian counterparts. It's hard to imagine what Parmenides would have thought had he known about the story of the *Vin Fiz*. Perhaps he would have thought that the aircraft had a "soul" that in some sense always existed, that the appearance of its creation, journey, and destruction in the world were illusory, and that its essence carried on forever. For Parmenides, there was no change, only identity.

Empedocles (who lived from roughly 490–430 BCE in Sicily) tried to find a compromise between these two views. Like Heraclitus (and unlike Parmenides) he accepted that the perception of change was valid. We can generally trust our senses, Empedocles thought, and accept that we live in an ever-changing world. But he posited that impermanent and unchanging objects like a human being or the *Vin Fiz* were made by the coming together of the four elements, Earth, Water, Air, and Fire. (According to Socrates, Empedocles was the first Greek to unite the four elements in a single theory.) It was the elements that were eternal and indestructible. Although they may combine to make various forms and then separate again when those forms cease to exist, the elements themselves are not born or destroyed. So there was a substratum to existence that did not change, and a real appearance that did change.

To Empedocles, the *Vin Fiz* itself would be *relatively* real, but not permanent, while the four elements that composed it were also real—but *absolutely* real—and eternal. Of these two realities, the elements were the more real. Change only happened in the sensory world where we perceive the objects that are created and destroyed through the combination of the elements. In the underlying reality, there is no change in the elements, and they are "ever and always the same."[7]

Empedocles attributed the coming together and separating of the elements to two forces, love and strife, which we could parse as attraction and repulsion, and which had a moral as well as a physical dimension. Love and strife, like the elements themselves, were part of the absolutely real world, and their operation was visible as the creation and destruction of forms. In Empedocles's cosmology, the forces of strife and love oscillated around a point of balance, producing periods of universal growth and universal destruction. He called this balance "The Vortex." You may notice a contradiction between the idea that the elements are unchanging and the idea that the elements are rearranged by strife and love. This points in fact to a fundamental problem with the idea of identity, which I see as fundamentally the tension between the reality of never-ending change, or "becoming," and the way our minds "fix" things by seeing them—if you recall our discussion of the verb "to be"—as "existing" and "remaining."

Democritus, if you can bear with me for one more Greek philosopher, actually *was* born in Greece—unlike the others just mentioned—and lived circa 460–370 BCE. Like Empedocles, he believed that there was an underlying reality composed of something unchanging, but he dispensed with the idea of the four elements and saw the world as being fundamentally composed of *atoms*—which were of different kinds—and *void,* or empty space. For Democritus, atoms were the smallest possible units of matter because they, in his view, did not contain void and were therefore indivisible. Democritus was a materialist, doing away with the notion that things happened "for a purpose," and denying that some creator or intelligent design was behind the universe. He even saw the "soul" as composed of a special type of atom, which dispersed upon an individual's death, only to be reconstituted in other individuals, much as the carbon in your body will re-enter the carbon cycle and ultimately become part of other living beings after your death. Like Heraclitus, Democritus held that everything "flows," but unlike Heraclitus he also held that behind the appearance of change there were unchanging and eternal atoms. We now know, of course, that there are atoms but that they are not unchanging or eternal. But Democritus, almost accidentally (he had no empirical data to support his theories), came very close to the modern scientific understanding of matter and to scientific materialism.

Compared to that of his Hellenic near-contemporaries, the Buddha's concern with the field of change and identity was substantially different. The Buddha had no interest in formulating theories that explained the nature of the universe around him. He believed that speculation about the origins and ultimate destiny of the physical world were pointless and a distraction from what he saw as the most meaningful inquiry we can engage in, which is why we suffer and how to end suffering. In a potent image, he said that speculating about whether the cosmos was infinite or finite, eternal or not eternal, or whether the body and soul were the same or different, is to be like a man shot with a poisoned arrow. By the time he found an answer to all his questions about who made the arrow, what the arrow was made of, what kind of bow it was fired with, and other such details, the poison would have taken effect and the man would have died. The important thing is to pull out the arrow.[8] The Buddha therefore did not teach chemistry, mathematics, or astronomy.[9] He did, however, have a keen interest in the field of change and identity, because he believed that views on such matters had a direct bearing on the amount and kind of suffering we experience in life. And he paid exquisite attention to the workings of the mind in pursuing and understanding the origins and the allaying of suffering.

One of the most well-known statements of the Buddha is that all compounded things are impermanent (*anicca*), that that all compounded things are unsatisfactory (*dukkha*), and that all phenomena lack inherent self-existence (*anatta*). This agrees with Heraclitus's position that everything is change—or at least that all compounded things are change. But this word "compounded" suggests something like Empedocles's view that the world of phenomena we experience is the result of the elements coming together, or Democritus's view that it is compounded of atoms. Buddhism appears at first glance to have a similar view. A human being, some Buddhist texts explain, is the coming together of different physical and mental factors, just as a chariot is the coming together of various pieces of wood and metal. You can point to no one part of the chariot—the pole, axle, wheels, frame, yoke, etc.—that is in itself the chariot. Nor is there some invisible chariot-y essence that exists outside the visible components. As we've seen, it's not just the coming together of these parts but their functioning as a means of transportation that would make them a chariot. Similarly, a human being is compounded of different things functioning as a human being. The Buddhist tradition thus finds many ways to dissect the idea of a person or self—including the Six Element Reflection. So far we have something that seems closely to resemble Empedocles's view of the underlying reality of the Four Elements. However, the Buddha did not posit any underlying substratum that was permanent and eternal. The point of the Six Element Practice is not to see a human being as made up of the Six Elements, because those elements too are impermanent phenomena. The point is to undermine any basis for clinging to an idea of a separate and unchanging self. To return to a water analogy, a river is made up of uncountable numbers of small currents and eddies. But each of these currents or eddies is in turn capable of being analyzed further, and so the currents and eddies too have no essence.

To the Buddha, the Six Elements did not represent an underlying and unchanging reality. The elements too were caught up in great cycles of creation and destruction. His understanding seems to have been that at the end of "world cycles" (which took place on a scale of billions of years), the elements we know will be destroyed and a new cycle of creation of the elements would begin afresh, in something resembling the "Big Bang" that created our universe. If you see in this a contradiction to my earlier assertion that the Buddha was not interested in things like the origin of the universe, you make a good point. What I would answer is that he was not interested in these things as religious teachings: he neither required his followers to believe in a particular cosmological theory nor was any such belief seen as affecting their spiritual progress. He was probably just using an existing cosmological myth to make a point about impermanence.

While many of the Buddha's contemporaries believed that the elements were eternal (i.e., they too had indestructible essences), it's clear that he saw them as no more than transient phenomena, with ultimately no more "essence" than a human being: "When even this external ... element, great as it is, is seen to be impermanent, subject to destruction, disappearance, and change, what of this body, which is clung to by craving and lasts but a little while? There can be no considering that as 'I' or 'mine' or 'I am.'"[10]

Young at Heart

We tend to think of the body as being relatively static and separate from the world around it. We know all too well that in order to stay alive we have to eat and excrete, but most people seem to think of this in terms of a relatively static body burning energy and of food and water passing through the body. We don't think so much in terms of a continuous replacement of the body. And yet the latter is what's really going on. The body, with variations from tissue to tissue, is in a constant state of turnover, with cells breaking down and being replaced on a constant basis. Like the *Vin Fiz,* the body's component parts are continually replaced. As we reflect on this, we can come to appreciate that the body is not a thing but a process, its identity or selfhood a mirage held together in the mind as a mere assumption.

The body is constantly changing. Some cells have a high turnover. Cells in the gut lining, for example, are replaced every five days because they're continually traumatized by exposure to corrosive gastric acids, harsh enzymes, and the mechanical stresses of passing roughage. Likewise, the cells in the skin's outer layer only last about two weeks, due to their exposure to the elements and because of damage from friction. These tissues have evolved as disposable coatings, sacrificed in order to protect underlying tissues. Red blood cells are similarly disposable; they get a pummeling as they slam through the body's blood vessels. Whirling in the turbulence of the heart and arteries, and squeezed through narrow capillaries, they last only 120 days. Your liver, roughly speaking, is just more than a year old. Cells in the liver, which is the body's detoxification plant, last about 300 to 500 days, according to Dr. Markus Grompe, who studies metabolic liver diseases at the Oregon Health and Science University.[11] Even your bones are subject to turnover and to constant remodeling. In your bones, cells called osteoclasts act as tiny demolition squads, deconstructing the bone around them, while other cells called osteoblasts are busy remodeling, allowing your bones to adapt to new mechanical stresses. The net result of this competition is that your entire skeleton is replaced every ten or so years. Your body is younger than you are.

All this has been known for some time, because the turnover of some parts of the body can be observed fairly easily. But for other tissues, the situation was less clear. A great deal of controversy has long centered, for example, on whether the brain creates new cells, or whether you march from childhood into adulthood with a steadily dwindling supply of gray matter. Interested in whether the brain could in fact generate new cells, Dr. Jonas Frisén, a stem-cell biologist at the Karolinska Institute, in Stockholm, Sweden, devised a new method of dating the body's tissues. He found that on average the cells in an adult's body might be as young as seven to ten years, but that there was considerable variation, from mere days almost to a lifetime.

Frisén realized that the radioactive carbon-14 produced by the superpowers' atmospheric nuclear tests between 1955 and 1963 acted as a marker that would allow the age of DNA within cells to be measured. Carbon-14 exists naturally at a steady level in the atmosphere, but the atmospheric nuclear tests of the fifties and sixties more than doubled the natural amount. This pulse of radioactive carbon was absorbed into plants, and through plants into animals, including ourselves. Because DNA is a stable compound, the amount of carbon-14 in the DNA of a tissue's cells can be used to determine the age, on average, of that tissue.

Frisén found that in people in their late thirties, the average cell age in the muscles between the ribs was 15.1 years. Ignoring the surface cells of the gut, with their high turnover rate, the average age of cells in the gut's main body was similar to rib muscle, at 15.9 years. Cells in the brain, however, were found to be about the same age as the individual being tested, suggesting that not many new brain cells are produced in adulthood. At the moment (and the science is very preliminary) it seems that the neurons of the cerebral cortex, the inner lens cells in the eye, and possibly the muscle cells in the heart are with us for life. These are the body's equivalent of the wing-strut and rudder that made it to the West Coast on the *Vin Fiz's* transcontinental journey. But the rest of the body is considerably younger than you are, and most of your body is around seven to ten years of age. In one sense you are a second-grader.

You may be wondering, why, if your skin is replaced every two weeks, are you getting older? Why, if the body is capable of regenerating itself, do you age? Oddly, the science of aging is still unclear. It seems that our mitochondria, the cells' powerhouses, have lost the ability to repair their DNA. Aging may happen because the mitochondria simply wear out and the body's ability to generate energy declines. Another theory has it that the DNA of our cells, despite the body's best attempts to repair mutations, eventually accumulates enough mistakes that we can no longer effectively produce new proteins. A third theory is that the stem cells upon which the body relies to produce new cells become feebler as they age. But whatever the reason, it's obvious that what's being replaced is not of the same quality as the original. Physiologically, it would seem that *"plus ça change, plus c'est la même chose"* does not apply. It's more the other way around: the more things try to stay the same, the more they change.

We can use the power of imagination to picture this constant change going on in the body, to have a sense that the body you're sensing right now—the body that you think is you, or that you inhabit—is in the process of dissolving and being rebuilt. The body is not static. It is not unchanging. It's an eddy, a whirlpool, a river, a waterfall. However we see the body, its essential characteristic is that it is transitional—always on the way to being something else. We may identify with it as being us. We may not wish it to change and be unhappy about it changing, but change it must. And as a changing process, it's essentially ungraspable. You can try to catch hold of water flowing in a river, but it simply slips through your fingers. In a deep sense there is no "thing" there for you to hold onto.

If the ego is grasping after some kind of "essence" in the body—something that is uniquely us and that endures unchanged over time—we may be tempted to latch onto those cerebral cortex cells Frisén identified as being with us for life. Perhaps we may think of them as being the locus of selfhood. The brain, after all, is where we store information about ourselves. It's where memories are formed and where they reside. It's where we ultimately perceive, and where we think. And so it's perhaps natural to look there for the physical correlate of our sense of self. But even here, there is change. Frisén's study looked just at the DNA of neurons and not the cells that surround them. It's not the neurons themselves that accompany us through life's journey, but the DNA they contain. The molecules comprising the cells housing that DNA are constantly being broken down and replaced, like the aircraft around Calbraith Rodgers as it flew across America. A neuron itself is a cellular *Vin Fiz,* with subcellular components being replaced as the cell traverses the continent of life. The cell membranes, the organelles where biochemical processes take place, the chemicals that transfer information around the cell and to the rest of the body—all are continually being replaced within the neuron.

The ego may yet grasp after the DNA that endures within the ever-changing matrix of our neurons. But everywhere we look there is change, and even the DNA at the heart of your neurons is no exception. DNA exists in a dangerous world full of unrelentingly corrosive metabolic processes and is subject to damage and repair. DNA breaks and is repaired. It becomes corrupted and either must be fixed or the cell will be damaged or die. Most of your DNA survives intact, but DNA itself is not entirely static, and you don't die with exactly the same DNA you started with. DNA itself is dynamic and is a process, not a thing. In any event, although our DNA is a crucial component of our bodies, it's clearly not sufficient in itself to make a self. DNA can't think, feel, remember, or have experiences.

In my own reflections during the Six Element Meditation, I don't find it necessary to consider the physiological fine print of all the details of tissue replacement. To do so would change a meditative experience into something more like a doctoral thesis defense. But the science that engrosses me outside meditation lingers in a general sense in the mind and nourishes my practice. I bear in mind at least the principle that this body I identify with is in a constant state of self-replacement, and specific examples often come to mind. Heraclitus's aphorism "Everything flows and nothing abides," encapsulates the feeling I get as I reflect on the body. In my imagination, I sense the body as flowing. From moment to moment, your body is changing. The body, with everything else in the universe, is in a constant state of death and rebirth. Heraclitus's river is always a different river, and your body is always a different body. This is the perspective I let sink into my mind as I meditate.

The effect of reflecting in this way is ultimately to experience a degree of liberation. Trying to identify ourselves with a body that is ultimately ungraspable is an inherently frustrating task, and we experience a kind of relief as we let go progressively. Really seeing and accepting the reality of constant change in the body frees us from some of our fear of aging and illness. The energy that would normally go into our clinging and into worrying about our own imperma-nence frees up and is available for more creative pursuits. Being less concerned about ourselves, our bodies, and how others might see us allows us to be more compassionate; the less we're concerned about ourselves, the more we can be concerned about others.

CHAPTER SIX

Trapped in the Elements

"Think not I am what I appear."
—Byron[1]

I once spent four months on an intensive retreat in the mountains near Alicante, Spain. In the limestone cliffs bounding the southern side of the retreat center was a natural amphitheater I loved to explore. At the back of the amphitheater, generations of goatherds had piled up fallen rocks to make a corral where they could protect their animals; to the left of the corral was the cave itself—a narrow fissure that plunged back diagonally into the cliff. High within this tight space were ledges covered in soft, dusty soil where the goatherds themselves slept, waking up to a glorious dawn view of the Mediterranean Sea. I've always been fascinated by caves, and I spent a fitful night up on one dusty ledge, in the impenetrable dark of a moonless and cloudy night, bats flitting overhead and the strange gnawing fear in the belly that comes from lying in a place that is not only unfamiliar but also wild, mythic, and primeval.

Halfway through the retreat, during a group meditation in which we were reflecting on the elements, I slipped into a waking dream. I was exploring the cave at the back of the amphitheater. I clambered through the ever-narrowing space to its very end and discovered something I'd missed on my previous excursions. At ground level, right at the narrow back of the underground chamber, was a low, slit-like opening. I was intrigued. I got down close to the earth, and peering though the cramped space was excited to see another cavern beyond, far grander than the one I was in. Driven by a compulsion to explore the unknown, I got down on my belly and started wiggling through the tight opening, commando-style, using my elbows for propulsion. I crawled through a long channel—longer than my body. I was most of the way through when I realized, to my alarm, that I'd become stuck, my shoulders gripped by the rough limestone. I tried to wriggle my way backward but couldn't move. My elbows were pinned by my sides, preventing me from moving either forward or backward. Panic overwhelmed me. My chest was tight and I could hardly breathe. My face was pressed almost into the earth. I was trapped in what was in effect a stone coffin. I was completely helpless, unable to move. And I was on my own. If I shouted, my voice would be swallowed up by the cavern. Worse, I hadn't told anyone where I was, and often no one came up here for days at a time. I knew I was going to die. Then, suddenly, I was back in the meditation hall, sitting quietly in a row of still figures, with incense smoking in silence and candles flickering, sweat trickling down my back. And my first conscious thought was this: *I'm stuck in the Earth Element. I'm trapped by my attachment to the body.*

It often seems as if the things we cling to own us. When we're caught up in compulsion, it seems that it's the object of our desire that has the power. A good film is "gripping." Drugs "have a hold" on an addict's life. We are "captivated" by beauty, "ensnared" by temptation. We see the object of our attraction as the active agent, ourselves as the victims. In my imagination, it was the elements that held onto me, but this was just a poetic way of saying that I clung to the elements, that my sense of self was entangled in the body. This is the whole point of reflecting on the elements—to realize how much we cling to them, to realize how much this clinging limits us, and to help us let go.

The first five reflections in the Six Element Practice are intended to help us recognize and let go of our clinging to the body. They're intended to help us free ourselves from fearfully clinging to a narrow identification with our physical form. This chapter and those that follow are offered as opportunities to reflect on our experience. You have an opportunity to engage imaginatively with the material. You have an opportunity to notice the thoughts and feelings that arise as you read, and you have the opportunity to engage with those thoughts and feelings in a process of exploration. I invite you to turn words into experience, and then to observe and learn from that experience.

Our Bodies, Our Selves?

As you're reading these words, become aware of your body. Pause to spend a few minutes feeling your body's weight, its substance. Observe the body not in a cold, distant, or critical way, but with appreciation and love. The two of you have been through a lot together. The body deserves your love. So, as best you can, adopt an attitude of kindly awareness as you notice your physical form. Feel the contact between different parts of the body. Notice, as the Discourse encourages us, the solid parts of this form: the skin, the muscles, the sense of the bones pushing down though the flesh, the teeth, the hair, the nails. Experience the solidity of all this. And let your mind imagine the parts of the body you can't directly feel: the heart, lungs, intestines, liver, kidneys. All of this, according to the "Discourse on the Elements," is clung-to.

As you observe the body, and as you imaginatively connect with it, ask yourself, what kind of relationship do you have with your body? Do you have a sense that your body is you? That you are the body? Is the body something you own? Do you exist in the body? Is the body just a part of you, so that it exists within you? Is your body your friend? A partner? Or even an enemy? Just sit with those questions and see what arises.

Continuing this reflection, we can conduct some thought experiments to determine the extent to which we cling to the body. So, imagine how you would feel if your front teeth were lost or damaged in an accident. How would you feel about losing your hair, or to be less extreme, about merely stepping outside on a bad hair day? How do you feel when you develop a blemish on your face? How do you feel when you see yourself naked in a mirror? How do you feel about aging? Does it matter to you what happens to your body after death? Do you have any resistance to the idea of your organs being donated after you die? If so, why would that be, given that you won't have need for them any more? How do you feel imagining your corpse being cremated or decaying underground?

As for our attitudes toward others, in what ways do you judge people by their bodies? Do you find yourself liking or disliking people purely on their appearance? Do you make negative assumptions about someone's personality if they are unattractive? Do you make positive assumptions if someone is conventionally attractive? Do some people simply look untrustworthy to you, even if you don't know them?

It may be that not all questions I've chosen resonate with you. Some strongly touch me, others less so. I like to think I'm not very caught up in my appearance, but then again I've had anxiety dreams in which I've lost my hair or teeth; it's a rare day that I don't wish I had a trimmer and slimmer body; and if I don't dye my hair, I'll find myself glancing toward the hair-coloring section in my local drugstore. I do not welcome aging. I sometimes feel anxious about the minor ways in which my body no longer functions as well as it once did, and I wish on some level that I could turn back the biological clock. I fear the death of the body. I'm by no means obsessed with these issues, but I have to admit I'm still emotionally caught up with my body, and I believe we all are to a greater or lesser extent.

So I have to admit I'm still stuck in the elements in the sense that my sense of well-being hinges, at least in part, upon my body's appearance. And I assume that you, unless you are an exceptional individual, also cling to the body. I'm stuck in the elements in that I see the body as "me" and as "mine." I identify with it and when I judge my body I feel I'm judging myself. I feel that when others judge my body they are judging me. Probably you're the same. We think that the body is us, and that we are in the body—not entirely perhaps, but substantially, enough for it to matter. Enough for us to suffer.

In many cases we get caught up in assuming that the body is the person, and the person is the body. Alexander Todorov, an assistant professor of psychology and public affairs at Princeton University, has studied how we make first impressions. He found that within a tenth of a second we make deep and long-lasting judgments about a person's character—whether they are likable or unlikable, trustworthy or devious, aggressive or friendly. Just by seeing a face for one hundred milliseconds.[2] And those snap judgments, as he discovered by comparing them with the actual personality profiles of the photographs' subjects, turn out to be staggeringly inaccurate. Worse, their accuracy declines the longer we look at photographs of people we don't know.

Todorov and his colleague Charles Ballew discovered that they were even able to predict, with a high degree of accuracy, the outcome of political races in the United States by noting how people responded to a brief glimpse of candidates' faces.[3] They were able to correctly predict the outcome in 68.6 percent of gubernatorial and 72.4 percent of senate races in this way. These figures give a sense of how much we believe the body is the person, and that the person is the body. We unconsciously assume we can know a person's interior world—their character—by means of a lightning assessment of their form. This is the kind of thing I mean when I say we are trapped in the elements. We think of our selves as being bound up with the body, and because we assume that's also true for others, when we see another person's physical form we think we are seeing the self.

These assumptions limit our ability to relate compassionately to others. When we judge others in this way, our assumptions trump reality. We can no longer see the other person for who he or she is, and instead we relate to our idea—usually false—of who he or she is. Freeing ourselves from the attachment to the elements is to free ourselves to be more compassionate, to treat people as people rather than opportunities to exercise our prejudices.

We may believe that we are the body, that the body is us, or that the body is one part of us, along with other non-physical parts like the mind or soul. We may believe that we are in the body, or that we own the body. We may even believe all these things at different times, even though some of these opinions contradict each other. We'll be dissecting these assumptions by reflecting on the body and our relationship to it. We'll use the traditional form of the reflection on the elements, but because our modern understandings of anatomy and physiology are far more sophisticated than in Gautama's time, and because we now have powerful tools for analyzing the body's makeup, we won't limit ourselves to a strictly traditional approach to the practice. We'll integrate contemporary knowledge of anatomy and physiology into the reflections on the elements.

CHAPTER SEVEN

The Communal Self

"No single event can awaken within us a stranger whose existence we had never suspected. To live is to be slowly born."
— Antoine de Saint Exupéry[1]

In 1995, Karen Keegan, a fifty-two-year-old mother of three who lived just outside Boston, Massachusetts, received an unsettling call from her hospital. Karen was told she had a disease eating away at her kidneys and needed a transplant as soon as possible. Because of the urgent nature of her condition, her doctors suggested she find who in her family might be willing to donate a kidney. Because children share half of any given parent's genetic code, there's a good chance that a child's cells will have matching cell surface proteins, meaning that a transplanted organ won't be rejected as foreign by the body's defenses. Karen's three sons, and, for good measure, her husband, went in for testing to discover whether they would make suitable donors.[2]

A couple of weeks later the lab results came in, and Karen received another call from the hospital, scarcely less unsettling than the first.

Her physician told her they had a "very unusual situation" to discuss: the DNA testing on her sons revealed that two of them didn't match her DNA. These sons shared DNA with their father, but were only distantly related to Karen. To be blunt, she could not be the mother of her own children. Naturally, hospitals conducting DNA tests uncover the opposite situation—where the presumed father turns out to be unrelated to a child—from time to time, but Karen's situation was something new. Karen was of course convinced the hospital had to be wrong. After all, she was *there* when her sons were born. She gave birth to them. She felt the pain. The results must have been wrong. So the hospital ran the tests again—only to get the same readings. There had been no laboratory error.

It would be natural to assume there must have been a mix-up with the babies at the hospital. But not only would it be unlikely that one woman would *twice* end up taking home the wrong child, Karen would have taken home the same woman's children both times. Plus, the sons' DNA *did* match the father's. Karen's husband was the father of all three boys, but Karen was not the mother of two of them. Things went crazy for Karen at that point. When her doctor cast around in the scientific community for explanations, there were suggestions that Karen might have implanted another woman's embryos into her womb, that she might have had fertility treatment with another woman's eggs, that she might have stolen the children. Many thought Karen must be at fault because their attitude was, as Karen put it, that "DNA is never wrong." Karen's family was plunged into sadness and confusion as they tried to make sense of information that was quite literally unbelievable.

Karen's doctor had a feeling that something didn't add up. After considering and discarding many theories, she realized that they'd done all the tests on Karen's blood. Maybe something about her blood was unusual? Perhaps they should test DNA from other parts of her body? This seemed absurd, but sometimes when nothing makes sense all you can do is something nonsensical. Karen went in for more tests. The inside of her mouth was scraped, hair samples were plucked, and biopsies of her liver, thyroid, bladder, and skin were taken. And that's when things began to get really strange. Karen, it transpired, had two sets of DNA. She was genetically not one person, but two people sharing the same body. And it was the other person— the stranger inside Karen—who was the mother of two of her boys.

Karen was a twin. She had had a nonidentical twin sister who had fused with her in the womb, with the two siblings becoming "one" individual—Karen. It's not even correct to say that Karen "was" a twin. She *is* a twin. Both sisters are alive, and Karen is both of them. Parts of Karen's body are her unnamed sister, while some are her own. The ovaries, thyroid, and bladder are a mixture of the sister's and Karen's tissue, while for some unexplained reason Karen's blood is entirely her own. Two of her sons had been born from the sister's ovarian tissue, while the third was from one of Karen's own eggs.[3]

Karen's condition is rare, but it has a name that she first learned from her doctor. Karen is a "chimera."

The Chimera

In Greek mythology, the Chimera was a creature—a monster—composed of various parts of many animals. Homer's *The Iliad* depicts the Chimera as "a thing of immortal make, not human, lion-fronted and snake behind, a goat in the middle, and snorting out the breath of the terrible flame of bright fire." Hesiod, somewhat later, envisaged the

Chimera as a "creature fearful, great, swift-footed and strong, who had three heads, one of a grim-eyed lion; in her hinderpart, a dragon; and in her middle, a goat, breathing forth a fearful blast of blazing fire." In Greek and Roman mythology, hybrid animals are often treated with great suspicion, and even fear. Medusa, the Gorgon, the woman with snake hair, was a monster. As was the Minotaur, who was half man and half bull. The half-horse, half-man Centaur was seen as barbaric and uncivilized, prone to raping and pillaging. The classic Chimera, being a composite of not two, or three, but *four* creatures—taking her fire-breathing as a sign that there is some dragon DNA in the mix—is particularly monstrous and fearful. (Pegasus, the winged horse, was the immortal offspring of the god Poseidon, and perhaps for that reason the Greeks looked on him favorably, as we still do.)

In modern scientific terms, a chimera is an animal with two or more genetically distinct cell populations. Biological chimeras sometimes arise naturally, but more often these days are deliberately induced in the laboratory via the fusion of two different fertilized ova. They have been useful in helping scientists understand the immunology and development of the embryo.

The first time I saw a photograph of a chimera—the fusion of a goat and a sheep—I felt disgust. The creature looked pitiful, with patchy hair that clearly belonged to two different species. It seemed sad, its head hanging, almost as if ashamed of its own monstrosity. Even the portmanteau name given to it by researchers—"geep" (a combination of goat and sheep)—seemed ugly and unnatural. The unease that we commonly experience in relation to chimeras may be a measure of our desire for a biologically tidy world. We like the idea of clearly defined species in their neat little conceptual boxes.

Karen Keegan is a "tetragametic" chimera. Her body arose from four sets of gametes—two eggs and two sperm—rather than the more conventional one sperm plus one egg. The condition of tetragametic chimerism is becoming better known, to the point where it's entered popular culture. A well-known *CSI: Crime Scene Investigation* television episode hinges on a rape case in which a suspect's DNA—taken from a cheek swab—doesn't match semen recovered from a victim. His semen is actually that of the vanished twin brother who shares his body. Eventually he's caught when cells from other parts of his body are tested. In 2004, after winning a gold at the Summer Olympics in Athens, the U.S. cyclist Tyler Hamilton was accused of "blood doping," or trying to boost his body's oxygen-carrying capacity by transfusing himself with another person's blood. He was allowed to keep his medal on a technicality, but at another sporting event two weeks later Hamilton was again accused of blood doping. When tests revealed that his blood contained two different cell types, his lawyers, with the aid of a Massachusetts Institute of Technology scientist, argued he was a chimera: the result of a "vanished twin" who had been absorbed into his body and was contributing cells to his blood. But this theory didn't fly with the U.S. Anti-Doping Agency, and Hamilton was given a two-year suspension. Hamilton has never admitted wrongdoing, but his case is an interesting instance of chimerism (or alleged chimerism) in popular culture. Chimeras: coming soon to a daytime soap near you.

A second case of questionable maternity—rivaling Karen Keegan's for peculiarity and with even more soap-opera potential—emerged in 2002, when Lydia Fairchild, who was pregnant with her third child, separated from her husband, Jaime Townsend, and applied for welfare support. The welfare department demanded a DNA test to prove that Townsend was in fact the father of the children. As with Karen Keegan, it turned out that the children were the father's but that the mother was unrelated to them. Fairchild was sued for fraud. It was assumed that she was claiming welfare for someone else's children or running some kind of surrogacy scam—and prosecutors demanded that her two children be taken into care. It was only when a sharp-eyed and impressively fair-minded lawyer for the prosecution found an article about the Keegan case that further testing was done and it was confirmed that Fairchild was a chimera. As Fairchild's third pregnancy came to term, the judge ordered that a witness be present to ensure that blood samples be taken directly from the mother and child. Two weeks later, DNA tests confirmed that Lydia Fairchild was not the biological mother of the third child either.[4]

Chimeric individuals may go their entire lives without discovering that they're composites of two different people. In some cases there may be subtle signs like each eye being a slightly different color or the body hair having asymmetrical patterns. Some chimeras have skin that is obviously of two different tones, and these can form Blaschko's Lines—V-shaped patterns formed by the skin being a mosaic of two different tissue types. In individuals where the two skin types are identical in color, these lines may only be observable under UV light. The chimeric individual may be male, female, or a hermaphrodite and may have organs with different sets of chromosomes. Since about half the chimeras formed by the fusing of two nonidentical siblings would be hermaphroditic, and since such conditions are rare, it's presumed that this type of chimerism is very uncommon. A *New Scientist* article from 2003 estimated that about thirty chimeras similar to Karen Keegan had been identified. But the true incidence is unknown; cases have only emerged in exceptional circumstances, like Karen Keegan's and Lydia Fairchild's.[5]

Chimeras are becoming more common as a result of in vitro fertilization procedures, or IVF. The drugs given to make a woman ovulate usually make her produce more than one egg at a time, and often several embryos are transplanted into the womb on the understanding that some won't survive. Because of the transplantation of multiple embryos, the chances of two of them merging increase, and it's thought that the embryos bumping into each other in the petri dish may encourage fusion. This apparent wastefulness is necessary because of the immense expense of IVF treatment—if you're going to spend tens of thousands of dollars on getting pregnant, you don't want a single embryo to be transplanted only to discover it's non-viable.

If it wasn't for Karen's acute need for a kidney transplant, and the subsequent DNA tests she and her family underwent, she never would have discovered that she was in fact twins. And had the embryonic reshuffling gone slightly differently and her blood and the three ova that gave rise to her sons belonged to the same sister, she would not know to this day. Karen later learned that had things gone differently in the womb—had the two fertilized ova fused *after* the first four days—she would have become a Siamese twin. "When you hear that," Karen says, "you immediately have a more concrete vision of two selves. It brought home the reality that I really was a twin." She now lives with a "shadow feeling of loss" at the fact she might have had a separate sister.[6]

Recently I gave a DNA sample, in the form of a cheek swab, as part of *National Geographic's* Genographic Project, which traces the wanderings of humanity's many branches back to our emergence from Africa. I could see my genetic ancestry laid out on a map, and follow the trail of my forebears as they wandered out of Ethiopia, through the Middle East, into Central Asia, Russia, the European mainland, and up into Scotland. As I looked at the report detailing my genetic heritage, I found myself wondering: How do I know that I am not a composite individual? How do I know there is not a stranger living silently within me? The simple answer is that I don't. And probably you don't either. Karen Keegan certainly didn't, and neither did Lydia Fairchild. Unless you've had extensive DNA tests of multiple tissues from your body, it's possible that half the human cells in your body belong to another individual—a vanished twin. Any one of us could be a twin, a composite individual, and not know it.

As part of our exploration of our sense of individuality, let's consider this. Imagine that your body is like a jigsaw, with half its pieces being you and half being a lost sibling. As you let that thought sink in, how do you feel about your "self"? Do you feel augmented or diminished? Or both? Is it an unsettling thought? How would you feel about the stranger within if he or she were sharing your body?

The thought that I may not be entirely "me" is one I find unsettling. If I imagine myself as a chimeric individual—and I'm unlikely ever to discover whether or not I actually am—I initially feel a sense of distaste to be sharing my body, as if I've been invaded, partly taken over. There's been a kind of partial *Invasion of the Body Snatchers.* The ownership of what I'd thought of as unequivocally me is now in question. I no longer "own" half my body. But as I continue to play this game of imagining that I am a chimera, I grow more curious. What would this twin have been like had he been born, had he not "vanished"? What would his name have been? What would it have been like for me, growing up as a twin? Which parts of me are me, and which parts are "him"? Does it even make sense to think of a "me" and a "him"—and which is which, anyway? I try to imagine what it would be like if "I" had been absorbed into "him" rather than the other way around. But that reflection brings up confusion: what difference would it make? Perhaps my brain comes from my vanished twin, in which case maybe I am him; and the genes identified by the Genographic Project, which I'd assumed were my genetic self, are "the other." My mind is tying itself in knots, and I then find myself grasping after the simplicity of thoughts such as "It doesn't matter. It's all me anyway." But that's not entirely satisfying, because half of what I'm claiming as my own, as my physical self, is not actually me at all. Disgust, curiosity, and confusion seem to be the three things I most strongly feel when I consider myself as a potential chimera. And those three responses seem to be how the Chimera of myth was regarded as well.

As we've seen, there's good reason to believe that tetragametic chimerism is very rare. You almost certainly—almost—are not one. But it turns out that you are a chimera of sorts. We all are.

The Human Commune

The classical Greek Chimera was considered to be female, which is appropriate given that many people—perhaps all of us—are chimeras of our own and our mother's cells. You may have been trying to break free from your mother's influence for years, but perhaps you never will: cells from your mother's body can cross the placental barrier and infiltrate your own body, in a process called "microchimerism." These maternal cells can settle down anywhere in the body, including the blood, heart, liver, and thymus gland. Your mother is quite literally inside your head, and I find myself wondering if this explains some of the times I hear a familiar voice from childhood lecturing me about my bad habits. These cellular interlopers have been shown to live within the offspring's body for decades, and they may be with us for life. You are not just you—you're your mother too.

And the reverse process takes place as well, with cells from the fetus making their way into the mother's body. Some 80 to 90 percent of women have been found to carry their children's cells in their blood during pregnancy, and it's been shown that they can carry them for decades afterward. If you're a woman who has been pregnant, you are in some sense your children. But this cellular promiscuity doesn't end there. If you have older siblings, cells from their bodies will have crossed over into your mother, and some of those cells may have migrated back into your body while you were a fetus. Since roughly one-third of pregnancies don't make it beyond the first three months, you may even have inside you cells from siblings you never knew you had. And since your mother may well be carrying cells from *her* mother, bits of your grandmother may be living inside you as well. And if your mother was a younger sibling, then cells from your aunts and uncles will have made the transplacental trip from their bodies to yours via your grandmother and mother.

Microchimerism seems to be implicated in some autoimmune disorders, such as lupus and rheumatoid arthritis. It's also suspected that some heart disease in children is caused by a reaction to maternal cardiac cells within the child's heart. But just as a mother picks up a fallen child and kisses a skinned knee to make it better, her cells may also come to the rescue of her injured child. When the immunologist Dr. J. Lee Nelson, of the Fred Hutchinson Cancer Research Center, in Seattle, looked in the pancreases of four individuals, including a diabetic patient, she found maternal insulin-producing beta cells in all of them. While mother's little helpers were found in even the healthy pancreases, twice as many beta cells were found in the diabetic pancreas. Mom was there to help heal a pancreatic "owie."[7] And some researchers, like Anne Stevens, then working with Dr. Nelson at the Fred Hutchinson Cancer Research Center, suspect that the maternal heart cells embedded in the cardiac tissue of the child may be trying to repair already damaged tissue.

Chimeric cells may also come from a fraternal (that is, nonidentical) twin, without the complete fusing of the embryos that created Karen's and Lydia's composite identities. Chimerism in humans was in fact first discovered when some individuals were found to have not one but two blood types. Studies revealed that blood cells had migrated from one twin to another when their blood supplies in the womb had become entangled, with cells taking up residence in the sibling and making him or her into a composite person, at least in terms of his or her blood. This kind of chimerism is more common than you may think. Although you may not have a twin now, it's possible that you had one in the womb, and that he or she donated his or her cells to you and was then reabsorbed. According to Charles Boklage, a professor in the Department of Pediatrics in the Brody School of Medicine and adjunct professor of biology at East Carolina University, a twin is quietly reabsorbed in up to an eighth of all pregnancies, with no suspicion that a sibling had ever existed. Other researchers, however, put the incidence of Vanishing Twin Syndrome at about 6 percent of all pregnancies.[8]

Any one of us may be a human menagerie—a commune of several individuals, including fraternal siblings, twins, mother, aunts, uncles, grandmother, and even all of the above—cohabiting under the guise of being a single individual. As one writer said, the thought of playing host to cells from all these different people "may offend your sense of individuality."[9]

Notice how you feel as you reflect on this. Become aware of your body both experientially and as an image in your mind. And then imagine that cells from your relatives are fluorescing from within like neon. They're a tiny glowing minority within your body, but they stand out like lights on a Christmas tree or nighttime cities seen from space. These are the strangers within. They are you, but they are not you. How is your sense of individuality affected by this thought? Do you feel differently about yourself when you consider that you may be a composite individual?

CHAPTER EIGHT

The Earth Element

"Teach your children what we have taught our children,
that the earth is our mother. Whatever befalls the earth befalls
the sons of the earth. If men spit upon the ground,
they spit upon themselves."
—CHIEF SEATTLE[1]

Voltaire noted that "Originality is nothing but judicious imitation."[2] There is nothing as creative as life, and life borrows without shame. There is not a single atom, not a single subatomic particle within your body that is self-originated. You did not create any of the matter of the body that you think of as yours and take to be you. The entire human body is borrowed from the outside world. The entire human body, as it is being created and sustained, is on loan from— and ultimately belongs to—that which is not you. An awareness of this can lead to a greater sense of humility, gratitude, and freedom.

In exploring the interconnected and impermanent nature of the body, we start with the Earth Element. Gautama's suggestion was to consider that "the internal Earth Element and the external element are simply Earth Element." In other words, the notion that there is a "you" Earth Element as opposed to an "other" Earth Element is a false one. All of the Earth Element—internal or external—is one, and is neither self nor other. The body exists only as a part of this one Earth Element. With our physical form in mind, we begin to reflect on where this body came from.

> "What, Bhikkhu, [i.e. monk] is the earth element? The earth element may be either internal or external. What is the internal earth element? Whatever internally, belonging to oneself, is solid, solidified, and clung-to, that is, head-hairs, body-hairs, nails, teeth, skin, flesh, sinews, bones, bone-marrow, kidneys, heart, liver, diaphragm, spleen, lungs, intestines, mesentery, contents of the stomach, feces, or whatever else internally, belonging to oneself, is solid, solidified, and clung-to: this is called the internal earth element. Now the internal earth element and the external element are simply earth element. And that should be seen as it actually is with proper wisdom thus: 'This is not mine, this I am not, this is not my self.' When one sees it thus as it actually is with proper wisdom, one becomes disenchanted with the earth element and makes the mind dispassionate toward the earth element."[3]

In the Beginning . . .

Where did this body begin, and was there anything at the beginning that I could call me or mine?

There's no mention of conception in the traditional outlines of the practice, but since the body begins there, that's where I tend to start my reflections. In my meditation practice I recollect that my life began with the fusion of an egg from my mother with a sperm from my father. I share with most people the reluctance to consider in any detail my parents' conjugal activities, and so in this particular exercise of the imagination I find it useful to indulge in a little vague generality. So there is an egg and a sperm, floating, as it were, in the midair of my imagination. Sperm and eggs are of course delivery vehicles for your parents' DNA. Note that it's *your parents'* DNA, not yours. In fact your parents' DNA was not theirs either. They both got their DNA from *their* parents, and so on and so forth back in time until the first common ancestor of all life. DNA perforce flows through time's river, or it ceases to exist. Like everything else in the body, our DNA is not owned, but only borrowed. We can look at the provenance of DNA from another angle as well. The atoms that constitute your DNA are borrowed from the outside world. Your DNA is doubly other, coming from your parental lineage and from food ingested by your progenitors.

I reflect that neither the sperm nor the egg was me. One was clearly part of my mother's body, while the other was likewise just one of the roughly one hundred trillion cells constituting my father's body at that moment in his life. Now, I can regard the product of the fusion of these two "not-me" cells as being, in some way, "me," but the knowledge that the parts were "not-me" rather undermines the notion of their sum being "me." Everything that made up that first "me" cell was borrowed. I have the sense, reflecting on this, of a disconcerting absence of "me" at the moment of my creation. I'd like to think that a "me" was created, but considering that "I" was made from stuff that was entirely "not-me" I experience the same dizzying sense of insubstantiality that arose in Chapter One, when we considered the possibility of another sperm having met the mother's egg.

Next I witness, in the mind's eye, the growth and development of this single-celled, half-mother/half-father/"not-me" entity in a series of mental snapshots and time-lapse movies taking me right up to the present day. In my reflections on the Earth Element, I'm not concerned with visualizing the specifics of the entire process of embryogenesis—one doesn't need a degree in embryology to reflect on it—but in a general sense I call to mind that the following events took place in my life: conception was followed by cell division and the development of an embryo, which became a fetus, and then a baby. This growth was possible because of the borrowing of the Earth Element from the outside world. The embryo at first got nutrition by absorbing secretions from the uterus, and it dumped waste products into my mother's uterine cavity, but it later grew by absorbing nutrition through the placenta. And what I took from my mother was in turn what she had borrowed. The flesh and other products of animals, crops that had grown in fields, and fruits that had been cultivated in orchards were all funneled through my mother's body to feed "me." That which is other (food) flowed through that which is other (my mother) into the body, which—remembering that the embryo began as a cell from each of my parents—is also other. When we look closely, it seems that there is no "me" to be found in the Earth Element that constitutes the developing embryo: "Now the internal Earth Element and the external element are simply Earth Element. And that should be seen as it actually is . . . ."

We can visualize ourselves being born and growing to the point where we ingest food ourselves. Rather than being channeled through the mother's body, food now flows directly into the body, being chewed, digested, and assimilated. We can imagine this process of growth, with its attendant flow and absorption of the Earth

Element, taking place right up to the present moment, right up to the arising of the form that is reading this book. In my meditation I picture this flow of the Earth Element. I call to mind fields and animals, seeing the Earth Element in the form of food flow from fields, along roads, into factories and stores, into my home, and into my body. The Earth Element flows like a river, and I am just one eddy amongst its countless currents. This is another opportunity to experience humility and gratitude. How many countless people have been involved in growing, transporting, processing, and selling the food we have eaten over our entire lifetimes? How many lives of plants and animals have helped sustain our small eddy? We can think of this and give thanks.

We are all part of a much vaster stream of the Earth Element, one that began at the birth of the universe and that will only cease when—or if—the universe ends. Our planet was itself born from the remains of a dead star. The chemical elements that make up the earth, and therefore our bodies, were forged in the center of high-mass stars that became unstable and exploded, scattering their seed across the cosmos. The resultant miasma collapsed, under the force of gravity, to give birth to new stars and planets, including ours. Neil deGrasse Tyson, the astrophysicist and irrepressibly enthusiastic communicator of science, declared, "It's quite literally true that we are star dust." This, he points out, needn't make us feel small and insignificant. Instead we can "bask in the majesty of the cosmos."[4] At the same time, in the raw intoxication of daily life our own petty concerns can seem to have epic scope, but when framed by the entirety of the universe it's easier to put them in perspective.

Our own particular eddy within the Earth Element continues as long as this body grows and develops, like an eddy in a river deepening and widening. But in essence there is in the body, well, no essence.

When we look at an eddy in a river, the mind imagines that there is some kind of separation between the eddy and the remainder of the water. In a way it's forced to do this by the very act of naming. We imagine there's a "thing" called an eddy, and that this thing is embedded in another "thing" called "water." But when we reflect more deeply we see there's only flow. The water that constitutes the eddy isn't the same from any one moment to the next. Imagine that we dropped some dye directly into an eddy in order to determine its exact form. The dye enters the water, spreads briefly through the water's swirling pattern, and in a moment is gone. The water that was the eddy is now simply river. The pattern of swirling water endures, but there is no enduring substance to the eddy. The eddy is nothing more than a self-organizing pattern within the greater flow of the element. So, just as the water in a river is continually flowing, creating the pattern we call an eddy, so too is the Earth Element flowing, creating the pattern of form we call "me."

As I observe the eddy that is my body I become aware that I am grasping after a sense of separateness and permanence. I think, or at least wordlessly assume, "This is me," but no sooner has the identification taken place than I become aware that what I've tried to hold onto has already passed by. The effect this produces is oddly liberating. It's liberating because to be static is, ultimately, to be dead. Aside from the inflow and the outflow, there is no eddy, and to see the body as static is to see it as being less than alive. To assume that the body is something relatively fixed, unchanging, and separate, is to miss its essential vitality, to see it as less than it truly is.

I sense my body in meditation, along with mental images of crops flowing toward and into my body, and I have a sense that I am the fields, I am the orchards, I am the soil. These things have all, transmuted, been incorporated into my body. Recognizing this, I am enlarged, no longer a small, disconnected thing but now something vastly more interesting and meaningful. My body is the cosmos made flesh. Paradoxically, at the same time as my sense of self becomes expanded, it also seems to have less importance. The skin of a balloon, when inflated, becomes thinner, less substantial, more translucent—it's no longer the small, solid, dull thing it was when deflated. If a balloon could keep enlarging without popping, it would eventually become infinitely thin, even invisible. This reflects something of how I feel about my body as I reflect on its interconnectedness with the outside world. The sense of expansiveness I feel is not the enlargement of self-importance, but a thinning out of the self.

When we have a sense that the world is known, that we know and understand ourselves, when we have a sense that the world is even *knowable,* we inflate ourselves in an unhelpful sense—in the sense of overestimating our own knowledge, mental capabilities, and importance. In sensing my body as a river—as a dynamic flow rather than as a relatively static object—I begin to realize that I do not know what I am. My body becomes a mystery to me. I become a mystery to myself. And I begin to realize that there is nothing—"no thing"—to cling to or to identify with. The desire to cling doesn't entirely vanish, but it seems that the universe is gently teaching me the futility of trying to grasp the ungraspable. One cannot hold onto a river.

The World as Self

As I emerge, blinking, into the dazzling sunlight of a June day in Paris, I look down and see that my suede shoes are coated in thick gray-brown dust. I try to brush it off with my fingers but it clings with remarkable stubbornness to the shoes' textured leather. It clings as I take backstreets, avoiding the heavy traffic, through the Luxembourg Gardens. It clings all the way to the square in front of Notre Dame cathedral. It's not until I scoop handfuls of clear, cold water from a fountain and pour them over my shoes that the dust is gone. But this is no ordinary dust. I have just been for a walk in the "Empire of Death"—the Catacombs of Paris. I have just strolled along underground tunnels packed with the mortal remains of thousands upon thousands of long-dead Parisians, their bones neatly stacked against the walls, often with the skulls forming crosses or arches. In 1786, the cemeteries of Paris having filled to the point that a spade could not be thrust into the putrid earth without hitting a bone, the authorities began to relocate the city's skeletal residents to a new home in the tunnels that had been created while mining limestone for the city's elegant buildings. The security guards at the Catacombs's exit checked our bags for stolen bones, but they didn't clean the dust of the dead from our feet.

The book of Genesis reminds us of the flow of the Earth Element: "In the sweat of thy face shalt thou eat bread, till thou return unto the ground; for out of it wast thou taken: for dust thou art, and unto dust shalt thou return." We come from the earth. We eat food from the earth. We return to the earth. This verse is best known in an adapted form used in funeral ceremonies—"Ashes to ashes, dust to dust"— but the body doesn't wait until death before earth returns to Earth. It's happening right now.

The river of earth flows both into and out of the eddy of form that we identify as "myself." While the body is in a constant state of self-replacement—on the leisurely order of a decade in the case of bones, to the more frenetic scale of a few days for the gut epithelium—something has to replace the attrition and something has to be lost. Earth in, Earth out.

The most obvious but least socially acceptable way in which the Earth Element leaves the body is through defecation. About one-third of our feces is composed of undigested food, such as cellulose, since we have no digestive enzymes to break down what is effectively the skeleton of the plants we eat. This roughage merely passes through the gut, helping move things along. It has been inside us, but has never really been a part of us. But most of our feces represents the body returning to the wider Earth Element. For ease of passage, our feces are lubricated with a layer of mucus, which is secreted by cells in the intestine. That's part of us. One of fecal matter's most notable attributes is its brown color, which comes from a combination of bile and bilirubin. These in turn come from the nearly one trillion dead red-blood cells broken down in the spleen every day. Blood cells of course contain iron, and it's oxygen reacting with this iron that creates the distinctive color of feces. That's you too. The remainder of feces is a mixture of fats such as cholesterol, inorganic salts like phosphates, dead cells shed from the lining of the gut, and protein. Every time you take a dump you're flushing part of yourself away. Somewhere, however, in the process between living blood cell and pulling the flush handle, we draw an arbitrary line separating our idea of self from our idea of other. Where do we draw that line? Can we even draw one that is actually meaningful? The boundary between self and other becomes hard to establish once we start to examine exactly where it lies.

Another notable characteristic of our feces is the odor, which comes from our symbiotic bacteria. They comprise about a third of the average poop. As we will see in Chapter Ten (The Fire Element), our gut bacteria form a kind of outsourced organ that has co-evolved with us and that performs vital functions, not just in the digestion of our food, but also in regulating our sugar metabolism and our immune response. It's scarcely possible to draw a line, metabolically speaking, between our "bacterial organ" and the rest of the body. So the presence of these bacteria can also be seen as a part of ourselves returning to the outside world. Your feces are part of the process of the internal Earth Element rejoining the outside world.

I reflect upon all this when I contemplate the Earth Element returning to the outside world. And I reflect upon where my feces go. Depending on the sanitary arrangements in the places you frequent, your stools will, in one way or another, return to the cycle of the elements. Much is gobbled up by grateful bacteria and other microorganisms, to whom it's a rich source of nutrition, and this forms an important part of the purification process as well as returning our feces to the food chain. Some human sewage, after suitable treatment, ends up as fertilizer pellets. A few cities now convert human feces into gas or burn the waste directly as a fuel. This all flows into the world at large and into other living organisms. There's no escaping the fact that much of the world around us is composed of secondhand human material. Think again now of the Earth Element outside you—that's you.

Similarly, we're always losing hair and skin cells. As we've seen, the skin's entire outer layer is replaced every few days, sacrificed to provide protection against wear and tear. Cells at the skin's base are living and have a blood supply, but after skin cells are produced they move up the strata toward the outside world, losing the nucleus and other organelles, and flattening out. As they near the body's exterior, they fill with the tough protein keratin, secrete waterproof oils, and die. Your skin's outer layer is quite literally a dead wrapper, enclosing living tissue. Because of these changes, keratinized skin cells are relatively waterproof, so that when you are submerged in water you don't suck up liquid like a sponge, and when you're in the relative dryness of a normal atmosphere you don't shrivel up like a raisin. Without your "dead skin," these unfortunate events would happen and you would quickly die.

The keratinized layer of the epidermis also protects against infection and mechanical trauma. In doing so, however, it has to be continuously replaced, with the outer cells being sloughed off in a process called desquamation. Every time you dress or undress, about half a million dead skin cells become airborne. Billions are lost each day. The gray dust that you see relentlessly accumulating on your home's furniture is dead bits of you. Your vacuum cleaner is full of you.

There are entire ecosystems devoted to dealing with this dead skin. Since your desquamated skin cells are close to being pure protein, they provide a rich source of food. Lurking in the sofa, in your mattress, and on carpets, dust mites (tiny arachnids related to spiders) happily chow down on your dead skin, breed, and defecate in your furnishings and carpets. No matter how hygienic your household, the mites are there. When people have dust allergies, it's not usually the dust they're actually sensitive to, but the feces produced by the mites. Think about that next time your nose itches. When you consider it, these dust mites are made of you; their main source of food is your skin. Mites are made of people. So are their feces.

Fungi have also adapted to eat dead skin. Some, unfortunately, don't wait until the cells have been shed before they start feasting.

If you've ever had a case of athlete's foot or thrush, you've experienced firsthand how unpleasant it is to be the prey of another species. The fungi that cause these itchy conditions are called dermatophytes (literally "skin-plants") and they feast on keratin. These fungi are, once again, you. The Earth Element that is in you becomes the Earth Element in them. They're sort of honorary members of the family—albeit of an irritating sort.

But most keratin-eating fungi prefer to dine alone, living in the soil and waiting until skin cells have been shed before tucking in. Probably all keratin-eating fungi, the athlete's foot- and thrush-inducing varieties included, began as soil-dwelling organisms that learned to hitch a ride on their food source. Keratin eaters perform the unlikely task of digesting a tissue that's evolved to be indigestible. We should be grateful this happens. Given that over a lifetime a human sheds more than a hundred pounds of skin cells, and given that there are more than six billion of us on the planet at present, we'd be knee-deep in scurf if something hadn't evolved to digest it. So those soil-dwelling, keratin-loving fungi—you can give them thanks even as you reflect that they're made up of you too.

All these dander-dining creatures are of course just one part of the cycle of the elements. They die natural deaths or are consumed by other creatures higher up the food chain. Eventually the Earth Element that was once part of your epithelial cells will become part of many organisms—insects, plants, fungi, animals, and even other people. All these creatures are, in part, you.

Our hair meets the same fate as our skin. Also made of keratin, we shed hairs at the rate of one hundred each day (that's counting only head hairs, not those on the rest of the body). Whether they're lost outdoors, washed down the drain, or dumped in a landfill, they'll meet the same fate as skin cells, being digested by voracious fungi. And again, this is a boon unless we relish drowning in our own keratinous jetsam. I think of all this while reflecting upon how my body is, right now, in the process of returning to the earth. Skin cells, right now, are floating away from my body. Every few minutes another hair falls and becomes the world around me—plants, fungi, animals, soil, and other human beings.

And my body is burning up. Although we're in danger of straying into the Air and Fire Elements here, another way the Earth Element leaves the body is combustion. The body stores energy as glycogen and fats, both of which are used to produce energy. Protein can also be used, but since this is akin to burning the furniture, it's the body's last resort. When the body breaks down its reserves in order to release energy, carbon dioxide is produced as a byproduct and is expelled from the lungs. Each time you breathe out you're literally exhaling your own body. The Earth Element within has become the Air Element outside you. And the carbon dioxide in the stale air you expel from your lungs continues into the carbon cycle, being absorbed by plants—by phytoplankton in the oceans (the basis of the food chain for all ocean life), by forests around the world (including the rainforest) and by grasses and crops.

When I reflect upon the internal Earth Element returning to the outside world, I have a sense that the rainforests; the grasses around the world and the animals that eat them; the crops in the fields and the people and animals that consume them; and the phytoplankton in the ocean and the entire pelagic food chain right up to the great blue whales are all in part me. Einstein's "optical delusion" of separateness leads me to think that I am small and limited and apart from the rest of the world. But reflecting on the cycle of the Earth

Element reminds me that I am an inseparable part of the great river of becoming. I am an eddy in a vast cycling flow of the Earth Element, and as with a literal eddy there is no boundary between me and the world. Rather than having sharply defined edges, my being blurs into the world around me. The sense I have of separateness is revealed to be a limitation of my senses, which are unable to trace the currents of the Earth Element as it flows into, through, and back out of the particular eddy that I cling to as myself. I begin to have a sense of my body dissolving under me. At times this is disorienting, as if the floor has suddenly vanished beneath my feet. At other times I feel freed of a burden, as if I've been unnecessarily carrying a crutch and have realized at last that I can lay down the unneeded support.

As I visualize the flow of the Earth Element and the small eddy that my being forms within it, I recall the words of the "Discourse on the Elements," where Gautama suggests we reflect "with proper wisdom" upon the thought, "This is not mine; this is not me; this is not my self." These words become a mantra, not repeated mindlessly but dropped like an offering into the mind. "This is not mine; this is not me; this is not my self." Over and over, I hear these words echo in the depths of my being. And the aim is simply to allow the depths to respond.

The assumptions I make about having a self, about owning a body, and about the body being the self are not likely to be overthrown all at once. The assumptions I make have an internal stability, and while they may be thrown off center while I reflect on the Element, they have a way of reasserting themselves. The temporary sense of openness and wonder that can arise during reflection dissolves over time, revealing my assumptions of solidity, continuity, and separateness to be still present; even openness and wonder are impermanent, transient phenomena. However, perhaps the remarkable thing is that such strongly held beliefs can be challenged in such a short time. My habitual assumptions have a lifetime's worth of momentum behind them, but even a few minutes spent reflecting upon the true nature of the Earth Element can make a noticeable difference in my sense of who I am and what my relation to the world is.

Eventually, as the Discourse says, "When one sees it thus as it actually is with proper wisdom, one becomes disenchanted with the Earth Element and makes the mind dispassionate toward the Earth Element." The mind clings less to the body, being less concerned about the inevitable changes that take place within it. Aging bothers us less. We're less concerned with how others perceive us. It's not that we cease caring, but we simply suffer less: we put less energy into resisting the inevitable physical changes that come about through aging and illness. We suffer less because we're less prone to judging ourselves and to obsessing over how we think others see us. Observing that everything we identify with is in a constant process of dying and being reborn, death seems less a catastrophe and more an integral part of life.

Although we've brought contemporary scientific knowledge into these reflections on the flow of the Earth Element, this approach is essentially the same as Gautama advocates—seeing that ultimately there is only one element. The internal and external Earth Element are one and inseparable. What we currently identify with as ourselves comes from the outside world. What currently constitutes us is in the process of returning to the outside world. In essence the distinction between the inside and outside worlds is a false one, produced by Einstein's "optical delusion of consciousness."

Letting Go into the River of Earth

The purpose of the reflections in this and the chapters on the other Elements is to challenge our sense of ourselves as static and separate beings, to change the sense we have of our selfhood being equated with or even identical to the body. The reflections help us move from a sense of the body being a static thing that we own to a sense of the body being a fluid and dynamic thing that is unknowable and ungraspable. They undermine our assumption that the body is a separate entity and help us appreciate that we are deeply interconnected with the so-called outside world.

In recognizing that the internal Earth Element is not separate in any way from the external Earth Element, in recognizing in fact that there is only one Earth Element, we become liberated. To have our sense of our selves tied to the body is a source of pain. The body changes. The body breaks down. Ultimately the body will fail us. If our sense of our selves is tied to the body, we will suffer, because we have no firm basis for a sense of security and well-being.

But upon what, then, is our sense of well-being to rest? What is to be the basis for our sense of security? The answer is paradoxical. It's letting go of clinging that leads to security. It's realizing that there is no possibility of finding security in a fundamentally insecure world that leads to a sense of calm and equanimity. Well-being comes from no longer desiring security, from simply allowing the elements to flow through us without clinging to them.

It takes confidence to let go. When we find this confidence in the midst of all-pervasive change, we no longer attempt to locate the self in the Earth Element. Changes in the body no longer trouble us. We have reached a state of equanimity. It's not that we don't care—we can cling less and still look after the body. Our physical form needs to be fed, exercised, and made presentable so that we can function in the social world. But we can become less neurotically caught up in those activities, better able to age gracefully without Botoxing, nipping and tucking, dyeing, and hair-transplanting our way to an artificial and sometimes grotesque parody of youth. We can groom and dress the body with less fear about how we will be judged. We can appreciate aging as a sign of growing experience and wisdom. We can be more forgiving toward the body, not seeing it as a traitor for changing. We can simply be more at ease with ourselves.

The Buddhist teacher Sangharakshita has observed that all insight meditation is a preparation for death. That's more than usually apparent in the case of the Six Element Practice. Upon death, the elements begin returning to nature. Whether the body is cremated or buried, the eddy of the body can no longer hold together. The internal Earth Element rejoins the external element—whether as particles of smoke and molecules of carbon dioxide, or whether absorbed into the bodies of soil-dwelling creatures—revealing that there really is only one Earth Element, which is neither self nor other.

We know that death is inevitable, but at the same time we need to be reminded because we don't like to think about the end of our current, known existence. We don't like to consider that we will enter an unknown realm, even if that realm is simply the unimaginable state of nonbeing. The practice of reflecting on the flow of the Earth Element reminds us that death is not unknown. It's taking place right here, right now. In every moment the body is dying and being reborn. Your bones are dissolving and being rebuilt, entire cells are self-destructing and being replaced by new cells, and within cells structures are being torn down and built anew. If we look closely, we can recognize that death is not unknown. We can see it here and now. And each time we reflect on the flow of the Earth Element we become a little more comfortable with our final passing.

There's a *mudra,* or symbolic gesture, that some Buddha statues make with the right hand. It's called the "Earth Touching Mudra." The fingertips of the seated Buddha's right hand reach down and lightly make contact with the earth. This gesture is seen as an expression of confidence. The hand does not grasp the earth, but merely touches it delicately, as your fingertips might graze the surface of a flowing stream, sensing the movement without trying to hold it back. The earth flows and the fingers merely trail in it as it passes. And the other hand—the left hand—rests on the lap in meditation. These two gestures—representing the calmness of meditation combined with a light, graceful, non-grasping appreciation of change in the Earth Element—are what we are attempting to emulate.

This doesn't come all at once. In one legend Gautama reaches down to touch the earth, and the earth—in the form of a goddess—testifies to the eons of practice he has done to reach the state of equanimity in which he lives. We don't need to take this literally, thinking in terms of countless lifetimes of practice, but we can take home the message that to let go of grasping after the Earth Element, to become comfortable with impermanence, is something that comes not all at once but with repeated reflection.

CHAPTER NINE

The Water Element

*"The least movement is of importance to all nature. The
entire ocean is affected by a pebble."*
—BLAISE PASCAL[1]

For the ancients, the Water Element was a living force to be respected, revered, or feared. To Hesiod in Greece in the late seventh century BCE, water was under the special care of the gods and was a purifying gift from them, to be treated with veneration. "Never cross the sweet-flowing water of ever-rolling rivers afoot," he entreated us, "until you have prayed, gazing into the soft flood, and washed your hands in the clear, lovely water."[2] Water rituals such as this were seen as having a morally as well as a physically hygienic effect, washing away a person's sins. Water offers purification, and to cross a river without ritually cleansing oneself would displease the gods: "Whoever crosses a river with hands unwashed of wickedness, the gods are angry with him and bring trouble upon him afterwards," Hesiod says. And waters themselves could be gods—living beings with wills of their own. Oceanus was the personification of the great ocean that encircled the world. His three thousand sons were river gods and his three thousand daughters were the spirits of streams, springs, lakes, and fountains. All bodies of water were therefore descendants of the ocean, suggesting that the Greeks had a good grasp of the hydrological cycle.

Achilles, in Homer's *The Iliad,* becomes caught up in the internal politics of the gods when, filled with bloodlust, he slaughters many enemy soldiers in the river Scamander, causing its waters to run red.[3] The river is angered by this pollution, but Achilles continues his sacrilege. As he kills a young soldier, Achilles mocks the futility of the sacrifices the young man had made to the river god in exchange for protection; Achilles then goes on to kill another warrior who is the son of a river god. There's only so much a river deity can take. Scamander takes human form, and to make a long epic short, the two battle, with Achilles facing mighty waves powerful enough to uproot great trees. It is only by the intercession of other gods that Achilles survives the confrontation at all.

This conception of the Water Element as a force outside our control could be taken as a mythologized reminder that, as the Buddha put it, water is "Not me, not mine" and that "I am not this." In the Six Element Meditation, the reflection on the Water Element involves recognizing that it, like all the other elements, is simply flowing through us, cannot be owned, and cannot be seen as a part of the self.

The early Greek thinker Thales of Miletus, who lived a century or so before the Buddha, saw the Water Element as the archetype of all others. The Earth floated on a vast body of water, and it was the movements of the supporting ocean that caused earthquakes. But more than this, water for Thales was the underlying materiality that gave form to all things. It was the universal substance, of which the other elements are merely variant forms. Water could exist in liquid, gaseous, and solid forms, and even heat could come from water: a dry pile of plant matter is cold, but add water and—voilà!—it generates heat. Water's archetypal quality of flowing into various forms may also have suggested that it was not just a metaphor for the other elements, but the basis of them—the underlying and unchanging essence in a world of becoming.

The most striking thing about the Water Element is its quality of flowing. It's because of this characteristic that I too think of water as being the archetype of all the other elements. The Earth Element does flow, to be sure. It flows in a literal sense, as with landslides or the movement of tectonic plates—but these movements are either rare enough that they spring to mind infrequently, or they happen on timescales that are remote from our day-to-day experience. We generally expect mountains to remain where they are and the ground beneath our feet to provide a reliable support. Fire (energy) and air also flow, but these aren't directly visible like the flow of water. On the other hand, it's part of my everyday experience to perceive water flowing. I see water flowing from the sky, flowing along the river that passes by my house, flowing from faucets, and flowing down drains. I hear the trickle of urine on my periodic trips to the bathroom. I can feel the blood pumping in my arteries and the saliva sloshing in my mouth. This ready familiarity means that the flow of water becomes a metaphor for the other elements that compose our bodies. As the Buddha once said: "Just as a mountain stream, coming from afar, swiftly flowing, carrying along much flotsam, will not stand still for a moment, an instant, a second, but will rush on, swirl and flow forward; even so . . . is human life like a mountain stream."[4]

When I meditate upon the various elements entering this human form, swirling around, and passing out again, it is in fact the image of a river that most often comes to mind. Sometimes I imagine that I'm sitting next to a six-foot stretch of river that represents my self—my body, feelings, thoughts, and memories. I sit on the bank, watching the waters flow by in this length of river that represents what is myself, me, and mine. As I watch the waters roll by I'm forced to recognize that what constitutes this "me" is forever changing. What I've just identified as "me" is now gone, and has been replaced. This is disconcerting, and I begin to realize more and more that I constantly grasp after a kind of self-definition and try to delimit the self, as if I fear that I will be lost in the flow of the elements. The grasping becomes more conscious, the identification more obvious. Yet as I continue to reflect on the transitory nature of the elements as they pass through my form, I realize that grasping is futile. One may as well try to hold onto flowing water as to claim the elements as one's own, or as oneself. The moment of identification is followed so closely by the moment of dis-identification that they are essentially the same moment, and the moment of grasping becomes the moment of letting go. I find myself experiencing a sense of ease, less compelled to try to grasp the ungraspable. I begin to feel liberated.

Sometimes the image is different. I imagine that I sit before a waterfall. The sheet of water is like a cinema screen, and on it is projected a photograph or movie of my body. I can see myself, and yet there is nothing static within the image. What makes up the representation of myself, what constitutes the substance, what is apparently "contained" within the image I see of myself, is not a thing but a flow, an endlessly changing current, an ever-moving wall of water. In no two moments am I the same person, because the waterfall is not the same waterfall. As with the image of the river, the contents of the form are forever being replaced. There is an appearance of substantiality—of something static—but there is no essence. And again, sitting with this image, as I continue to observe the transitoriness of my self, I have a sense that there's nothing to grasp. Indeed I begin to sense that there's no one to do any grasping, since it's my *self* that is void of substance.

Being the River

Early in my introduction to Buddhist practice, I had an opportunity to participate in a *puja,* the collective chanting of some inspirational and philosophical texts. Most of what I heard went straight over my head because I found the idiom foreign and the concepts abstruse. But it was one of the more baffling texts that I also found most intriguing: a work called the *Heart Sutra.* The *Heart Sutra* is so named because it explains the core philosophical teaching of the Mahayana school: a teaching known as *shunyata,* or emptiness. Actually, the word "explains" is not entirely accurate because of the highly paradoxical nature of the text, which combines two different perspectives on the world in order to illuminate the self's indefinable nature. And so we have statements such as:

> Form is emptiness,
> Emptiness is form.
> Form is only emptiness,
> Emptiness is only form.

This kind of statement is in effect saying, "Look we have something we call a 'self' (which includes a 'form' or body), but when we look

closely at that self we find that it lacks (or is *empty of*) the characteristics we assume it to have: characteristics such as permanence and
separateness. The self is made up of stuff that is/was/will be 'not self.'
And when we say it is 'made up' of this not-self stuff, that's not to
imply that it's static. The not-self stuff that makes up the self is simply
flowing through." As you'll see, it's hard to talk about the *Heart Sutra,*
or the teaching of emptiness, without lapsing into the same kind of
paradoxical talk it employs.

The words of the *Heart Sutra* rattled around in my young mind (I
was in my early twenties at the time, and coming toward the end of
a grueling degree in veterinary medicine), both fascinating and frustrating me. To some extent I intellectually understood the teachings
it summarized, but I knew that a direct appreciation of the teachings
eluded me. It was as if I'd been studying the geography of France
in textbooks but had never set foot on the country's soil. Then, one
day, as I was hoeing a patch of ground in the West End of Glasgow
(I was spending part of my summer vacation working in a Buddhist
gardening cooperative), an image appeared to me that explained the
Heart Sutra in a way that went deeper than mere intellectual appreciation. I hadn't exactly set foot in France, but it was if I'd found myself
flying low over the French countryside, finally getting a clear view of
it through a gap in the clouds. It was a direct experience, albeit a brief
and distant one.

The image involved water. Specifically, I had an inner vision of an
eddy in a river. Like many boys who had access to country streams,
I'd grown up fascinated by water—the way it flows, its textures, its
sounds, and the way in which it ultimately defied all my attempts
with dams made of mud and stone and branches to hold back its flow.
Eddies particularly fascinated me. I was intrigued by how they held

their form in the midst of constant motion, and by the fact that it was their motion that allowed that form to exist. It's also quite astonishing that water can have a hole in it, which is essentially what an eddy is—a restless hole in the water.

An eddy never holds exactly the same form for two consecutive moments, but there is often a relative constancy of location and shape that give it, to the human mind, a sense of permanence. The kind of relatively static eddy that forms at the edge of a stream looks more or less the same over a period of time. It may change, but I have a sense that it is the same eddy. The mind in fact names this thing "the eddy," implicitly assuming that this eddy is a "thing." But when I look more closely, what do I see? There is no clear boundary to the eddy. Where does it stop and the river begin? It's impossible to say. Although I still perceive a form there, it's a form without a boundary or, to put it paradoxically, a form without a form. Even wondering where the eddy stops and the river begins implies an assumption that the eddy and the river are in some way separate, as if the eddy could be extracted from the river. That of course is nonsense, but it's a nonsense that in some way my mind creates by regarding "river" as one thing and "eddy" as another. Even if I edit the question to read, "Where does the eddy stop and *the rest* of the river begin?" there's still a mental sense of separation that I find impossible to avoid. The fission of the concept of a river into "eddy" and "rest of the river" inevitably implies a real division. I can't help but look for the eddy's edge, and every time I fail.

What's the eddy made of? Obviously it's made of the same stuff as the rest of the river—water. But just as Heraclitus's river isn't the same river in two separate moments because the waters that form it have changed, so—and for the same reason—is the eddy not the same eddy in two consecutive moments. Do we then have a succession of eddies, one following another in rapid succession? If I assume this then I'm forced to ask when one eddy ends and the next begins, and I'm faced with the same situation that I encounter when I look for the eddy's edge. I'm looking for boundaries in a situation where there is only continuity. Our imagined eddy has an apparent form, but that form, when we look for it, is elusive; the eddy is not permanent and neither does it have any separateness, even though my mind expects to find both of these characteristics.

All of this came to me, as I was gardening, in a few brief moments, rather like a bolt of lightning; and it occurred to me that the metaphor encapsulated what the *Heart Sutra* was expressing, and that this applied to all forms, including ourselves. I too am a kind of eddy in the flow of elements. I have an apparent form, but that form has neither permanence nor separateness. The eddy that I call myself is made up of stuff that is not-self, and that "not-self stuff" is simply flowing. When I look for the boundary between myself and the world, I can't find one. When I look for some defining "stuff" that is in me and constitutes the essence of me, I can't find that either, because *everything* is in motion. I can see my self, but I can't pin down what it is. My self seems to be indefinable.

The Traditional Reflection

The Six Element Reflection gives us a sense of the indefinability of the self because it helps us to strip away everything with which we identify. In the reflection on the Water Element we're taking one more step along the path of self-analysis and "dis-identification." We start with reflecting upon the Water Element inside the body—something we may be tempted to regard as ourselves, or part of ourselves, or as belonging to ourselves.

In the context of the traditional reflective practice, the Water Element is simply everything liquid within the body. How much water there is varies depending on gender and body weight, as well as the time of day and how hot it is, but for men the figure tends to be about 60 percent, and for women about 55 percent. The traditional list for reflection upon our bodily fluids includes "bile, phlegm, pus, blood, sweat, fat, tears, grease, saliva, nasal mucus, synovial fluid, urine, or whatever else internally, belonging to oneself, is water, watery, and clung-to." That's what we call to mind in the practice: as many watery aspects of the body as we can envision—those named above as well, perhaps, as semen, vaginal mucus, cerebrospinal fluid, lymph, the fluids in and around cells, and any other bodily liquids or quasi-liquids.

While meditating, I can directly perceive many aspects of the Water Element. I notice the saliva in my mouth. I feel my eyelids sliding over the teary fluids that coat my eyeballs. I sense the moistness of the out-breath compared to the dryness of the in-breath. I observe the beating of my heart as it sends blood coursing through arteries and veins, as well as the resultant pulses in various extremities. Sometimes I'm aware of the pressure of urine in my bladder. I can sense moistness in the armpits, groin, and other intimate parts of the body. On hot New England days, I can't help but feel sweat trickling over my skin and feel wet fabric clinging to my body. In winter I can sometimes feel my nose run.

I resort to my imagination in order to call to mind the Water Element in the body that's not directly perceptible. I recall that every cell in my body is full of liquid, that each cell is surrounded by and bathed in liquid. Synovial and cerebrospinal fluids come readily to mind, as do lymph and the mucus that covers not just the nasal membranes, but all mucosal membranes throughout the body, including the respiratory system, the esophagus, and the intestines. If I were a woman I'd also include the vaginal and uterine mucosae. Additionally, I might remind myself that all the food in my digestive tract is moist, and that this water is within my body and "clung-to" as mine. I might think of the eyeballs, plump and swollen like two ripe fruits.

I also call to mind the Water Element in the outside world. There's water within the food and drink stored in the house, water filling the water mains, ready to pour from faucets, water soaking the earth, water in plants and in the bodies of animals, water flowing in sewerage pipes and in storm drains, and perhaps rain or mist or other precipitation. There are streams, rivers, ponds, lakes, and the oceans; more than seven-tenths of our planet is covered in water. Deep below, water percolates in aquifers. We live on a planet saturated perhaps to the core with water. High above, there are droplets of water suspended in clouds, raindrops on their way to earth.

Having considered the Water Element inside the body and the Water Element outside ourselves, we move on to reflecting on how the two are really the same thing. In other words, we reflect on how the Water Element enters and leaves our bodies. So we consider how liquid enters, as moist foods and as beverages: every molecule of water within the body just part of the great cycle of water on the planet, each molecule simply borrowed for a brief time before it's returned.

In reality there is just one Water Element, the traditional teachings remind us, not a "me" Water Element and a "not-me" Water Element. The human body is almost literally a river—a conduit through which flows a tiny portion of Earth's 1.3 billion cubic kilometers of water.

There is one water cycle, as we could put it in more contemporary terms. We talk in terms of a "body" of water, and perhaps we could think of the world's water supply as being one literal body in which we are all cells. The water outside individual beings is like the fluid bathing the cells in our more literal body. Perhaps more poetically we could think of all life as being the "Children of Oceanus," especially since life may well have begun in a volcanic vent in some ocean trench.

At any one time, one-millionth of the world's water is inside living organisms, according to Dr. Peter H. Gleick, co-founder and president of the Pacific Institute for Studies in Development, Environment, and Security, in Oakland, California, and a world-renowned expert on global water issues.[5] This may seem like a tiny proportion, but there have been living organisms on the earth for something like 3.8 billion years, and given the rapid rate of turnover of water within living organisms, we can imagine that virtually all of the water on our planet has passed through countless beings. To say that it has "passed through" is an understatement, however. Photosynthesis combines water and carbon dioxide to create carbohydrates, while the breakdown of fats, carbohydrates, and proteins produces water. At any one time, much water is not found in the form of anything resembling water. This is one way in which the elements are revealed to be "empty." Water itself is a conditioned phenomenon, coming into being and passing away. The water absorbed by the root of the plant becomes starch and ceases to be water. I digest the starch, and water is created once again. The Water Element has no essence.

I invite you to become aware right now of the saliva in your mouth. Where did this fluid come from? The water forming this tiny quantity of spittle comes from every ocean in the world, from every lake, and from every river; water constantly circulates and flows, in liquid or gaseous form, around the planet. And these few teaspoons of spit come not just from the oceans and other bodies and channels that exist *today*. Every river that has ever flowed, every ocean that has ever existed in the 4.5 billion years of our planet's existence in is your mouth right now. How many other living beings have these water molecules passed through? The number could only be a guess, but it would surely be in the billions. Within your veins flows the sap of redwood trees, the blood of dinosaurs, and the steaming breath of every volcano that has ever existed.

All this water on our planet came, at some point, from outside the earth. It's likely that as our planet began to coalesce from a cloud or ring of dust and rubble around the newborn sun, water was already present in the form of ice. The water that permeated the rubble around the new-formed sun was actually created in a previous star— one that had come to the end of its life, exploding violently, leaving a vast cloud of gas and dust out of which our solar system condensed. Even after the earth formed, vast quantities of water (although probably only a small proportion compared to what was already there) arrived in the form of plummeting comets, meteors, and asteroids. From the point of view of early life-forms, these would have been a mixed blessing. Incoming rocks and comets brought precious water and organic molecules needed for the very existence of life, but they also wrought havoc with the massive collisions they caused: the impact point vaporized down to the bedrock, and plumes of dust cut off sunlight—all the catastrophes familiar to us from disaster movies and end-of-the-dinosaur-era documentaries. These waters are in your mouth right now and all through your body, in blood and bile and in and around every cell. These comets, some of them, may have traveled from other star systems, ejected by the gravitational slingshots caused by near-misses with gas giants. You are, in the very water of your being, an interstellar child. You are a recycled star, become aware. And the same is true for every living organism on Earth. We all share the same water and participate in the same water cycle. That redwood sap flowing in your veins is also in countless other living things: bacteria, frogs, and the cat next door. We are, on a physical level, each other. And each of us is everything.

In the traditional reflection we recall, and experience, the Water Element returning to the outside world. Those sensations of moistness in the armpits and groin, the dribbles of sweat, the wetness of the out-breath—all are perceptible examples of the Water Element cycling through and out of us. We urinate and defecate, relinquishing the Water Element in even more earthy ways. About half the water lost from the body is in the form of urine; the rest is sweat, feces, and our breathing. We experience or visualize all these ways that we surrender the Water Element, aware that this is just one tiny part of a vast process. These few pints of water that we return to the outside world each day drift in the air until, raised to the atmosphere's cooler heights, they coalesce as clouds, or are flushed down waste pipes where, after suitable treatment, they rejoin rivers, lakes, and oceans, continuing the cycle.

And so we come to a sense that there is just one Water Element, by recalling the flow of water, from the vast cycle of the wider Water Element, through this human form and back to the outside world again—endlessly flowing, on and on. And as we imagine and experience this flow, we reflect that the Water Element never belonged to us. We can never possess it. We can never hold onto it. Our very lives depend on the Water Element flowing through us. And so we repeat, drumming the message of non-attachment into the depths of the mind: "This is not me; this is not mine; I am not this." But when we talk about relinquishing the Water Element, or surrendering it, these words are just imperfect and misleading metaphors. How can we relinquish something we never possessed in the first place? The Water Element is a force that is, essentially, outside our control, like the gods of old.

The Preciousness of Water

The ancient reverence for water in Hesiod's *Works and Days* is one that we seem almost entirely to have lost. Although our world is drenched in water, we rarely appreciate just how little water there actually is. As we look at a globe and see 71 percent of the world's surface covered in water, we rarely consider that it is spread in an incredibly thin film over the planet's surface, less than a thousandth of the diameter of the earth at its deepest point, and on average three ten-thousandths. If the earth were shrunk to the size of a soccer ball, the average depth of the ocean covering it would be sixty-five microns, or about twice the thickness of a grocery-store plastic bag.

The image on the next page gives a graphic representation of the size of Earth, its total water supply (the white sphere), and the accessible freshwater reserves (the tiny, dark sphere at nine o'clock within the white sphere). Some 97 percent of the total water on Earth is saltwater; roughly 1.7 percent is locked up in the ice caps, glaciers, and permanent snow; and a similar amount is soaked deep into the earth. Approximately 0.007 percent of the planet's water is available for direct human use, including water in rivers, lakes, reservoirs, and accessible aquifers. You may have to look very closely at the diagram above to notice the tiny dot representing this.

Based on "Global water and air volume"
(Adam Nieman, Science Photo Library).[6]

Looked at this way, we can see that usable fresh water is a rare and precious commodity. And yet we don't treat it as such. So much water is being removed from our world's rivers that many of them do not reach the sea anymore, or at best they terminate in a sludgy trickle, while inland lakes are vanishing. These changes are driven mainly by human overuse, although climate change also contributes. For graphic illustrations of what we're doing to the world's rivers, we can consider the fates of the peoples dependent upon the Euphrates River in Iraq and the Kamayurá of the Brazilian Amazon.

Iraq is facing the worst drought in living memory, and the Euphrates is a shadow of what it once was.[7] Fishers and farmers are fleeing to the cities, crops are withering in the fields, and children grow sick drinking from the dwindling supplies of ever-more polluted waters. Sheep graze where the river once flowed. Boats lie stranded on dry land. The hoses of irrigation pumps dangle impotent over brown mud where ponds and lakes stood for centuries.

Many factors are contributing to this catastrophe. Iraqi agriculture withdraws too much water from the river; rainfall is well below historic averages; and perhaps most importantly, Iraq's upstream neighbors, Turkey and Syria, are able to siphon from the Euphrates before it reaches Iraq. The worst may yet be to come: some Iraqi officials predict that the river's flow could soon be half of what it is now. Modern civilization arose in Mesopotamia because of the regularity of the water supply there. So constant were the waters, in fact, that the Book of Revelation prophesies the drying up of the Euphrates as one sign of the end times.

The indigenous Kamayurá of the Amazon are facing the extinction of their culture.[8] Fish is their staple diet, but men now return with empty nets from rivers that once teemed with fish. The children now eat ants to get protein, but even the ants are becoming scarce. Because of the disappearance of the fish, the Kamayurá now have nothing with which to barter for other foods like rice and beans. If, as seems likely, the Kamayura have to move from their traditional lands, their native language and cultural traditions will be lost forever.

What is causing this? About thirteen thousand square kilometers of forest are felled in the Amazon each year. The cleared land is drier, and the reduction of moisture in the local environment means bigger fluctuations in the rains and in the flow of the rivers. Tribes plant crops only to watch them wither. Medicinal plants are becoming rare or are vanishing altogether as the climate changes. And in a place that was once too moist for fire to take hold, forest fires are a growing danger. The destruction of additional hectares of forest by fire will of course only add to the environmental catastrophe the Kamayurá face.

Recounting these stories, I think of the myth of Achilles fighting the river Scamander and wonder if we are in some sense at war with the environment that supports us. Achilles was attacked by the river for polluting its waters and also for mocking the blessings it bestows on life. Are we not guilty of the same offenses? Achilles only won his fight because he had other gods on his side. But we appear to be on our own.

Although overuse may account for much or even most of the decline in river flows, it's certain that climate change is what's causing glaciers to shrink all over the world. The glaciers of the Himalayas are shrinking at an accelerating rate, which is worrying when we consider they supply water to a billion people. Climate change, to be sure, can also increase rainfall, because warm air holds more moisture. But it also alters weather patterns and causes the rains to fall in different places and at different times compared to historical patterns. In the old days, they might have said that the gods were angry with us and were punishing us by meddling with the weather. If we think of ourselves, as I have suggested, as "Children of Oceanus," then his traditional offspring—the rivers, streams, springs, mists, and rains— are the victims of a family feud. We have tapped into the lifeblood of our brothers, sisters, and cousins—the fresh water resources on our planet—and are mightily vanquishing them. But in doing so we are fighting a Pyrrhic battle, in which we and our children too become victims. In a battle with the environment, no one wins.

Children of the Ocean God

In the reflection on the elements, we are ultimately meant to let go of the identification with anything as being the self. The goal is a complete liberation from all clinging and from self-limiting definitions. But on the way to that goal it seems we can usefully expand our sense of self. When I look at myself as a son of Oceanus, embodying waters from every era, from every ocean and stream, and from countless beings, my sense of who I am changes. I have less of a sense of myself as a deracinated being, existing without connections to the wider world. I see myself as more significant, as an inseparable current in life's stream. When I consider the waters that have passed through my body—that I have at some time considered as me, mine, and myself—and see how they have permeated the global body of Oceanus and his children, I start to see the world itself as being me, mine, and myself. I want to protect the planet's waters. I want to guard the family of Oceanus.

This extension of the self, while not the ultimate goal of practice, is still spiritually and materially healthy; it extends our circle of concern beyond our narrow selves and thus dilutes our sense of clinging. It's a return to the reverence for nature that Hesiod enjoined when he told us, "Never cross the sweet-flowing water of ever-rolling rivers afoot until you have prayed, gazing into the soft flood, and washed your hands in the clear, lovely water." Contemplating the soft flood of the ever-rolling self can, perhaps, be a form of prayer, and to contemplate the waters of the flowing elements perhaps a form of purification.

CHAPTER TEN

The Fire Element

"Nothing is ever at rest—wood, iron, water, everything is alive, everything is raging, whirling, whizzing, day and night and night and day, nothing is dead, there is no such thing as death, everything is full of bristling life, tremendous life, even the bones of the crusader that perished before Jerusalem eight centuries ago."
—Mark Twain.[1]

Let us for a moment step into the experience of Antoine Lavoisier's hapless guinea pig. You've been confined for hours in a dark metal tube. You hear only the faintest of muffled sounds from outside, which you can barely identify as the voices of your master and his assistant. You have no idea why you're there. All you know is that it's dark—that the nice human who feeds you has picked you up, placed your palpitating body in this metal box, and then taken away the light. And it's cold. You sniff for food, but there is none. There's no straw or wood to stand on, and your little paws are becoming chilled. But yours is a phlegmatic race, and true to your kind you settle down and wait, patiently, shivering in the dark and cold. You don't know this, but the box is surrounded by melting ice. And the ice is in turn surrounded by snow that keeps the ice at a constant 0°C.

The purpose of this 1782 experiment was to confirm Lavoisier's hunch that the respiration of living things was similar in some way to the combustion of non-living substances like coal, wood, or charcoal. The French scientist and tax collector had already established that combustion involved the removal of oxygen from the atmosphere, and by measuring the amount of ice melted by the guinea pig's metabolism he was able to conclude that respiration was indeed another form of combustion, with organic matter being slowly "burned" using inhaled oxygen.

As it happens, the relationship Lavoisier discovered between ordinary combustion and metabolism is one paralleled in the Six Element Practice. The Fire Element *externally* is energy in all its forms, including fire in the literal sense. But *internally*—as a constituent of the human body—it's specifically considered to be the energy of metabolism. In the "Discourse on the Elements" it is defined as, "That by which one is warmed, ages, and is consumed, and that by which what is eaten, drunk, consumed, and tasted gets completely digested, or whatever else internally, belonging to oneself, is fire, fiery, and clung-to: this is called the internal Fire Element."[2]

The Buddha, like Lavoisier after him, recognized that combustion and metabolism were essentially the same. While the Fire Element outside the body can be considered as the sum total of energy in the universe, we could consider the internal Fire Element to be life itself.

Early Indian texts from long before the time of the Buddha describe fire as being hidden in all things, even in water and in plants. It's not hard to think of this as an intuition, poetically expressed, that there is energy bound up in all matter. The *Rig Veda,* the most ancient of Indian religious texts, describes fire (metaphorically seen as the god Agni) as the "embryo of waters, embryo of woods, embryo of all things that move and do not move,"[3] suggesting that energy is inherent in all things, and suggesting also that it's essentially the same energy that is found in living and non-living things. Fire is declared to be omnipresent: "You [Agni] have filled earth, heaven, and the air between, and follow the whole cosmos like a shadow."[4] Fire declares itself to be the source of all life: "In plants and herbs, in all existent beings, I [Agni] have deposited the embryo of increase. I have engendered all progeny on earth, and sons in women hereafter."[5] Life is the sustainable self-organization of energy within the material world.

As it happens, it was Lavoisier who was the first to publish, in his *Traité Élementaire de Chimie,* a list of chemical—as opposed to classical—elements. He also helped clarify that an element was a substance that could not be further broken down chemically. And interestingly, among the thirty-three elements he identified, he included both light and heat (or "caloric"), which he considered to be subtle forms of matter. He wasn't alone in this view: until the nineteenth century, many scientists believed heat to be a rarefied and elemental liquid that flowed from hot to cold bodies. Even for the father of the chemical elements, fire was itself an element.

Because we're accustomed to thinking in terms of the 117 (or so) modern chemical elements, the idea of fire as an element can seem primitive. But in the schema of the four traditional elements, it's an effective way of making sense of the world. Consider it in this way: Earth is solid matter, Water is liquid, Air is gas of any sort, and Fire is energy. These are the three phases of matter (solid, liquid, gas), plus energy, which is more or less how the average person thinks of the physical world as being constituted. We should perhaps give the Ancients credit for having evolved a sound, if basic, grasp of how the physical world was organized.

Reflecting on the Fire Element

In the context of the meditation practice, we become aware of any heat and movement in the body. When I'm sitting, I notice the warmth of the body, which is most obvious under my clothing and where different parts of the body contact each other. I also feel the warmth of the out-breath compared to the coolness of the in-breath. The very movement of the body as we breathe is an aspect of the Fire Element, since breathing is a biological process; the movement of the breath is metabolic energy in action. Similarly, I can feel the beating of the heart and the living pulse of blood in my extremities. I pay attention to the aliveness of my muscles, the sense of energy on alert, awaiting the instructions that will initiate movement. In my hands in particular I can feel a tingling sensation like electricity, especially if they are touching.

On a more imaginative level, I call to mind the sparks of electricity flowing along nerve fibers and jumping across synapses, and fields of electrical energy pulsing in the brain. I can see in my mind's eye the combustion taking place in the tiny mitochondria: the furnaces within each of the trillions of cells in my body. I can be aware that there are stores of chemical energy in the body in the form of fats and carbohydrates. I can visualize the digestive processes taking place in the gut: the secretion of acid and enzymes, the oozing of bile into the intestines, propulsive waves of peristaltic contraction mas-saging digesta along the gut. I can imagine the never-ending repair processes: specialized cells degrading and rebuilding the bones, the constant regeneration of cells throughout the body, and the pro-cesses taking place within the cells as membranes and organelles are repaired and replaced. There are enzymes hard at work even within your cells' nuclei, repairing strands of DNA that have been shattered by radiation and chemical damage. This is the Fire Element within the body—the organization of energy to build and maintain the human form.

These reflections, incidentally, don't need to be cold and clinical; a healthy dose of appreciation and wonder is both desirable and beneficial. To observe this living body is to be aware of the most complex known structure in the universe. Just this brain alone has 100 billion neurons, and these neurons are supported and maintained by ten times that number of glial cells, whose functions are still being uncovered. Each neuron is connected to ten thousand others, forming an unbelievably complex network of living tissue. A gray, gelatinous mass of fat and protein that can sense, think, and feel: how amazing this is! And that's just the brain. The body as a whole is phenomenally complex, buzzing with electrical and chemical activity. This is something to be noted not in a cold and distant way, but with relish, wonder, and an appreciation of marvels.

Casting the mind outside, I recall the various forms of energy in the rest of the world: the energy upon which life ultimately depends. Typically I tend to begin (and I invite you to join me) by calling to mind those forms of energy that are closest at hand and directly perceptible. As I write this chapter, I'm sitting in the guesthouse of an orphanage in Ethiopia, where I'm adopting a baby boy. I appreciate the light penetrating my eyes. I appreciate the warmth in the space around me—the warmth in the air, heat radiating from the sun, re-radiating from the courtyard outside. I notice the sounds of living beings. A bluebottle makes liquid thudding sounds as it smacks repeatedly against the window. I hear the barking of dogs, the singing of birds, the voices of people (including my nine-month-old son, babbling and wriggling on the bed beside me). Farther afield, I sense the ecosystems around me: the peppers and false bananas growing in tiny city gardens just outside my window, the trees that shade this hot and dusty city, and the eucalyptus forests that blanket the surrounding hills. The Fire Element is embodied in innumerable living beings beyond my direct perception: the millions of people in this city and billions more around the world, uncountable living creatures both large and small, down to the tiniest single-celled organisms, the plants that blanket the earth and drift near the surface of the seas. There are even living organisms penetrating the rocks of the earth itself. So far, organisms have been found thriving at depths of 3.5 kilometers (more than two miles) and they probably go much deeper.[6]

I notice the roar of Addis Ababa's traffic and the drone of a distant aircraft coming in to land at Bole Airport. I hear the whir of my laptop's fans and feel the heat from its battery as electricity flows through its complex circuits. I can hear the buzz of a generator from a local business (the power outage that struck early this morning is a common occurrence, and the local bars and restaurants are well-prepared). All these are the perceptible signs of the external Fire Element. I'm also mindful that there is gas hissing along pipes in the kitchen downstairs, that usually (although not today) there is energy flowing in electrical wiring around me, that despite the power outage there is still heat in the water tank in the bathroom. There is chemical energy stored in foodstuffs in the guesthouse—the guavas and bananas in the fruit bowl, the lentils, vegetables, and rice that our Ethiopian cook is preparing for lunch, the many other fresh, dried, and canned goods in the kitchen cupboards.

Imaginatively, I connect with the hot rocks convulsing in the depths of the earth below me, with the heat and light streaming from the sun, making our planet habitable. I recall lightning crackling, the sun-driven breezes, running water, and the never-ending swell of the distant oceans. Just to the north is the Gulf of Arabia and some of the world's largest oil reserves: these are the fossilized remains of the sunlight of eons past. These are all forms of the Fire Element outside my body.

Having embraced in my mind the Fire Element within and outside my body, I see the essential unity of the two, recalling the ways in which the Fire Element flows into the body and then out again. The Fire Element is one, indivisible except in my mind. Right now, my body is absorbing the heat of the sun's rays. Later, I plan to have a brief shower in the dwindling supply of hot water that remains in our bathroom's immersion tank. The energy in that water will warm my skin, being carried by my bloodstream to all parts of my body. I'm probably still digesting last night's dinner—*injera* (a sour pancake made from a grain called *teff*), and various lentil, bean, and vegetable dishes—and my stomach is still breaking down the guava I just snacked on. My body is absorbing and redistributing the heat of the Ethiopian coffee (espresso-strong, just the way I like it) I sipped a few minutes ago. All this is the Fire Element entering my body.

And in every moment, the Fire Element is flowing out of my body. Although my eyes are not equipped to see them, clouds of warm air billow from my body, and body-temperature gas streams every few seconds from my airways, mixing with the cooler air of the room. Heat radiates from my body, warming my surroundings. When I move, I can feel the warmth where I've been sitting: more heat that has left the body. It's because all this energy is pouring out of me that I have to constantly replenish the Fire Element.

In this reflection we sense that life itself is a flow of energy, that the metabolic energy animating the other elements is itself borrowed from the outside world. This heat and movement—this life—that I sense within myself is not me, not mine, not my self. I am not this. It's only by letting go of the Fire Element, by letting it flow through us, that we can live. Although in reality there's no question of "letting" the Fire Element flow through us: we can't but do otherwise. We can't hold onto "our" energy. It's not "my" life. Life itself is flow, and the energy of life cannot be grasped or possessed.

This is the reflection on the Fire Element, conducted more or less along traditional lines, although enhanced by some basic scientific understandings. But science can do more than just embellish our appreciation of the way in which the Fire Element flows through the the body as part of a self-sustaining pattern of energy. A key problem in science can help us appreciate the Fire Element, and its non-self nature, in another way.

The Mystery of Life

First we can consider life itself. What is it, after all? We've been using the term "life" without defining it, and it turns out, in fact, that coming up with an airtight definition of life is surprisingly difficult. Most scientists agree that for something to be living it must show the following abilities:

To extract nutrients from the environment
To release and use energy from those nutrients
To excrete waste products
To make copies of itself through reproduction

These defining characteristics sound fine until you consider, say, whether a postmenopausal woman is alive. Obviously the answer is yes, but this dents our definition, because a postmenopausal woman cannot reproduce. A postmenopausal woman, it could be argued, had the ability to reproduce earlier in her life cycle, so the definition could be adjusted to take account of the entirety of an organism's life span. But what about an individual who is sterile for his, her, or its entire life cycle? In many insect species, for example, reproduction is limited to certain individuals in a colony. Is the queen bee (the one female in a swarm of honeybees capable of laying eggs) the only living female in the hive? Or should we consider the entire swarm—but not all its constituent parts—to be living? Defining life is getting to be confusing.

And what of the living dead? Ice samples up to eight million years old from Antarctica have been found to contain deep-frozen bacteria.[7] When thawed, these organisms took months to reproduce; possibly their systems had been damaged in storage. Organisms that were a "mere" hundred thousand years old cranked back into reproductive activity in just a week. What of those bacteria when they were in the long sleep of cold storage? They didn't feed, release energy, excrete, or reproduce. Were they then non-living? When we try to define life, the situation quickly becomes messy. Life in fact has multiple competing definitions, none that is universally accepted, and none that is problem-free.

In recent years, tiny cell-like structures called "nanobes" have been found. These miniscule structures, 20 to 150 nanometers in diameter and exuding tendril-like structures, are far smaller than bacteria, and approach the size of viruses. Discovered in sandstone three miles below the seabed, they appear to contain DNA and to reproduce. Yet many scientists don't accept that these "organisms" are in fact living. "There's no way a free-living cell is going to be less than 100 nanometers," claims John A. Baross, a biologist at the University of Washington, in Seattle. And his skepticism seems justified; a cell of such tiny dimensions should be unable to contain the machinery needed for life. Baross points out that "biological entities" could possibly be that small, but couldn't be free-living and self-replicating. Some scientists wonder perhaps these organisms (if they are organisms) have a massively distributed form of life, living as a network. Again, this challenges the definition of life, as "individual" nanobes might not perform all the functions associated with life, even if the network as a whole did.[8]

This lack of an adequate definition of life isn't a deficit in the thinking of scientists—it's not that if we wait long enough some smart young graduate will come up with a tidy definition. It seems more likely that the phenomenon we call life will never be adequately defined, precisely because life is indefinable. We can't even all agree on whether a particular thing is living or not—most scientists say that viruses are non-living because they need the reproductive apparatuses of other beings to reproduce. Others would hold out for viruses being living organisms. As the French Nobel Laureate André Lwoff wryly commented, "Whether or not viruses should be regarded as organisms is a matter of taste."[9] Viruses require other living organisms for reproduction, but many organisms live in symbiotic relationships, each requiring the other to perform functions that are essential for life. All this fits well with the Buddhist position that the self (atta) is essentially indefinable. Our selves are examples of life, and we simply can't say exactly what life is.

I want to be clear that I'm not criticizing science or scientists for being unable to come up with ironclad definitions. The problem is not with scientists' thinking, but with the mind's attempts to deal with an untidy, boundaryless universe. Biologists' field of study is living organisms. If we go back to the literal meaning of the word "field," we can see that it represents something with no clear edge. We may think of a field as having a defined boundary, marked by a fence, but of course not all fields are like that. The word originally just meant a "felled" area, or forest clearing, and some fields even today are simply clearings in the wilderness, with no clearly defined boundary. In the center is a denser concentration of crops, and you know unequivocally that you are in the field. But walk toward the margins and the situation is less clear. The field merges into the surrounding territory in a gradual way. Exactly where does the field end and the wilderness begin? Perhaps no two people would agree on exactly the same boundary. Like a literal field, life seems to have no clear boundaries and shades off into territory that we consider non-living. Life is, again, essentially indefinable.

And yet a huge amount of emotional energy can be invested in the idea that there is a boundary around the field of life that can be clearly defined. It's as if the human mind insists on there being no uncertainty, no unclarity, as if having named something "the field" means that we *must* therefore establish exactly where the field ends. Once again we're faced with the human mind insisting on separation, on definition, in a universe where there is continuity, connectedness, and imprecision. In scientific circles, discussions about definitions are often the most heated; much hate mail has been generated over the question of whether Pluto is a planet, to give one recent example. The problem of defining life brings us right back to the problem of the self and how we tend to see ourselves as being, in some sense, absolutely separate. When we look for the boundaries of the self we find no clear line, just as when we look at the boundaries of what constitutes life we find no clear delineation between the living and non-living worlds.

None of this means that we need throw up our hands and declare it impossible to compose useful definitions. As thinking beings we need to name, and those who are interested in studying the world scientifically have to define—or at least attempt to define—their terms. But as we create definitions, we need to recognize their provisional nature and the inherent fluidity of the world on which we try to foist our neat divisions. We need to hold definitions lightly, remembering that they are the map rather than the territory. When we find ourselves caught up in heated discussions about whether viruses are or are not living, or whether Pluto is a planet, the very heatedness of the debate should cause us to stand back and observe how the mind is trying to pin down something that's essentially "un-pin-downable."

Ecosystems as the Flow of Energy

Science offers yet other ways of looking at life that, like the Six Element Practice, challenge our notion of a separate self: ways going beyond the fact that the energy and raw materials that sustain a self come from outside the self and are therefore ultimately not the self. One such way of seeing life is the concept of the ecosystem. From one particular perspective, an ecosystem is a flow of energy (or as we might say, a flow of the Fire Element) through living beings. Sustaining an ecosystem—a network of interrelated species—requires the transfer of energy from one organism to another. We also know this energy-transfer system as a "food chain," although the metaphor of a chain is far too literal, since energy flows in many directions, not linearly, as from one link of a chain to the next. We need to think more of a "food web."

For a sustainable ecosystem to exist, there must first be some kind of primary extraction of energy from non-living sources—the external Fire Element becoming the internal Fire Element. Some organisms extract energy from the water issuing from hot springs, and a few even extract energy from radioactivity. But the main source of energy in our planet's biosphere—the sum total of all ecosystems—is the sun, with plants doing most of the extraction through photosynthesis.

Organisms that extract energy from non-living systems in this way are known as "autotrophs." Some of the energy an autotroph extracts is stored within the organism's body in the form of the chemical bonds that hold together the organic substances that comprise the autotroph's very body. In the case of plants, this includes stems, roots, seeds, leaves, etc, which all contain usable energy. This energy can be exploited by "heterotrophs" such as animals, insects, and fungi, which cannot chemically capture energy from non-living sources but can only extract energy by breaking down the complex organic chemicals crafted by autotrophs or by other heterotrophs. A sheep eating grass is an example of a heterotrophic organism eating an autotrophic one. A human eating mutton is an example of one heterotrophic organism extracting energy from another. A mosquito sucking the blood of the human as he or she eats mutton is another such example, and a useful one since it helps dispel the myth that humans represent the top of the food chain. The food chain is actually a web without top or bottom. The point of discussing all this is that we can think of energy as another form of flow, and ourselves as merely one part of it. An ecosystem is a flow of energy within a network of living organisms. It is in fact the flow of energy amongst organisms that *constitutes* an ecosystem.

The sun is like a rain cloud, hurling a cascade of photons, or light particles, in all directions, including toward Earth. We can imagine the world's fields and forests as a vast series of catchment lakes, trapping a small quantity of these photons. (The rest are either absorbed by inorganic matter or "evaporate" by bouncing off living things and re-radiating into the environment.) The energy of the sun that is usefully captured by photosynthesis becomes trapped in the chemical bonds of the molecules that constitute grass, grain, trees, and other plants. A tiny fraction of this trapped energy is what we call our food supply. Some plants we will eat directly, such as the wheat that goes to make my morning toast, or the sugar and plums in the jam that I spread on it. Other plants, like grasses, will be eaten by farm animals, and the energy of the former will help form chemical bonds in molecules within the animals' bodies—protein in muscles, fats, and a small amount of carbohydrate. Our food, in the form of meat or edible plants, flows along rivers of dirt and asphalt toward towns and cities. It is dammed temporarily in the reservoirs that we call supermarkets, and then sent coursing along rivulets of asphalt into our homes and our bodies. Energy flows, much as water does.

Of course this flow isn't tidy. There's considerable "evaporation" of energy at each linkage in the food web. Energy is lost as radiated body heat, as feces, and as locomotive energy. And many food crops are in fact food for non-food animals such as insects and rodents. And some food turns out to be inedible due to spoilage and is dumped or plowed back into the land. The flow of energy, on its way from the sun to the bodies of living beings, is turbulent and wasteful. Perhaps the remarkable thing is that any energy is left for us to consume.

The flow of energy does not stop with us. We are part the food web, which has no end. Our various wastes, including the carbon dioxide we exhale, the skin and hair we shed, and our feces and urine, all end up becoming sources of energy for other creatures in the food web. The heat from our bodies simply radiates outward, making a small but significant contribution to the warmth of our environment; each of us radiates as much heat as a hundred-watt light bulb. This "lost" energy leads to a slight increase in the jostling of the molecules in the atmosphere, water, and land around us.

Energy simply flows through us, just as water and the other elements do. And an individual organism is just an eddy in this larger flow of energy. A living being, seen in this way, is a self-organizing vortex of energy and matter, not separate in any real way from the surrounding flow of the elements. Each of us, in terms of the Fire Element, is merely a tiny current in a vast torrent that begins in the heart of the sun and that ends as the random jostling of non-living matter. We do not own any of this energy. Neither do we create any of it. We merely borrow it for a while and then pass it on.

I find it humbling to consider the extent to which we merely lap at the edges of the great torrent that is the Fire Element. Of all the energy that the sun showers into space, only a tiny amount (perhaps one photon in a hundred billion) lands on Earth. And of all the energy in the uncountable billions of photons constantly drenching the earth, only a tiny amount will find its way into living systems, and of that only a tiny amount will be consumed by human beings. Despite Copernicus, we tend to think that we are at the center of the universe—that it all exists in order to serve us. But rather, we are scavengers of energy, peripheral to the vast processes unfolding around us. Considering this, we can perhaps appreciate why the Six Element Reflection is said to be an antidote to conceit.

On Being a Human-Microbial Hybrid

Yet another way we can appreciate our interconnected nature is to consider our status as walking, talking, thinking ecosystems; each of us is a human-bacterial-fungal-viral hybrid. Some 90 percent of the cells in your body are bacterial; you are a staggeringly cosmopolitan society of cells.[10] Considering this can help undermine the sense of separateness that we have. In fact we receive considerable help from other living organisms in order to maintain our status as living beings.

Some of the non-human parts of ourselves are unsavory hitchhikers, such as the organisms that cause thrush, athlete's foot, or food poisoning, but many are intimately woven into the body's metabolic pathways, carrying out essential functions for the human host. Some are protectors. Microscopic flora such as *Lactobacilli* help protect against infection. *Lactobacilli* are the body's partners, carrying out immigration and policing roles that the body alone can't handle, and which it doesn't in fact need to handle because the role has been delegated for so long. *Lactobacilli* are arguably as much a part of us as our skin cells or pancreatic cells.

But there are many other ways in which bacteria play a role in human metabolism, to the extent that we cannot function properly without them. Bacteria help protect us against infection, digest our food, make vitamins, moisturize our skin, help us to metabolize fats and sugars, help regulate our body's immune system, and manufacture chemicals that protect the heart from disease. We even have an organ that has evolved specifically to provide a home for friendly bacteria. Consider the following ways in which we are dependent upon microorganisms:

There are about 3.3 pounds of bacterial inhabitants in the small and long intestines, consisting of at least five hundred and possibly as many as a thousand species. They help break down carbohydrates and also make nutrients such as vitamins K and B12. Our metabolic pathways are incomplete without these bacteria and the chemicals they produce for us.[11] The bacteria in your gut also help with digestion. The human body lacks the enzymes necessary for us to break down plant sugars, such as xylan and cellobiose (similar to cellulose), which humans could not otherwise digest. Cellobiose is a key component of plant cell walls and is therefore found in most edible plants, such as apples and carrots. Bacteria allow us to extract energy from our food that would otherwise be unavailable.[12] Gut microbes also promote fat storage by suppressing the gut's production of a protein, called Fasting-Induced Adipocyte Factor, that helps cells close the "gates" that allow fat to enter. By disabling the gatekeeper, microbes help fats stream into the body's cells, providing us with more energy. In fact these "bugs" control humans at a cellular level.[13]

As well as helping with fat metabolism, bacteria play a role in the body's handling of sugars. Takeshi Matsuzaki and other researchers working at the Yakult Central Institute for Microbiological Research, Tokyo, Japan, found that introducing *Lactobacillus casei* into the diet of mice with non-insulin-dependent diabetes led to a decrease in their blood glucose compared to a control group.[14]

Your skin supports roughly one trillion bacteria. Again, these perform useful functions, not just preventing pathogens from invading but also moisturizing the skin and keeping it healthy by metabolizing the raw fats your skin produces. These bacteria are essential to the health of the skin—the largest organ in the human body: "I would hate to live without them," says the New York University microbiologist Dr. Martin Blaser.[15]

Biologists have long puzzled over the function of the humble vermiform appendix. Many animals live mainly on hard-to-digest plant matter, like leaves or grass, have a long pouch—known as the cecum—at the junction of the small and large intestines. Bacteria hosted in the cecum break down the plants' tough lignin and cellulose, turning them into chemicals that the animals' digestive enzymes can tackle. You and I have a cecum, too, but since we have evolved to eat foods that are more easily digestible, our version of this organ is smaller. The human appendix dangles ineffectually from the end of the cecum, and is the vestigial remnant of what would have been, in our leaf-eating ancestors, a much larger organ. However, since the appendix is prone to life-threatening infection, why haven't we lost it altogether? The answer seems to be that the appendix is the digestive system's backup storage device—a bacterial sanctuary that allows for the rapid restoration of the gut's microflora after a catastrophic event such as an infection or treatment with antibiotics. The narrow opening of the appendix prevents gut contents from entering. And yet it is more than wide enough to allow bacteria to move back into the gut after a bacteria-depleting diarrheal illnesses like salmonella. As immunologist and biochemist William Parker, who first hypothesized the role of the appendix, says, "If you don't have something like the appendix to harbor safe bacteria, you have less of a survival advantage." This, then, may be why evolution has not dispensed with the appendix.[16]

Because we're dependent upon bacteria for digestion and other essential functions, some scientists say that a person is a "superorganism" consisting of his or her own cells as well as our microscopic brethren. Royston Goodacre—of the School of Chemistry, and Manchester Interdisciplinary Biocentre, at the University of Manchester in England—says that "the human can be thought of as a human-microbe hybrid."[17]

Now that the entire human genome has been decoded, researchers are starting to understand that the human and microbiome genomes are one collaborative system. Rather than simply talking about genomics—the study of a single genome—they now refer to metagenomics, or the science of studying a collection of genes from multiple organisms almost as if they were part of one genome. "Over their millions of years of coevolution with us, microbes have learned to manipulate networks of human genes," says Jeffrey Gordon, director of the Center for Genome Sciences at the Washington University School of Medicine. "The genomes of our gut microbes probably contain 100 times more genes than our own genome, providing us with traits we haven't needed to develop on our own."[18] Only 1 percent of the genes in the human body are human.

"The human genome is an amalgam of human genes and the genes of our microbial 'selves,'" says Steven Gill, a molecular biologist formerly at The Institute for Genomic Research (TIGR) and now at the State University of New York at Buffalo. "Without understanding the interactions between our human and microbial genomes, it is impossible to obtain a complete picture of our biology."[19] The human genome lacks some essential enzymes that break down the food we eat into energy critical to survival, a situation that prompts Gill to point out that while bacteria could survive perfectly well without their human hosts, humans would be doomed without their bacterial partners. We are not biologically complete without our bugs: "The microbiota and its collective genomes . . . provide us with genetic and metabolic attributes we have not been required to evolve on our own," as the authors of one paper on human-bacterial mutualism put it.[20]

We inevitably think of our lives as being, well, *our* lives. We think of life—the Fire Element—as something that we own. We think of ourselves as being separate. But if we imagine the body, including the 90 percent of our cells that are microorganisms, working as a system, we begin to see the human body as a collaborative enterprise. Your metabolism is an "open loop" requiring countless other organisms to complete metabolic and regulatory pathways. We require microorganisms to produce chemicals we need, to digest foodstuffs we can't handle alone, to transform waste chemicals we can't dispose of ourselves, and even to control the body's defense mechanisms. These organisms have co-evolved with us over millions of years. We and they, together, are one system. Can we think of them as being ourselves? This challenges our normal way of seeing ourselves, which assumes a kind of independence and separateness that just doesn't exist in reality. A sense of humility can come from considering the extent to which we are dependent upon "humble" microorganisms.

Accepting our bacteria as part of us may seem contradictory to the reflection we've been considering: "This is not me; this is not mine; I am not this." We seem to be saying here something more like "This *is* me; this *is* mine; I *am* this." But the contradiction is only apparent. As we expand the sense of the self to include (technically) non-human life forms, the sense of self begins to dissipate. We begin no longer to see ourselves as separate. We see ourselves as connected, and so our sense of self is held onto less tightly.

You, the Virus

If knowing that microbes extend the human genome helps under-mine our sense of separateness, it's worth considering that our very

DNA is a collaborative project. Since the human genome was first sequenced in 2001, more than a hundred thousand viral elements have been found embedded in it. Most viruses simply infect a cell, hijack the cell's metabolic pathways in order to reproduce itself, and then leave (with or without killing the host). But certain kinds of viruses are able to insert their DNA into our genome. Scientists studying the genome were astonished to find that viral genes vastly outnumber human ones. Only about 1.5 percent of the genome is made up of human genes, while clearly identifiable viral genes account for 9 percent. But in total, virus-like genes represent an astonishing 90 percent of the human genome.[21] We are more virus than we are human; or to put it another way, to be human is to be mostly viral. At a genetic level, you are mostly not you.

It turns out that we could not in fact be human without the viral contribution to our genome. While most of our viral DNA has no apparent purpose, some of it has taken on important roles. The repurposing of formerly viral DNA—the hijacking of the hijacker—is thought to have played a vital role in the evolution of life, including human life. "There is a growing body of evidence that [these] elements have contributed to the evolution and genome structure in many species . . . and may have contributed to the genetic changes that led to the emergence of the human species," says John McDonald, of the University of Georgia, who has studied the relative ages of viral DNA in the human genome.[22] The extra material that viruses add to the genome becomes raw material for the creation of new functionality within the host organism. In fact, wherever scientists find a new burst of speciation, they also find a burst of genetic invasion by viruses. Clearly virus infection is tied up with the emergence of new species in important ways, although the details aren't clear.[23]

But one example of how viruses may have created what we are today is found in the very human realm of intimate relationships. Human behaviors such as monogamy—which is remarkably rare in the animal world (think of dogs, cats, farm animals, and chimps)— may be the result of viral influences. Viruses have been shown to alter complex behaviors such as egg laying and host selection in parasitic wasps, and there is suggestive evidence (although no conclusive proof) that viruses may have given rise to the tendency in some mammals to form family units through emotional bonding. A relatively small change in the DNA of the notably promiscuous montane vole made it behave more like its monogamous cousin, the prairie vole. Humans, unlike our closest relative, the chimpanzee, have a propensity (although obviously not an absolute one) to monogamy and joint child-rearing. Could this have arisen as the result of a viral infection? It's an interesting possibility, especially considering that the researchers in the montane vole study did in fact use a virus to alter the animals' genome. Many other changes in our genome may have been instigated by viral interlopers, and the most significant differences between you and a chimpanzee may well come down to some viral DNA changing the activities of a few receptors in the brain.[24] Is it possible that the warm feelings you get when you look at a loved one are due to viral DNA lurking in your genome?

The evolution of gestation—the maturation of the young inside a womb—is now known to have been helped along by viruses. A fertilized egg contains surface proteins different from those of the mother, and by rights the egg should be attacked by the mother's immune system. But one thing viruses are good at is suppressing the immune system. What we see when we look in the womb during pregnancy is an environment swarming with viral proteins. These are produced in the outer layers of the egg, forcing the mother's body into tolerating it. When the genes giving rise to these viral proteins are disabled, the egg is unable to implant.[25] Even the placenta itself—thin enough to allow the transfer of nutrients, but largely impenetrable to infecting organisms—is believed to result from the actions of genes that were formerly viral.[26]

This is something to reflect on. Imagine the DNA in the nuclei of your cells, coiled like a rope. Look closely, and imagine that the truly human DNA is pink, while the viral and virus-like DNA is blue. The blue constitutes about half the genome, the pink just a tiny smattering amounting to about one or two parts per hundred. The rest of the genome is what's often called "junk DNA," and its function, if any, isn't yet known—you could visualize that portion as a mysterious black color. Your human lineage is a minority in your own body. How is your sense of self affected by this thought? How do you feel knowing that you are a composite being, right down to your genome? How is your sense of yourself affected by knowing that essential parts of "you" come from outside the human lineage? As you visualize your genome in this way, try repeating the words, "This is not me; this is not mine; I am not this." Notice what effect this has.

Considering these examples of our interdependence can help us expand our sense of what the self is. While we may habitually tend to assume that we are separate from the world around us, we in fact are not and cannot be separate. We are totally dependent upon other organisms for harnessing energy from non-living sources and for channeling that energy into the food web. But we can't even properly harness that energy *within our own bodies* without the help of other organisms. It's both more accurate and more interesting to embrace a more expansive view of ourselves—one that sees the human body not as a disconnected object but a dynamic, incomplete, and interdependent set of living processes—a vortex of energy and matter in a river of life.

We do not create any of the energy we use. All the energy used in the human body is borrowed from the outside world. Ultimately it returns there. We are part of a great vortex of living energy far greater than ourselves. The Fire Element flows through us, and we are unable to hold onto it. In fact we live by not holding onto it. This energy, as it flows through us, animates matter, which in turn has also been borrowed from the outside world. Where, in all this, are we? We're left with an interesting paradox—we are living organisms, and yet life is not ours. Our life is a thing on loan.

CHAPTER ELEVEN

The Air Element

"For hundreds of thousands of years I have been
dust-grains floating and flying in the will of the air,
often forgetting ever being in that state."
—Jalāl al-Dīn Rūmī[1]

It's midwinter 1982, and I'm in a lodge perched on a cliff overlooking the undulating quicksilver of the Atlantic Ocean on Scotland's wild and rugged west coast. In the company of about two-dozen others, I'm on my first intensive meditation retreat. The days consist of long sessions of sitting and walking meditation interspersed with simple meals. Sometimes in the meditation room I long to sleep, but every time my head begins to nod I'm jerked back into reluctant wakefulness. Other times it's as if I've tapped into a wellspring of joy; intensely alive and content to focus on the breath, I realize there's nowhere else I'd rather be or anything else I'd rather be doing.

Outside, the weather is as changeable as my inner experience. Although a few days are mild and almost springlike in a chilly, Northern European way, with rich sunlight slanting from behind towering masses of cloud, the winter also brings days and nights of ferocious storms in which the wind howls and—to my alarm—makes the glass in the windows of our lodge buckle visibly, the reflections snapping back and forth in time with the more powerful gusts. The air seems like a living force, and not one that is friendly. As soon as we settle down to meditate, it seems that the winds redouble their assault on the lodge, as if the elements are unhappy with our activities.

On the last full day of the retreat, however, the elements subside, the air stills, and the skies turn a brilliant azure. The retreat leaders announce the day's pilgrimage to a particularly beautiful *lochan*— a small mountain lake—nestled amongst craggy peaks. And so we hike across the rugged landscape, and it's good to be out in the wilderness after so much time in the meditation hall. All the sitting we've done has apparently had its effects on my perceptions. I'm stunned by the hallucinatory quality of the lichens covering the boulders, their yellows and gray-greens almost impossibly vibrant and their fractal patterns preternaturally vivid. Dead bracken is the color of copper; the branches of distant birches appear purple. The whole world explodes with color, and is alive. We walk in near-silence, the sound of our breathing accompanied only by the hollow sound of feet on rocks and mossy moorland. Tiny streams seem to be chuckling as we step over them.

At last we reach the lochan. The beauty is astonishing, especially to senses opened wide by two weeks of intense stillness and reflection. In the presence of this rugged majesty, all we can do is stand and look, hushed and awestruck, and there's so much beauty it seems that the heart will burst trying to take it all in. But Robert, who is a talented amateur photographer, dashes forward, wanting to capture images of the landscape uncluttered by human forms. He reaches the water's edge and places a camera between his face and the surrounding beauty. As we watch him squint through his viewfinder, searching for the perfect composition, a waterspout rises from the center of the lochan. For a moment it rises skyward but then starts to race in Robert's direction. At first there had been a sense of fascinated bafflement. I've never seen anything like this before. But now there's a sense of inevitability, as if what's to come is preordained. Focused on what he can see through his camera viewfinder, Robert is unaware of the vortex racing toward him. He presses the shutter button and captures another shot of water and mountain. The column of water rushes for the shore. We watch, enthralled, as the drama unfolds. The waterspout, breaking as it hits the gravelly beach, hurls its payload earthward and drenches Robert, who leaps backward in surprise.

In this moment it really does seem as if the elements are alive, and that air, water, and earth have taken offense at my fellow retreatant's lack of reverence. And then, that night, after the final meditation and ritual chanting, the gong rings out to signal the end of the retreat, to be followed moments later by a peal of thunder—the only one we've heard in the fortnight of the retreat—which rolls around the bay, echoing and re-echoing. It feels like it's time to go.

I like to consider myself a rationalist, dedicated to empirical explanations of the world. In retrospect I have no doubt that the storms only appeared to increase in power whenever we sat to meditate because we were quieter and more attentive at those times. I have no doubt also that the water sprite I saw attacking my photographer friend was a case of his being in the wrong time at the wrong place, combined with the sun's rapidly warming the air over a mass of cold water. And thunder happens—if enough people go on enough retreats, there's bound to be a peal of thunder on at least one occasion just after the final bell. No deities are required. And yet the experience had the goose-bump-inducing quality of a supernatural event. It *felt* like an encounter with a personification of natural forces. And if a modern rationalist can fall prey to such sentiments and feel the ripples of superstitious thought patterns, it's not surprising that for premodern cultures, the elements were often gods.

The Sky as God

For the Mesopotamian cultures living on the fertile plains between the Tigris and Euphrates rivers, the universe was alive with gods. The genesis of all things was the great ocean, Nammu, "the mother who gave birth to heaven and earth." Where Nammu came from is a mystery unwritten, but it is recorded that she gave birth to An and Ki—the gods of heaven and earth. An and Ki made incestuous holy love and begat Enlil, the god of air, who separated the vast emptiness of space from the firmness of earth, creating the atmosphere. Having literally moved heaven and earth—in order to give the seed of the land space in which to grow, we're told—Enlil went on to father the god of cattle and the goddess of grain. He even invented the pick-axe[2]—obviously a much-appreciated farm tool for the Sumerians to have attributed to it a divine origin. Enlil is a very agricultural god.

We tend now to look at agriculture as a lowly occupation, but agriculture was and is the foundation of civilized life; and so Enlil was not just any god, and not even just any powerful god—he was the supreme deity. Enlil, as the air god, bridged heaven and earth and so controlled the crossroads of the known universe. He represented the Air Element that brought rain and allowed people and animals to eat, live, and breathe. He was all-powerful. And like many a powerful god, he was not all sweetness and light. Once, annoyed at being kept from sleep by the noisy proliferation of human beings on the earth below him, he decided to send a massive flood to wipe out the clamorous masses. Fortunately, one man (Atrakhasis in the Akkadian version) was given advance warning of the impending deluge. Constructing a massive boat, he took aboard many different kinds of animals and was able to ride out the flood. In one rendition of the tale, his boat came to rest on a mountain as the waters subsided. After waiting a week he sent out a dove, which soon returned, unable to find a perch. Eventually a raven was released and, able to find land and eat, it never returned. After the flood, a sacrifice was made, a rainbow appeared, and the goddess Ishtar invited all the gods but Enlil to gather round.[3] In this obvious precursor of the familiar tale of Noah's Ark, Enlil is the equivalent of Jehovah, who likewise is a sky god prone to both creation and destruction.

Sky gods—Zeus, Jupiter, Enlil, Jehovah—tend to be the supreme deities in their respective pantheons. No doubt this is largely because the sky is above us and affords a spectacular view of what's transpiring below. It is an ideal vantage point for a deity who wants to keep an eye on creation. The sky also brings the weather patterns that provide life-giving sun and rain. But the preeminence of sky deities may symbolize too the immediate need we have for air. We can live without food for weeks or months, and without water for days, but it only takes a few minutes without air to bring life to an abrupt halt.

Air as Lifeforce

Air allows the "seed of the land" to grow. It is necessary for life and is a symbol for life. In Genesis we are told that "The Lord God formed man of dust from the ground, and breathed into his nostrils the breath of life; and man became a living being" (Genesis 2:7).

What makes the human body different from dead matter, in the biblical view, is the divine breath of the creator god, which is the living force within us. In Sanskrit, Air and breath are synonymous, and both are the names of a single god, Vayu or Prana—*prana* being the life force. For the Greeks, *pneuma* meant not just "air," but also "breath" and "spirit." To the Romans, *spiritus* meant not just the breath but the living essence, so that the phrase "give up the ghost" ("ghost" is a translation of *spiritus*) has the dual meaning of ceasing respiration and surrendering one's soul. In Taoism, the *chi,* or life force, is literally "breath," and the universe was created from nine streams of breath. The breath is, in mystical terms, that which makes the difference between a sentient being and a lump of dead meat.

For centuries, the cessation of breathing was the diagnosis of death. Using mirrors or a feather it could be confirmed that the *spiritus* had stopped flowing or that the ghost had departed. It was therefore not surprising for people to conclude that breathing is essential to life, but that the breath is life itself—a vital substance flowing within the body. But the Air Element can also destroy, as with Enlil's deluge, and as with Katrina, Andrew, Wilma, and their violent hurricane siblings. (Perhaps the modern convention of naming hurricanes, cyclones, and tropical storms is a nod to the concept of the Air Element as an angry deity.) Like all the other elements, Air is a force outside of ourselves, and a power ultimately outside of our control.

Often the breath is equated not just with a life force but with the essence of the individual—with the soul. In the *Brihadaranyaka Upanishad*—one of the oldest Indian (and pre-Buddhist) sacred texts—the mental and physical faculties have a competition to see which is most important to the body. Each of the Faculties takes a year off in turn, then returns to see how the others fared in its absence. Vision, hearing, and the others take their vacation, and yet the remainder of the body somehow gets by. Even when the mind returns from his sojourn, the other faculties report that they have muddled through: "Like fools, not knowing with their mind, but breathing with the breath, seeing with the eye, hearing with the ear, generating with seed; thus have we lived."[4] But when the breath simply *begins* to depart, the other faculties panic and realize that the game has gone too far: "The vital breath, when on the point of departing, tore up these senses, as a great excellent horse of the Sindhu country might tear up the pegs to which he is tethered. They said to him: 'Sir, do not depart. We will not be able to live without thee.'" This description reminds me of the terror described by the writer Christopher Hitchens when he volunteered to be waterboarded, to see for himself whether it was in fact a form of torture. He described the experience as being "flooded more with sheer panic than with mere water," and despite his determination to endure the experience for as long as possible, he seems to have lasted only a few seconds.[5] Being unable to breathe makes one feel as if one were being ripped apart.

The *Brihadaranyaka Upanishad* also contains a passage in which the breath is described as a string holding the self together: "By air, as by a thread . . . this world and the other world, and all creatures are strung together. Therefore . . . people say of a dead person that his limbs have become unstrung; for by air, as by a thread . . . they were strung together."[6] We're also told that the immortal Self (*atman*—this is the Sanskrit version of the Pali, *atta*) is the puppet master who pulls that string: "He who dwells in the air, and within the air, whom the air does not know, whose body the air is, and who pulls the air within, he is thy Self, the puller within, the immortal." Here the breath is seen as something like the physical essence of the self—that which holds everything together—and the atman as the essence of the essence, the non-material power that causes the breath to move. So the unchanging soul is closely connected with the breath, being a kind of non-material accompaniment to it, and in fact the word "atman" itself comes from a root meaning "breath."

The Restless Spirit

The Air Element Reflection reminds us not only that the element is ultimately outside our control, but that it's ultimately outside what we consider to be "us." It dispels any notion that the breath—or any other aspect of the Air Element—comprises an essence, so that we cease to define ourselves in terms of the physical body. Having worked in the earlier stages of the reflection at freeing ourselves from identification with the solid and liquid matter that comprises the body, as well as the living fire that powers it, we now free ourselves from identification with the breath as well.

For the Buddha, the Air Element was neither a god nor a mystical force within the body, but simply a natural phenomenon. It was the breath and the wind. He observed that the wind—the external Air Element—was a potentially violent force that could cause widespread havoc: "It sweeps away villages, towns, cities, districts, and countries." But like all the other elements it's "impermanent, subject to destruction, disappearance, and change." In the hot season of India, when "they seek wind by means of a fan or bellows," we are told that "even the strands of straw in the drip-fringe of the thatch do not stir." As well as being an evocative description of an airless and sultry day in rural India, this is a reminder that the Buddha's view of the elements is not always in accord with our own. He did not think of the Air Element as being air as we understand the word today, but as being "wind." The Air Element was by definition something in motion, and if it wasn't moving, the element had ceased. And it's true that our bodies can't detect air unless the air is moving or we're moving in relation to it. My use of the word "airless," above, suggests that these notions of air as something that exists only when it's in motion are embedded in our culture too.

The Air Element is described in a stock passage: "What is the internal air element? Whatever, internally, belonging to oneself, is air, airy, and clung-to; that is, up-going winds, down-going winds, winds in the belly, winds in the bowels, winds that course through the limbs, in-breath and out-breath."[7] And to cover all bases, the description concludes by throwing in the catchall phrase, "and whatever else, internally, belonging to oneself, is air, airy, and clung-to."

This list strikes me as being a curious mixture of earthy observation and early Indian mystical physiology. Up-going winds are simple belches, down-going winds are farts, and "winds in the bowels" is a term that needs no explanation. (I can imagine this part of the teaching provoking unmindful giggling among the younger monks.) The in-breath and out-breath are part of our daily experience and need no elaboration. The concept of "winds that course through the limbs," however, is one of the more "poetic" interpretations of how the Air Element was thought to function in the body. According to physiological science at the time of the Buddha, our limbs move because the heart pumps air through the veins of the body. The human body, rather charmingly, was seen as a kind of pneumatic device, a mannequin powered by compressed air. This idea that the arteries carried air rather than blood was to persist in Europe right up to the early 1600s, because blood tends to pool in the veins after death, making it appear that the arteries are filled with air. Even when, in 1616, William Harvey demonstrated that blood flowed from the heart via the arteries and returned to the heart via the veins, he still hadn't a clue how blood from the arterial system found its way back into the veins; the discovery of capillaries was still several decades off.

The Traditional Reflection

The traditional refection follows the same pattern as with the previous elements:

1. We notice the air in the body, imagining that which we can't directly experience.

2. We notice and reflect upon the Air Element in the outside world.

3. We reflect that there is in fact only one Air Element, that the Air in the body has come from outside, returns to outside,

4. And that it is therefore not us, not owned by us, and that we are not to be identified with the Air Element.

The Air Element is just one more river flowing through the human form, a river of transient gases that ebbs and flows like the waters in an estuary, the body filling and emptying with its innate rhythms, the breath rising and falling in time with the tidal forces of the body's physiology.

When reflecting on the flow of the Air Element, we start with our direct physical experience. We can of course follow the advice of the Discourse and notice any intestinal rumblings. More often, though, we start by becoming aware of the flow of the breath in and out of the body. You can do this now, starting by noticing the sensation of the breath flowing through the nostrils, up into the airways, down the throat, through the trachea, and into the lungs. Of course as soon as we've done this we're aware that the lungs are full and that we need to exhale again, and we observe the reverse process. With the Air Element, the giving and taking are so much more closely linked than with the earlier elements that we can't observe one phase of the breath without immediately noticing the other.

To anyone with even a passing acquaintance with the techniques of meditation, watching the breath is a familiar tool of mental training. Many of the more common methods of meditation involve observing the breath in order to cultivate mindfulness—a quality of present and non-attached observation. Observing the breath is more difficult than it might sound. Typically, after a brief period of observing the sensations of the breath in the practice of mindful breathing, or *anapanasati*, the mind starts to wander and gets lost in thought. We become focused on something we're worried about, or are annoyed about, or we simply daydream. And, oddly, there's no awareness that this is happening—the mind is on "automatic pilot." But at some point we return to mindful awareness, realize that the mind has been wandering, and bring the focus of our awareness back to the breath again. This cycle is repeated over and over, because the mind wanders again and again. At first it can be hard to keep the mind focused on the breathing for more than one or two breaths. But with practice we become more attentive and focused. What happens is that we are training the mind to pay continuous attention to one object—which in this case just happens to be the breath. Because we are spending less time ruminating—i.e., being immersed in thoughts that are anxious, irritable, undermining, or concerned with fantasies—we begin to feel calmer and happier. In time we find that this skill of detaching ourselves from unhelpful rumination carries over into our daily lives, and we find ourselves experiencing more equanimity, not becoming upset by things that would normally push our buttons. We also find it easier to sustain focused attention on whatever we happen to be doing. Among other things, this makes it easier to do reflections such as recollection of the Six Elements.

But classic mindfulness of breathing, as described above, isn't quite what we're doing in the Six Element Reflection on the breath. We do of course bring our attention back to the breathing, but the aim is not simply to notice the sensations of the breath. We are also aware that it is the air *as an element* that we are observing, and we notice the cycle of acceptance and surrender of that element. As we're following the sensations of the air flowing in and out of the body, we're aware that this is Air flowing in, and Air flowing out. In the Six Element Practice, the mind is encouraged to wander in a mindful and reflective way as we consider the various ways in which the element passes through the body. We're becoming aware of the breath as a connection between what we think of as ourselves and what we think of as the outside world. We're reflecting on the essential identity of the inner and outer Air Elements. And in doing so, we begin to let go of any sense that the Air Element within the body is "me, mine, myself."

There are, as we all know, physiological processes in the body connecting the in-breath with the out-breath. In India twenty-five hundred years ago it was known, of course, that air flowed in and out of the lungs, and people entertained that charming notion of the body as a pneumatically powered marionette. But there was no real understanding of why we breathe. Hippocrates, a century or so after the Buddha, thought that breathing cooled the heart, and from the time of Galen in the second century, up to the time of William Harvey in the seventeenth, doctors in the West continued to believe that the function of breathing was to cool the body by removing excess heat from the blood. Breathing was imagined to be a biological air-conditioning system, and why people died so quickly in the absence of air was a great mystery. At the time of the Buddha, there was no understanding of the circulatory system, the exchange of oxygen and carbon dioxide in the alveoli of the lungs, or of the circulation of gases in the bloodstream. There was no understanding of the existence of oxygen or its role in combustion in the cells' mitochondria. But we now know all this, and so we can incorporate into our reflection an awareness of the entire process of gaseous exchange and circulation within the body. Again, we don't need to have a doctoral level of knowledge about these processes, but the principles are relatively straightforward and a general understanding will help us appreciate the ways in which the Air Element flows through the body.

And so we can notice once again the beating of the heart and any pulses that we feel in the body, since these (although not traditionally part of the practice) represent the Air Element flowing around the blood vessels as oxygen, carbon dioxide, and inert nitrogen. We can be aware that the Air Element (although not necessarily in gaseous form) permeates the entire body. Every cell in the body receives oxygen and emits carbon dioxide, and so every cell in the body is a minute part of the river of Air flowing through us. Respiration involves the entire body, not just the lungs.

But the Air Element does not simply flow through the body, re-emerging in a changed form upon exhalation. The Air Element is an integral part of every molecule in the human body. Fats, carbohydrates, proteins, and the inorganic compounds that form teeth and bones all contain oxygen, which ultimately comes from the atmosphere, entering the biosphere when cyanobacteria, green algae, and terrestrial plants photosynthesize. Proteins also contain nitrogen, and that too is of atmospheric origin, being captured when lightning strikes "fix" this otherwise unreactive gas by fusing it with oxygen. Atmospheric nitrogen is fixed too when bacteria (sometimes living symbiotically with plants) convert it to ammonia, which they then use to make organic compounds. When you look at the composition of the human body, a 70 kg person contains about 43 kg of oxygen and 1.8 kg nitrogen. We are, in a certain sense, largely creatures of the air.

In reflecting on the Air Element within the body, we have already begun considering how the internal Air Element comes entirely from the external Air Element—our atmosphere. Let's now fully switch our attention to the outside world. We can feel the out-breath stream away from the body. We can feel the intimate contact that the air makes with our skin, feeling its temperature and movements as it swirls by us. We can recall our experience of breezes and storms, evoking our stored memories of the element. We can call to mind the shell of gas that circulates above the planet—that sliver of space, between solid earth and the cold vacuum of the heavens, where life can flourish. Sometimes in my meditations I call to mind photographs of the earth from space—those astonishing images that reveal the tenuous-ness of our atmosphere as it fades out into hard vacuum, and the beauty of the massive swirling cloud formations that sprawl across the globe. Ulf Merbold, a German astronaut who flew on the space shuttle, was struck by the sheer frailty of our atmosphere: "For the first time in my life I saw the horizon as a curved line. It was accentu-ated by a thin seam of dark blue light—our atmosphere. Obviously this was not the ocean of air I had been told it was so many times in my life. I was terrified by its fragile appearance."[8]

We all share this precious and fragile resource. There are, in real-ity, no borders. The first Syrian in space, Muhammad Ahmad Faris, commented on the absence of the demarcations with which we're so familiar from maps and globes. "From space I saw Earth—inde-scribably beautiful with the scars of national boundaries gone."[9] And it's true; after seeing the earth as an unblemished whole, a map of nation-states does make our planet look like a surgical patient who has been crudely sliced and stitched up. The first Saudi Arabian to orbit the earth, Sultan Bin Salman al-Saud, made a similar comment about losing a sense of the world's artificial divisions: "The first day or so we all pointed to our countries. The third or fourth day we were pointing to our continents. By the fifth day we were aware of only one Earth."[10]

From space, it is easier to see that our atmosphere is not a static thing, but a dynamic process. Astronauts can see massive vortices of cloud being born, spinning across oceans and continents, and dis-solving back into the greater flow of the element. They can witness the red stain of dust storms stretching from the Sahara Desert to the Philippines. They can see the gray smoke from Asian forest fires smeared across the globe, all the way to Alaska. They can see brown plumes of volcanic dust blowing from Etna, in Italy, over to Libya, in northern Africa. In nature there are no nations, and the Air Element reminds us how we like to impose boundaries, whether between nations or between ourselves and the world.

Even from space, however, it is impossible to appreciate the full fact of the interconnected nature of the atmosphere. Science talks of Earth's systems as composed of the geosphere (the planet's solid parts), the atmosphere, hydrosphere, and biosphere (the total ecology of all living beings and their relationships). Interestingly, these four spheres mirror almost exactly the four classical elements. The geosphere is the Earth Element, the hydrosphere is Water, the biosphere is Fire (or at least the energy captured in living systems), and the atmosphere is of course the Air Element. Each of the four spheres affects and is affected by all the others. They work together in an interdependent way, so that the atmosphere is produced through interactions with the geosphere, hydrosphere, and biosphere. The earth below our feet is not just affected by, but is actually formed by the other three spheres.

To take just one example, vast areas of the earth's crust are comprised of limestone. Limestone is composed of the compressed shells of long-dead creatures (biosphere) such as mussels, clams, oysters, corals, and microscopic plankton that lived in shallow waters (hydrosphere), dropping their shells to the seabed when they died. These organisms were able to create their shells by combining the calcium with carbonates formed by carbon dioxide (atmosphere) dissolving in the sea.[11] Over time, these deposits build up and become rock, which becomes part of the earth's crust (geosphere).

Ultimately we can draw no line demarcating the Air Element from the other physical elements. And that's appropriate, given the fact that we're reflecting on the boundaryless nature of the self. The "selves," as it were, of the elements are lacking defined boundaries, as are all things. The concept of the elements is once again a series of labels imposed on our experience of the world, attempts to define as static processes that are actually dynamic. The elements too are empty of selfhood. We mentally break down our bodies into the four physical elements not because these categorizations are somehow more real. They are simply convenient classifications that allow us to mentally deconstruct our self-definitions, and the hold that these self-definitions have on us. Just as we are empty of any inherent selfhood, so too are the elements themselves empty.

Having contemplated the Air Element externally, we bring the internal and external together. We appreciate the coming and going of the breath, its circulation around the body and its circulation around the globe, and we recognize that there is only one Air Element. There is no "other" Air Element or "me" Air Element, but just *the* Air Element. We reflect that we can't possess the Air Element that's within the body; it's simply passing through. We can't hold onto the Air Element, because to hold onto it would be to die. Life is letting go. And so we can come to see the Air Element as yet one more river—an endlessly circulating vortex of matter. Each of us is just a current in the stream, inseparable from other currents, our beings entangled at multiple levels with the solid earth, the oceans and other waters, the atmosphere, and all living things. It is only in fact by sharing in the Air Element that we are able to exist. To be alive is to be connected, and our existence is contingent upon the flow of the elements. Reflecting on the Air Element in this way can help us overcome our sense of separateness, permanence, and specialness. It opens us up to appreciating the small part we play in the great cycle of the Air Element and allows us to experience a sense of wonder. We are part of a greater whole, and there's a sense of grandeur about this fact that is the opposite of egoism and yet greatly affirming.

The One Breath We Share

If you have a sense that you actually do exist separate from the world around you, try holding your breath. As the Hindu *Upanishad,* quoted earlier, said, "By air . . . all creatures are strung together." Our atmosphere is—as one at least *hopes* every schoolchild knows—dependent upon plants and other photosynthesizing organisms, but we tend to forget just how life-driven it actually is. Sometimes when I'm meditating on the Air Element in the depths of a New England winter, I realize that there is virtually no photosynthesis taking place in the Northern Hemisphere outside the tropics. At those times, each breath I take is "legacy" air, the oxygen coming either from previous years of photosynthesis or having been produced on the sunnier side of the globe. When I breathe, I breathe the rainforest. I breathe the prairies and the tundra. I breath the ocean's plankton. As a measure of the rate of turnover of our atmosphere's oxygen, it's been estimated that it takes only two thousand years of photosynthesis to replenish all the oxygen currently in the air.[12] This may *seem* like a long time, but in geological and evolutionary time this is nothing: at this timescale the oxygen in our atmosphere would have been completely replaced one hundred times since modern humans originated in east Africa, about two hundred thousand years ago. We live in complete dependence upon other organisms. When I notice the air I am breathing and repeat the words, "This is not me; this is not mine; I am not this," I experience a profound sense of gratitude. Without other beings to create this atmosphere I simply could not exist.

The breath connects us intimately with all beings. In May 1996, a column in *New Scientist* magazine discussed whether it was true that each breath we took included atoms breathed by Leonardo da Vinci and other historical figures.[13] One contributor calculated—admittedly based on a measure of guesswork about the degree of mixing and recycling of the atmosphere—that each time we breathe in, we inhale 4.3×10^9 molecules that Leonardo had exhaled. Even if his estimate is off by several orders of magnitude, that still has us inhaling an unimaginable number of Leonardo's exhaled molecules with each breath. It was further reckoned that with each breath we take we inhale an average of five molecules that were part of Leonardo's dying gasp. This would be true for any historical figure you happen to choose, assuming that they lived at least a few decades ago—long enough that their exhalations have had time to mix completely with the Earth's atmosphere. Each time you inhale, you breathe in an unimaginably large number of molecules previously exhaled by the Buddha, Plato, Christ, Mohammed, and Confucius. The same of course is true with history's greatest sinners: the slave-traders, the murderers, and the torturers. With each breath, I breathe all humanity and I am all beings, living and dead. I am them. The air that has passed through my body will in the future be breathed and become part of the body of all humanity. I will become them, and they will be me.

I find something very intimate about this thought, that we each penetrate the being of every living thing on the planet, not just now but for all time, entering each other's lungs and leaves, bones and stems, blood and sap, joining with the very molecules, suffusing the entire body. And

you *are* the atmosphere. As we've seen, the body is thoroughly permeated by and even composed of stuff that has been or will be atmospheric
gases. When any organism breathes, the earth breathes. The carbon
dioxide that we exhale is food for plants, which build it into complex
carbohydrates. Our exhalations circle the globe, swept by winds, being
scattered randomly, and being captured by grasses, ferns, mosses, forests, crops, and algae. What was you becomes them. Sometimes, driving
along New England roads, surrounded by trees and fields, I reflect that
these organisms are composed in part of me, and I of them. Sometimes
I have the thought that I am driving through myself, and at other times
it seems as if I am the forest, driving through itself.

From the humblest of single-celled organisms to the blue whale
and the redwood, there is a sense that the entire biosphere breathes
as one. There is only one Air Element. We are of one breath, inhaling
and exhaling one another in a mutual interdependence that benefits
us all. Our breath mingles in the atmosphere, which is nothing more
than the combined breaths of billions of beings, improbably created
over billions of years from an archetypal atmosphere that would, if we
breathed it now, kill us stone dead. Without living beings we would
not have this atmosphere, which is "a biological contrivance," as James
Lovelock put it.[14] We can think, metaphorically, of our planet having
a respiratory system, and as you and I as parts of that system. We help
create this atmosphere, you and I. The air in which we live is us in a
dilute form. It's all other beings too—plant, animal, and microscopic.

There is a sense in which the earth does literally breathe. As Antoine
de Saint Exupéry said in his classic work of children's fiction, *The
Little Prince,* "What is essential is invisible to the eye."[15] Imagination,
as we've seen, can help us visualize what is invisible to our physical senses, but sometimes to see the essential you need satellites and

supercomputers. Scientists from NASA's Goddard Space Flight Center, using data from the Sea-viewing Wide Field-of-view Sensor (SeaWiFS) satellite, have made visible the planet's respiratory cycle by imaging the extent of photosynthesis in both the oceans and over land. The work of photosynthesis is visualized as bands of color, pulsating in concert with the seasons. The resulting images provide a stunning view of the earth breathing, showing the expansion and contraction of photosynthesis over a period of years and allowing us to appreciate the earth as a living organism.[16]

I look again and again with wonder upon these animations, where dry data representing millions of measurements are translated into beautiful bands of shifting color over the oceans and the land. I see something that resembles a breathing child. The Southern Hemisphere is like the child's belly, while the Northern is like the chest. The flowing patterns in each hemisphere differ, but move synchronously, one rising as the other falls. I feel a sense of tenderness and a powerful desire to protect this small sphere. These animations take us beyond the capabilities of our unaided senses, allowing us to see patterns too subtle and on too long a timescale for even an astronaut in space to discern with the naked eye. And watching these images, there comes a sense of belonging. If the earth is seen as a breathing organism, then you and I are the cells in its body.

In losing my sense of myself as a separate being, I find myself to be something grander. I find myself to be part of a living global system of miraculous complexity, where water becomes air, where air becomes living creatures, where living creatures become rock, where rock again becomes air. I find myself to be part of an astonishingly complex web of mutual dependencies powerful enough to shape the destiny of an entire planet, powerful enough to create an atmosphere and separate—as the god Enlil did—heaven and earth. I find that I am Gaia and Oceanus and Enlil. In losing my sense of myself as separate I am not diminished, but augmented. I am augmented physically—seeing myself as part of a greater whole—and also filled with an expansive sense of wonder and appreciation and compassion.

Images of the Invisible

It seems particularly appropriate that the simultaneous attenuation and expansion of the self I've described above comes from reflecting upon the most attenuated and expansive of the physical elements. Air becomes a metaphor for the insubstantiality of the self. And indeed, metaphors connected with the Air Element have often been used to communicate a deeper awareness of impermanence and of lack of inherent selfhood, or emptiness. Air itself is invisible and therefore doesn't make a very promising topic for imagery. But many Buddhist verses compare the body to foam,[17] or to a mirage or bubble[18]—all aeriform phenomena that are both transient and insubstantial. Later poetry from the Buddhist tradition uses the image of clouds and spindrift:

"Mists on a lake, clouds across a southern sky,
  Spray blown by wind above the sea . . .
  Meditate on their illusion, do not think of them
  as permanent!"[19]

All of these images have in common the sense that there is an appearance perceptible to the senses, and yet there is no "thing" that can be grasped. There is a form apparent to the senses, but no substance. To try to take hold of a bubble or foam is to destroy the thing we grasp, and to try to take hold of a mirage is utterly pointless since there is no object there at all—just light refracted by layers of air.

Some years ago, I went to a meadow in the French Alps to relax with a good book. When I arrived, the meadow was shaded by a few small clouds in an otherwise intense azure sky. Grumbling over my bad luck, but anticipating the speedy return of the sun, I settled down to my reading. A few pages later I noticed the sun still hadn't arrived, and when I looked up the cloud was still there, stubbornly blocking the sunlight. This seemed most strange, since I could see that the other clouds were scudding quite quickly across the blue. I was puzzled by this strange and immobile cloud, and so I studied it closely. I came to realize that the cloud was being formed by the updraft from the mountain on whose lower slopes I lay. As air rose up the mountainside, carrying moisture from the fields and forests, the moisture cooled and condensed out, forming the cloud—behind which the sun just happened to be at that time of day. As the current of air continued to rise, the droplets of moisture it contained evaporated and dispersed into the wind. I could actually see the cloud materialize at its own base. And again, at the top of the cloud, I could see wisps of water vapor attenuating into empty sky.

This seemed like a beautiful illustration of emptiness. Although I was seeing a form—one my mind took to be permanent—what constituted the form was constantly changing. A human being is like that too, although on a slower scale of change. What's more, although the cloud appeared to have a definite shape, that too was changing. It had no sharp boundary—there was just an irregular, fuzzy layer of moisture droplets dissipating into empty sky. And although the cloud was opaque and appeared solid, there was of course nothing there that could be held onto.

Clouds make a good analogy for the illusory nature of the self. There's nothing permanent in a cloud, just as there's nothing permanent to be found in the self. The cloud is not separate from its environment, just as my self has no separateness. Just as the cloud lacks the essential qualities I assume a "thing" has, so too does my self lack the qualities I assume a self has. In looking at mists or a cloud, we can see a form, often with an apparently well-defined edge, and yet there's nothing there that can be grasped. The fact that we name something a "cloud" often seems to create in the mind the assumption that the thing that's being named is as static as the label applied to it. Often we'll glance at a particular cloud and then look at it a short while later. Nothing much seems to have changed, because the human mind is not well-equipped to perceive change—especially not in something as amorphous as a cloud.

It's an interesting exercise to spend some time simply gazing nonstop at an isolated cloud, observing the changes that take place in it. What we see is constant, although often slow, change. The cloud is forever re-forming itself as currents of air circulate in the sky. The shape constantly evolves. Sometimes we'll see that in one place new cloud is forming, while in another place the cloud is evaporating. There may be an overall balance, so that the cloud appears to maintain roughly the same shape and size over the period of time we're watching. Sometimes new wisps will appear from nowhere and merge with the cloud. Sometimes the cloud will fission, calving new clouds. Unless we watch closely we miss all this and assume that the cloud hasn't changed. All of this makes a cloud a very good metaphor for the false ideas of separateness and permanence that we impute to our selves.

As far as I'm aware, the Buddha never used the rainbow—another phenomenon connected with the Air Element—as an analogy for non-self, but contemporary Buddhists often have. The Insight Meditation Society founder Joseph Goldstein, for example, uses the rainbow as an illustration of how things lack inherent existence:

"What is a rainbow? A rainbow is an appearance, arising out of the coming together of certain conditions of moisture and air and light in a certain configuration. When those conditions come together, a rainbow appears. There's no such thing as a rainbow in and of itself. A rainbow is simply an appearance arising out of those conditions. Now this doesn't mean that we don't see what we see. We all see the rainbow. And we can name it; we can use the concept. But if we don't look deeper, to see the inherent insubstantiality—there is no "thing" called rainbow, it's simply an appearance—then we go chasing after the pot of gold at the end of it. We take the concept to be real. And this is what we do in our lives: we're chasing the various pots of gold that we think are at the end of our various concepts and ideas."[20]

Like a cloud, a rainbow has the appearance of being a thing—something self-existent. And yet as Goldstein points out, what we see as a rainbow is the coming together of a number of conditions: direct sunlight, raindrops, the air, an eye, and a perceiving consciousness. A rainbow may appear to have a particular location in space, but it doesn't. The rainbow arises in dependence upon those who observe it. Each observer sees the rainbow in a slightly different place, because each observer stands in a slightly different relationship to the sun and to the raindrops falling through the air. So each of us sees a different rainbow. When we move, we create a new rainbow in a new apparent location, and so we can never hope to find the mythical pot of gold at its end. There's no "thing" there that exists independently of us, making the rainbow a powerful aerial metaphor for not-self.

Goldstein talks about how we chase the pots of gold at the ends of our various concepts and ideas. We take our concepts to be real, to the point where we (as a species) are sometimes prepared to kill and be killed in order to defend them. But all concepts are simply labels superimposed upon the reality we perceive. Our concepts chop our mental representation of the world into this and that, and yet the world itself is not similarly chopped up. The world is a continuum. Our definitions divide, and yet reality is indivisible.

How we perceive the rainbow's spectrum reveals how we impose our divisive concepts on the unbroken world of flow and change. A rainbow is produced by light moving from the air, through water-drops, and back into the air again, giving rise to a continuous spectrum of wavelengths. But we do not perceive a rainbow's colors as a continuum. Instead, the mind skips over intermediate colors in order to see only red, orange, yellow, green, blue, indigo, and (some-times) violet. It hasn't always been the case that people have seen seven colors, however. Xenophanes only described three and saw the rainbow as "a cloud that is purple and red and yellow." Aristotle too saw the rainbow as three colored, although he perceived purple, red, and green.[21] The notion of the tri-colored rainbow long persisted in Europe, probably because of the correspondences that could be made with the Holy Trinity. Milton, for example, described the rainbow as "Conspicuous with three listed [i.e., striped] colors." Sometimes four colors were described, and these were correlated with the four elements. Newton originally described only five hues—red, yellow, green, blue, and violet—and may have included orange and indigo in order to make a parallel with the seven notes of the musical scale.[22] And there is evidence that when he did later describe the sevenfold rainbow, those colors did not correspond exactly to the modern red-orange-yellow-green-blue-indigo-violet version we know today. In fact the notion of the seven-colored rainbow is vanishing; indigo is now often dropped, and so we're back to the six-colored rainbow (which, I suppose, could be correlated with the Six Elements). But when I look closely at high-resolution photographs of rainbows I find that I can, with only minimal effort to overcome my habitual division of the rainbow into seven colors, convince myself that I see a dozen or more distinct bands. Perhaps in the future we'll evolve specific words for those colors and have a decimal or duodecimal rainbow.

A rainbow is a continuous spectrum of color rather than separate bands of distinct hues—which is why our cultural conditioning can affect how many colors we see. It's that underlying unity and continuity that I'd like to highlight, since it seems to point to something very real about our own situation. We too are part of a continuity of phenomena. We are currents in the great cycles of the physical elements. We are woven into the fabric of nature. And yet we persist in seeing ourselves as separate from nature. We treat nature as if what we do to it will have no effect on us. We pump massive amounts of carbon dioxide into the air and risk upsetting delicate and infinitely complex balances that have evolved over the billions of years of life's existence on earth. We abuse our atmosphere, forgetting that in some sense we *are* the atmosphere, and that the atmosphere is us. In the myth of Enlil's deluge, human pollution of the atmosphere precipitated a catastrophic flood that all but destroyed civilization. In modern times, our tampering with the atmosphere risks inducing dramatic rises in sea levels through the melting of ice caps, and altered weather patterns across the globe, with drought in some places and flooding in others. It's unlikely we'll destroy the planet, but we may well come close to destroying ourselves. Nature always wins in the end.

In the *Epic of Gilgamesh,* the Great Mother lifted her jeweled necklace into the sky as a reminder that she would never forget the flood Enlil had visited upon the world. The rainbow here is a symbol of completeness and harmony, and a reminder that mind-made separations such as self and other are resolved into a greater unity. Appreciating the way that the Air Element connects and unites us with the physical world is not just a psychological or spiritual act, but the germ of a geopolitical one. Once the realization of our interconnectedness begins to dawn, it's hard, if not impossible, to ignore its implications. We are connected, and this brings with it responsibilities.

The reflections on the four classical elements were not originally intended to lead to greater environmental awareness, because at the time the practice was devised the last thing on anyone's mind was that a puny creature like man could seriously threaten the powerful forces of nature. But it strikes me that when we consider our interconnectedness with the elements, we can't help but become more responsible for how we act. As we move toward abandoning the idea of a separate selfhood, we may need to go through a phase of treating the whole of creation as if it were us. We need to extend our self-cherishing outward so that it embraces our entire world. And by enlarging ourselves through expanding the circle of our compassion, we can perhaps loosen the sense of ourselves as a tight, separate, and unchanging knot of being. Extend the idea of the self out far enough, and the idea of the self becomes meaningless. Perhaps we can lose ourselves and gain—and hopefully save—our world.

CHAPTER TWELVE

The Space Element

*"There is nothing in a caterpillar that tells you
it's going to be a butterfly."*
—R. BUCKMINSTER FULLER (ATTRIBUTED)

Andrew, an American student who has volunteered to participate in a psychology study, walks into Dr. Henrik Ehrsson's laboratory in the Karolinska Institute, in Stockholm, and stands opposite a plastic mannequin. Ehrsson's colleague, doctoral student Valeria Petkova, attaches electrodes to the middle and index fingers of Andrew's left hand, and then slips a video headset over his eyes. Through the headset, Andrew sees the images generated by two video cameras that are fixed to the mannequin's head and pointed down at its feet.[1]

Andrew is now seeing what the mannequin sees, so when he tilts his head forward and matches the mannequin's downward gaze, he immediately starts to have a sense that the mannequin is "him." That feeling becomes even more convincing when Petkova takes a marker and simultaneously strokes Andrew's belly and that of the mannequin. Andrew can see only the mannequin's abdomen being touched, but he can feel the pen brushing against his own body. The moment that the touch happens, Andrew, with a kind of jolt, feels that he's actually inside the mannequin's body. His sense of identification with his own body "snapped," he'll say later. Next, Petkova pulls the blade of a sharp knife across the belly of the mannequin. Although he knows the researchers wouldn't harm him, Andrew still feels the desire to pull away, and the electrodes on his fingertips register increased electrical activity—a clear indication of anxiety.

In a later experiment, Andrew stands opposite Petkova herself. She's now wearing the mannequin's video cameras, so that Andrew sees himself from her perspective. As before, he quickly begins to feel that he is in another body—her body—seeing himself from the outside. The two hold hands, and Andrew experiences Petkova's grip as his own. She squeezes his hand, and he feels that he's doing the squeezing. The fact that the two people are of different genders has no effect on the illusion, Ehrsson and Petkova find. A man can easily identify with a female body and vice versa. Typically, it only takes ten to twelve seconds for a volunteer to abandon his or her body and to identify with that of their partner or a mannequin; 70 to 80 percent of volunteers experience the illusion very strongly.[2]

The Space Element brings together the first four elements, with the internal element representing the human body as a whole—the shape, form, or appearance with which we identify. Although we undoubtedly cling to our bodies, the identification we have with them turns out to be surprisingly flexible.

It's even possible to persuade people that they are outside of their bodies altogether. In another experiment, Ehrsson filmed volunteer's backs with stereo video cameras. As in the experiment above, the volunteers wore headsets that allowed them to see themselves. They reported feeling as if they were outside and about two meters behind their bodies. When Ehrsson swung a hammer in the direction of the cameras, which were safely behind the participants' actual bodies, the volunteers experienced anxiety and showed measurable signs of emotional and physiological stress.[3]

Electrical stimulation to specific spots in the brain can also produce out-of-body experiences. A Swiss team at the Federal Institute of Technology of Lausanne, led by Bigna Lenggenhager, found with one woman that stimulating a brain region called the temporal parietal junction induced the illusion that she was hanging from the ceiling, looking down at her body. The woman had a normal psychiatric history and was reportedly stunned by the bizarre nature of her experience.[4]

At first sight it seems extraordinary that the location of our sense of self can be so easily manipulated. With only ten to twelve seconds of seeing our own body from the outside, or a tiny jolt of electricity to the brain, we can be induced to abandon our lifelong sense of inhabiting the body with which we have grown up. Then again, perhaps this isn't so surprising. Imagine yourself as a newborn baby. You have to learn to coordinate the movements of your body. You have to learn what arms, hands, and legs are for, how to move them in a coordinated way, and how to keep track of where they are. But most fundamentally, you have to learn that these *are* your body parts. We've all been through the stage of having to learn to initially identify *something* as our bodies. And that process of identification is ongoing—we have to continually adjust our sense of what the body is, because the body changes. As we grow, the size, proportions, and strength of the body change, meaning that we continually undergo a shift in our sense of what constitutes the physical self. If we couldn't make rapid adjustments to our sense of what our body is and how it functions, it would be hard to adapt our style of walking when we'd injured a foot, or adjust the amount of effort we make when carrying something heavy up stairs, never mind to adapt to dramatic changes like losing a limb.

The current thinking is that we create a mental map of the body—called a "schema"—and that this map is updated as the body changes. One fascinating discovery with regard to schemas is that the mental map includes not just organic body parts but also tools, which the mind treats as honorary body parts for the time they're being used. Lucilla Cardinali, of the National Institute of Health and Medical Research (INSERM) in France, and Alessandro Farnè, also of INSERM, and of the Université Claude Bernard Lyon, studied the effect of tool use on the perception of the body. They gave participants a gripping tool, similar to those used to pick up trash, and asked them to repeatedly pick up and replace a small block. This appeared to change the participants' inner body maps. After the exercise was over, the researchers found that the participants handled their bodies differently. For example, when asked to pick up and replace the blocks with their own hands, the participants' movements accelerated and decelerated more slowly than before, so that the task overall took longer. The body appeared to be struggling to adapt to the arms having their normal reach.[5]

This effect was more pronounced when participants were asked to do similar tasks blindfolded. No longer able to correct the body's movements based on what they were seeing, participants consistently overestimated the distance when asked to indicate particular lengths, acting as if their arms were longer than they really were. Again, the body's schema had been updated to include the tools the participants had previously used. The brain seems quite happy to alter its sense of what the physical self consists of.

I don't know whether fiddler crabs have a mental map of their bodies, but they too experience a change in their sense of selfhood when they use unfamiliar tools, although in this case the tools are natural body parts of the opposite sex. Female marsh fiddler crabs (*Uga pugilator*) have two feeding claws, both of which are equipped with chemical sensors and designed to probe the soil. The male, on the other hand, has one feeding claw and a second large claw, the latter used in aggressive displays aimed at warding off competing males. Marc Weissburg, a biologist at the Georgia Institute of Technology, in Atlanta, replaced the large male claw with a more delicate feeding claw from a female. Rather than using the female claw in an aggressive or defensive manner, as you might expect, the males started to use the new claw in a typically female way, probing the mud for food. And somehow, the part of the male brain that had been responsible for processing vibration and pressure was reconfigured to make sense of the chemical signals it was now receiving. Changing the body changed the brain. This extraordinary result shows how powerfully malleable the sense of self can be—at least in marsh fiddler crabs.[6]

How about Ehrsson's body-swappers? Did any of them behave differently when inhabiting a body of the opposite sex? Sadly, the experiments were brief, and none of the women reported feeling more "manly" while identifying with the male mannequin form they felt themselves to possess—although some reported being proud of the six-pack abs they had effortlessly acquired. "The issues of gender body and body identity are clearly important questions that could deserve further investigation," Ehrsson told me.

With the human subjects in Ehrsson's body-swap experiments, and with Lucilla Cardinali's grabber-tool tests, the adaptation of the schema, the brain's body-map, is rapid. This is not too surprising for anyone who's watched a pro athlete at one with a bicycle or skis or tennis racquet, equipment that seems to be an extension of the body. But it may strike us as being a big step from the brain's assuming, for example, that a bicycle is temporarily part of the body, to assuming that a mannequin *is* the body. It seems we simply assume that whatever body we see out of must needs be "our" body, no matter how unlikely that may be. "We feel that our self is located where the eyes are," said Ehrsson, in a BBC interview.[7] Or as the title of Lenggenhager's *Science* paper describing an artificially induced out-of-body experience puts it, "Video ergo sum"—I see, therefore I am.[8] If the new body is made of plastic or has suddenly changed gender, that doesn't prevent our identifying with it, so long as we have the illusion that we see out of that body's eyes. As in Andrew's case, if we're looking down at where the body usually is, what else could we be seeing there *but* the body? If there's something there, then it must be the body, and I must therefore have the feeling that it's *my* body. Once we can both see something touching the body and feel a corresponding contact, the illusion is complete.

The Illusion of Having a Body

Even if we've never set foot in a neuroscience laboratory or worn virtual-reality goggles, we have all had, nightly, the experience of inhabiting another body, because we all dream. In our dreams we inhabit a body that is entirely fantasized, and yet we have a sense of ownership of this phantom figure. While I'm immersed in my nighttime reveries, I fear for the dream-body's safety, am horrified when I discover that its teeth or hair are falling out, and get embarrassed when I discover the illusory body is naked in front of an illusory public. (Your neuroses may vary.)

The illusion of inhabiting this dream-body is as utterly compelling as Andrew's experience with the mannequin. In the dreaming state we are totally convinced of the reality of what we're experiencing, and yet the dream-body is an illusion. Sometimes the body we inhabit in dreams may not even be a representation of our "real" body, but that of a child, a person much older than ourselves, someone of the opposite sex, or an animal. And yet we think we "own" each of these bodies for as long as the dream exists. It seems that dream experiences are in a way a "rehearsal" for the experimentally induced body-swapping and out-of-body experiences about which we've been reading.

This is all directly relevant to the Space Element, because reflecting on this element involves becoming aware of the *entirety* of the physical form that we inhabit and identify with. The purpose of the reflections on the first four elements—Earth, Water, Fire, and Air—is to remind us that all the matter and energy we think of as constituting our bodies is actually "not-self." The stuff that makes up the body, and the energy that allows that stuff to be alive, all come from outside. But this takes an extremely analytical approach, using categories foreign to our day-to-day experience. While analyzing the body via the four elements can be a useful tool for deconstructing our sense of self, our primary identification in day-to-day life is not with abstractions called "elements" but with the concrete reality of the body. So the Space Element brings together all the elements we've been reflecting on and considers them in the more experiential terms of our appearance or form.

It's clear to anyone that Andrew had an illusory experience of a mannequin's body being his own, and that later he was fooled into thinking he inhabited a female researcher's body. And we all understand that the body we experience ourselves having in dreams is an illusion too. The Six Element Reflection, however, encourages us to see that it's also an illusion for Andrew to think that the body he *usually* inhabits is *his* body, and an illusion for you and I to do likewise. The Space Element reflection encourages us to see that this form we inhabit is "Not me, not mine, not myself."

The Traditional Reflection

The approach I'll be taking in this practice is, for the first time, rather different from that in the classic description of the Six Element Practice:

> "What is the space element? The space element may be either internal or external. What is internal space? Whatever, internally, belonging to oneself, is space, spatial, and clung-to, that is, the holes in the ears, the nostrils, the door of the mouth, and that [aperture] whereby what is eaten, drunk, consumed, and tasted gets swallowed, and where it collects, and whereby it is excreted from below, or whatever else internally, belonging to oneself, is space, spatial, and clung-to; this is called the internal space element."[9]

Reflecting on the body's orifices and alimentary canal doesn't, to me anyway, have the same level of existential significance as reflecting on the impermanent nature of the stuff that makes up the body, and

I suspect that an error has crept into the description of the practice. Elsewhere, the Space Element is defined as having "the characteristic of delimiting matter . . . it is manifested as the confines of matter."[10] This is a later text, but a text from the time of the Buddha conveys the same sense: "Just as when a space is enclosed by timber and creepers, grass and clay, it comes to be termed 'house,' so too, when a space is enclosed by bones and sinews, flesh and skin, it comes to be termed 'material form.'"[11]

We should think of the internal Space Element, I'd suggest, as being *the material form of the body,* or, to put it in a more experiential way, the body's appearance. This is the interpretation I have found most valuable in my own reflections. It's our shape, our form, our appearance—rather than the hollow spaces within the body—that we're likely to become attached to. And it's our attachment to our physical form and its appearance that we need to work on if we're to become free of the burden of self. We do this by becoming aware of the impermanent nature of the form we occupy, and also by reflecting on the essential identity of our "inner space" with the external Space Element, which of course is everything outside the body's boundary—everything with which we normally don't identify as being "my form."

The first point for reflection is how exactly we think of the boundary between internal space and external space. We all have a basic assumption that there's an inside that is "us" and that is surrounded by an external space that is "not us." But how do we decide exactly where to draw the line? Is it even possible to clearly demarcate where the body ends and external space begins?

In reflecting in my meditation practice upon the internal Space Element, I tend to become aware first of the shape of my body. Sensing the shape of the body from within is an interesting exercise.

If you close your eyes, which we often do in meditation, and bring your awareness into the body, what shape do you notice? I can feel my hands, for example, but unless I move each of the fingers in turn I have no sense of there being five fingers on each hand. I can feel my calf muscles, but they don't seem to have a distinct "edge" to them. In fact my entire body seems to be characterized by a fuzzy sensation. It's only where my skin contacts some hard surface that I have a clear sense of boundaries. Even where skin touches skin—for example where the arms lie against the sides of the chest—I find it impossible to have a clear sense of where the sensations from one part of the body end and those from the other part begin. Between the arms and chest there is an area of warmth, and those warm sensations seem almost to meld those two parts of my body together, like two toffees that have fused into a single sticky mass on a hot day. If all I had to go on was my proprioceptive senses, I would have a very strange idea of what my body was like, at least when it's at rest. Sensing the raw internal sensory data of the body this way, unaccompanied by the reassuringly clear-cut image our eyes provide, helps loosen up our sense of identification with our particular form. We realize that there are other ways to perceive the body, and that in some ways the form we have is indeterminate.

Where does the "outside" start? If I try to analyze exactly where the boundary of my visible form is, I quickly find myself with problems of definition. Looked at crudely, I could say that the skin forms the boundary of my physical self. But when we look closely at the skin—closely as in microscopically—we see a ragged layer of dead epithelial cells, flaking off into space. There's no clear-cut boundary to be found there. When we look even more closely, down at the atomic level, boundaries are even less clear-cut. The distances between the atomic nuclei in the molecules comprising my skin's cells are immense. Atoms are in fact about 99.9999999999999 percent empty space. An observer, shrunk to the size of an electron and shot like a tiny bullet toward my body, would have difficulty telling where outside ends and inside begins. The nuclei of my body's atoms would appear to be almost infinitely distant—as far apart from each other as stars in space. There would therefore be little indication, for the tiny observer crossing my body's putative boundary, of having moved from being outside to being inside. It wouldn't feel like crossing a border or entering a building.

As I sit breathing in my meditation practice, I might find myself wondering exactly at what point a particular molecule of air could be said to be "in" the body. Is it when it crosses some arbitrarily drawn plane enclosed by the rims of my nostrils? Is it once it's crossed into the bloodstream? Or bonded to a molecule of hemoglobin? Any line I choose to draw would be purely arbitrary. I look for the boundary of my physical self and can't find one. The closer I look, the more elusive it is.

The Ever-Changing Body

In my meditation practice I also recollect that the form I identify as being myself is not fixed and unchanging. From the moment of conception, the size, shape, and appearance of my body have been metamorphosing. To become more acutely aware of the imperma-nence of my body I sometimes imagine a miles-long queue of all the physical selves I have inhabited or will inhabit in this lifetime, from the fertilized egg to my moldering corpse. At the start of this queue I see a nondescript fetus and a baby I would pass on the street without recoginizing, but a little farther along I see a progression of forms that I have identified with as being "me" at various times. Ah! There I am in primary school, skinny, blond, and quite handsome, if I say so myself. But what's this? Here I am aged thirteen, with straggly hair darkened to brown, geeky spectacles, and incipient teenage acne. Then—what happened?!—there I am in my twenties, still surprisingly thin and having finally found a hairstyle that doesn't make me look like I'm an aspiring mad scientist. As I progress along this succession of physical selves I eventually see myself as I currently am—my hair receding, body becoming fatter—followed by a line of progressively older and frailer bodies heading toward oblivion. This succession of selves is another river—a form flowing through time and space, endlessly changing. At every stage of my life, I have identified with one of these past forms that I see in my mind's eye. There has been a sense of ownership—a form of mental grasping in which I have often been reluctant to accept the reality of change.

Here's a curious thing: as I've aged, I've found that I cling not so much to my current physical form, but to a somewhat younger version of it. I'm often surprised, looking in the mirror, to see how old I look, and in my mind's eye I fancy myself to be some five or six years younger than I actually am. The mirror seems biased, prone to catching me at my worst moments—when I'm tired and drawn. The real me, I'm sure, is just a little slimmer, with more of a lively twinkle in the eye. I admit that I'd hold back the flow of change if I could—stop myself aging, freeze my appearance as it is. Few wouldn't. But the river of self flows on, and clinging to a river is pointless, because there is no "thing" there to cling to. I attempt to cling to my form, but find that I slip through my own fingers. The body moves on, changing and aging, and I suffer again and again, unable to hold back the process of change. Contemplating the inevitability of impermanence, I practice letting go, again and again.

This sense I have of identifying more strongly with an earlier and more aesthetically pleasing model of myself is a common one. Research has shown that we often quite literally cannot recognize our own faces in a lineup. Nicholas Epley and Erin Whitchurch, in a study published in the journal *Personality and Social Psychology Bulletin,* photographed undergraduate students and then invited them back a few weeks later to identify their own images.[12] The researchers, however, had used computer software to produce a swatch of eleven photographs. Some of the images had been blended, to varying degrees, with an idealized composite face based on social norms of physical attractiveness. The results were a series of increasingly "improved" faces, based on the original. The researchers also used the software to create a series of less attractive images, morphing the originals to look more like faces with craniofacial deformities.

Interestingly, participants were far more likely to identify one of the "improved" faces as representing what they looked like, passing over the genuine image of themselves. It seems that our brains perform a kind of "mental Photoshopping," creating an inner representation of our appearance that improves substantially on reality. The authors pointed out that it wasn't surprising that people so often dislike photographs of themselves: "The image captured by the camera lens just doesn't match up to the image captured in the mind's eye," they were quoted as saying.[13] What we identify with, often, is an idealized notion of ourselves—slimmer, fitter, better looking. The fact that we are unable even to acknowledge the sensory reality of our own appearance is perhaps rather surprising or even shocking. But as T. S. Eliot said, "Humankind cannot bear very much reality."

The Body as a Probability Function

In order to promote the habit of letting go, I often explore in meditation how a "temporal delusion of consciousness" limits my perception of myself. I typically see my body only as it is here and now, limited in space, and cut off from the rest of the world. Unable to see past and future, I tend to think of my body as being a thing, stuck in the present, separate from the world around it, and not as the interconnected process it actually is. What has been in my body I no longer cling to. That which is to become my body, I also do not cling to as myself.

Because of the limitations of my mind and senses, I have to use the power of imagination to see the essential truth that my body is a river of matter and energy, with my present self as just one small part of the watercourse. I do not tend to look at the grass and trees around me and think that, because my exhaled carbon dioxide has been converted to starches in their bodies, they are a part of me. I don't tend to look at fields of corn, or clouds, or snow on a mountaintop, and think that they are me because I may ingest and incorporate them into my body in the future. But what if we were to compress past and future into this present moment? What if we were to imagine not just the matter that *is* in our bodies but all the matter that *has been* and *will be* part of our bodies? It's not just a question of imagining, say, all the food I've eaten or the water I've drunk, although that's interesting in itself. We can ask ourselves where that food and water came from. Very quickly we enter the immense and boundaryless web of complex relationships that forms our world. As we're well aware from our earlier reflections, my food was formerly soil and carbon dioxide and atmospheric nitrogen. The soil contains the mingled remains of dozens of mountain ranges, and fragments of countless living beings. It contains dust blown from continents on the other side of the globe, as well as dust that has rained down from space. The carbon and nitrogen in my food lead us back to the totality of our atmosphere, and that in turn connects us with all living beings from all times, as well as to the very rocks beneath our feet. If my body is a stretch of a river, then what is "upstream" approximates in volume our entire planet.

Where then is all the matter that used to be part of us? When we trace back all the matter that formerly constituted these bodies we inhabit, we find that it's distributed around all the world's oceans and rivers, fills the atmosphere, and is a part of virtually every living organism. What we have been—the "downstream" part of the river of our being—once again approximates, in a dilute way, the volume of the entire hydrosphere, atmosphere, and biosphere, as well as the very soil and much of the crust of the earth.

This is our reality: that the world becomes us and we will become the world. And contemplating this, I ask myself again, where in all this vast complexity am I? The answer is that I am everywhere. The 80 kg of matter currently in my body represents just a tiny fraction of what I have been and will be. The 80 liters I currently occupy is a minuscule portion of the volume I have and will occupy. With the flow of the elements from my entire lifetime compressed into the present moment, I see the entire world above me, representing what has yet to enter my body, and the entire world below me, similarly representing what has been me. My current form stands between these two as a vortex through which the world passes into itself. The worlds I visualize above and below me are not solid because of the dilute nature of what has been me and what will be me; instead they are hazy and cloud-like, representing the uncertainty of the location of all this present/future matter.

Accepting this model, for the moment, as myself, I see not a discrete entity, but rather something more akin to a subatomic particle, which does not occupy a definite point in space but which is "blurred" over a probability function that indicates the likelihood of its being found at any given point in space at any moment. We may think of an electron, say, as being like a small planet orbiting the sun-like nucleus of an atom, but this is not the case. An electron has no position unless we force it to have one by observing it. An electron is more like a dancing cloud that exists in many places in space at one time. This is how certain electrons are visually depicted—as twin clouds together forming an infinity symbol (∞), representing the probability that an electron may be found in any given spot at any one time. Likewise, with our vision corrected for temporal delusions of consciousness, we can see ourselves too as being spread out in a probability field, appropriately shaped like infinity. We are everywhere at once, and therefore are nowhere.

And all this is true for other living things as well (lest we should fall into thinking that the vortex of the world revolves only around ourselves). All beings are vortices through which the world pours. All beings pass through each other. One being contains innumerable others. If we could free ourselves from our temporal blindness, we would see ourselves not as individual units, but as interconnected nodes within a cloud of matter and energy. The idea that the sixty or seventy or eighty liters of space that our limited body occupies is "our" space is hopelessly myopic. In reality we occupy the world and each other. This, in a sense, is our true form.

Coming back to the limited form that I perceive with my physical senses, I contemplate also that my internal space is continually changing. The space enclosed by my skin (if that indeed is the outer boundary of my self) is moving because I am moving. Not only do I travel across the surface of the earth, but the earth itself is rotating on its axis at 1,600 kilometers per hour (kph) at the equator, and revolving around the sun at 107,000 kph. The sun is revolving with the galaxy at 792,000 kph, and that in turn is racing away from all other galaxies at an astonishing rate of 2.1 million kilometers every hour. Just taking that last figure in isolation means that even when you're sitting still you're moving at a rate that would take you from New York to London in nine seconds. The volume that your body has carved out of space in just the time it took you to read this paragraph is truly mind-boggling.[14]

.The "external" space that we are zooming through, we reflect, is the same space "we" occupy and think of as being "us." Space is not something we can own. At best it is something that we borrow. The Space Element is simply flowing through this form I habitually identify with. Given the time it takes for perceptions to move from the senses to the brain, by the time I have claimed any given space my body currently occupies as me and mine, it has already been relinquished. Realizing that the space my body occupies is the same space I identify with, I repeat the traditional words, "This is not me; this is not mine; I am not this."

Personal Space

Of course I *do* try to claim as me or mine not only the internal space of the body, but space around me as well. In daily life I find that I have a sense of having a "personal space" extending beyond my physical body. An indeterminate zone seems to extend around me, like a science-fiction force field, and entry to this volume of space is strictly monitored and controlled by my consciousness. Should a stranger seek to put a hand on my arm or even stand too close, I feel uncomfortable.

I once had a friend, Peter, who spent much of his childhood living in Turkey, where notions of personal space are different from those in my native Scotland. In his long sojourn abroad, Peter had picked up Turkish notions of what constituted an adequate recognition of personal space, and they were different from mine. Peter would often stand so close to me in conversation that I'd almost feel like I couldn't breathe properly. My chest would tighten, I'd feel anxious, and I'd experience a powerful desire to step away. And so I'd back off a pace, only to find a few moments later that he'd shuffled closer once more, back to the place where *he* felt comfortable. We socialized a lot and so we spent many hours like this in conversation, me shuffling slowly backward across a room, with him in oblivious pursuit. This pattern continued until Peter's sense of personal space had re-calibrated with the Northern European norm, and a "proper" sense of distance had been restored between us.

I notice in daily life that volumes of space not physically close to me can become identified as extensions of my personal space. When I'm driving around a busy parking lot, I'll sometimes see a space and immediately see it as "mine," only to discover moments later that some other driver has laid claim to it. "My" space has been stolen; I feel aggrieved. My car itself becomes an extension of my bodily space. The Colorado State University social psychologist William Szlemko found that drivers who plaster their cars with bumper stickers and other signs of "personalization" are more ready to treat their cars— and the road around them—as their personal space, being quicker to take offense at other drivers and engage in honking, tailgating, and other aggressive behavior.[15] In one experiment a researcher would sit at a light after it had turned green, while another researcher would observe whether the car behind had bumper stickers or other territorial markings. After the light had changed, those drivers who had personalized their vehicles were a full two seconds faster to sound their horns than those who hadn't.

One interesting manifestation of how external space can become part of what we identify with is the way in which we quickly adopt favorite seats. This is a more profound phenomenon than it might at first appear. We often feel a powerful sense of discomfort when we can't sit in "our" place. David J. Pollay, a syndicated columnist and leadership consultant, wrote about an experience of trying to "shake things up" by moving seats when he attended a conference involving about a hundred people. On the second day of the conference he switched seats in order to meet new people, but found that he was the only person to do so. The next day Pollay arrived just in time for the start of the meeting and discovered that the attendee he had displaced was back in "his" seat, complete with a triumphant smile at having regained what he presumably saw as his rightful position.[16]

John Suler, PhD, a lecturer in the Department of Psychology at Rider University, New Jersey, has matched the places where his clinical psychology students sit in the classroom with their personality types.[17] Loners, not surprisingly, like to sit away from other people, while people who sit in the middle like to be inconspicuous and to blend in with the crowd. The choice of a seat becomes an exercise in reinforcing our sense of who we are. As an exercise in self-awareness, Suler will ask students to sit in seats that are the complete opposite of those they would normally choose—to find a chair, in fact, where they feel positively uncomfortable. When he asks them how the change in position makes them feel, he often gets very strong responses. Sometimes people can't articulate the powerful emotions they experience when "displaced," and they resort to saying they feel "weird." These strong responses indicate that the students' sense of self is being disrupted simply by moving the location of their bodies.

These examples of identifying with external spaces as if they were our property—or even extensions of ourselves—highlight one of the reasons why Buddhist practice suggests that we try to let go of our identification with space. Clinging, Buddhist psychological theory tells us, leads inevitably to suffering. When our sense of self is dependent upon something that is impermanent, change is liable to pull the rug from under our feet. I side with David J. Pollay in habitually varying the seat I choose in order to shake up the dynamics of groups, to meet new people, and to experience myself differently. Presumably that's just my personality type expressing itself, but at least I know I won't be made to feel insecure just because I can't sit where I want to. I'd recommend moving seats as a practice in order to discover how attached you are to your chosen room positions.

When our cars are simply machines for getting from one place to another, then there is no problem. When a seat is just a seat, or when a change in seating arrangements is taken as an opportunity to have a new experience, then change can be positively beneficial. When we see our cars as extensions of our selves, we feel impelled to protect that extended self. Other "selves" (whether cars, drivers, or pedestrians) are seen as opposing and obstructing *our* selves, and so frustration, stress, and defensiveness ensue. When we identify so much with a seating position that our sense of well-being depends upon it, we suffer when "our" seat is unavailable.

Similarly, identification with the body itself leads to suffering. Seeing ourselves as our bodies, and our bodies as ourselves, we suffer. We see the body failing and we feel that it is *we* who fail. We see the body as imperfect and we feel that it is *we* who are imperfect. When our bodies are judged by others we think it is *we* who are being judged. We see injury to the body as being an injury to ourselves. And we see the body's aging as something more akin to a personality flaw than to a fact of nature. In order to develop equanimity in the face of the impermanence of our individual human form, we need to fully accept the reality of change. And the only way we can accept change is to cease from clinging. We have to cease from clinging to the body as it is or as it was or how we would like it to be. We have to accept impermanence in order not to suffer.

The Neurophysiology of Space

Sometimes in meditation the sense of there being an "inside" and an "outside" breaks down completely. The first time this happened to me was, oddly enough, in a dream. In this dream I found myself lying on my belly on a grassy bank on a university campus. People were walking back and forth. It was a warm and pleasant day, and I felt very relaxed and happy. With childlike curiosity I looked down into the grass and saw a tiny mushroom, which I knew to be hallucinogenic. I've never actually taken mushrooms or other hallucinogens, and I had no intention of tripping then. But in squeezing the mushroom lightly between my thumb and forefinger I'd evidently smeared some of its juices onto my skin, and when I inadvertently touched my right eyelid I started hallucinating, if one can talk of hallucinating in a dream.

What I experienced was hard to put into words. My experience was no longer divided into inner (my thoughts, feelings, and bodily sensations) and outer (the lawn, the students, the buildings). Instead there was simply a field of awareness rather like a Buddhist *mandala*. A mandala is a circular and symmetrical image symbolizing completeness, but the mandala of my experience included not just the visual but all sensory modalities. Here was the feeling of the grass on my skin. Over there was a sense of wonder. There the thought "What's going on?" Everything in my experience was present simultaneously. What was missing was any discrimination of these experiences into the categories of "internal" and "external." After perhaps thirty seconds of my world having dissolved its boundaries, a sense of anxiety ensued and the familiar world came back into focus. I relaxed; the mandala of perceptions reappeared once more, then vanished again; and the dream moved on.

Later, in my meditation practice, essentially the same experience would recur. I would experience the same mandala-like field of awareness, woven from various types of sensory experience, with no sense of there being an inner and an outer component to those experiences. There was no compartmentalization of experiences into the categories of self and other. While the dream had been in the end disorienting, in my meditation experience there was instead a feeling of complete acceptance. Everything I experienced was perfect as it was—with the proviso that nothing "was"—everything was becoming. The sense I had was that as long as my experiences were imbued with awareness, they would of their own inner dynamic evolve in the direction of completeness, wholesomeness, and happiness. These have been the most deeply satisfying experiences of my life.

There was also no longer any sense of my moving along a time line. Time was no longer a path with the past behind me and the future before me, as we commonly conceive of it. Instead there was a sense of an eternally unfolding present moment. Rather than time being a journey along a linear path, change appeared to be mandala-like. It seemed to be like a flower seen from above, endlessly unfolding from within, or like a kaleidoscope's image forever rearranging itself. It struck me as highly misleading to think in terms of there being a past behind us and a future ahead of us. Instead there was only this one present moment, eternally unfolding according to its nature. I found myself in an eternal, timeless present.

I'm not alone in having such experiences, or in valuing them as pivotal moments in my spiritual practice. And increasingly they're being studied by scientists, using new tools that can probe and map the activity of the mind. Researchers have shown that in meditation—both that of Buddhist monks and Franciscan nuns—the parietal lobes of the brain, responsible for orienting us in time and space, become less active.[18] Dr. Andrew Newberg, neuroscientist and author of *How God Changes Your Brain,* hypothesizes that "blocking all sensory and cognitive input into this area during meditation results in the sense of no space and no time which is so often described in meditation."[19] It seems that the parietal lobes of the brain have the function of creating a sense of time and space, and when that part of the brain goes offline, we lose our sense of there being an inside and an outside to our experience. The parietal lobes, incidentally, are the same area of the brain where electrical stimulation can induce out-of-body experiences.

It's tempting to describe the loss of a sense of time and space as an aberrant perception, a delusion brought on by part of the brain powering down, but we should remember that all experience takes place in the brain. When we see a sunset, the colors and shapes we perceive are created in the brain. They don't exist in the outside world. The sun, in reality, has no color—it simply emits photons of various wavelengths, and those photons are selectively filtered as they pass obliquely through the atmosphere. When we touch a hot steering wheel on a sunny day, or taste ice cream, those sensations too arise in the brain. We know nothing in fact of the outside world, except through the mediation of the sensations that arise in the three pounds of gelatinous, cellular computer inside our skulls. We can't know anything directly about what's "out there." All of our experience is internal. Perhaps the strange thing is that we take it for granted that some qualities exist "out there," given that they all arise "in here."

We think of the senses as being like windows through which the external world can be viewed, but this is far from the case. First our receptors can only respond to certain stimuli. Examples of receptors are the cones in the retina, which respond to light: you have three different types of cones, each responding to a specific range of wavelengths (one kind peaking at yellow, another at green, and a third at violet). Another example would be the specialized receptors in your skin that respond to heat (a separate class of receptors respond to cold). When receptors are triggered, they send a cascade of electrical "clicks" (called action potentials) down the nerves that lead to the various sensory areas of the brain. The action potentials for the color red and for the feeling of heat on your skin are essentially identical. Between all the sense organs in your body—for sight, sound, smell, taste, touch, heat, cold, and all the other many sensations you have—and the brain, there are just these tiny clicks flowing along nerves. That alone should tell us that our sense of the world is created internally. If there is, in the conduction of sensory data toward the brain, no difference between sound and color or between heat and the flavor of a plum, then the differences between various senses must arise in the brain. Which is exactly what happens. Our perceptions of external space all arise in the inner space of the body and mind.

It's the brain's parietal lobes that seem to have the effect of assigning "exteriority" to certain sensations, while assigning others (our thoughts, our internal body sensations) to the world of "interiority." In terms of raw sensory processing, there is no inside or outside. There are just perceptions, which are all internally generated, but are then divided by the brain into those it considers coming from outside and those that it considers coming from inside. In reality there is merely a field of awareness. It is the division into internal and external sensations, arguably, that is the illusion. Presumably it's a useful delusion, but it's a delusion nonetheless.

Further research of relevance to the separation of our experience into the internal and external hinges on what's called the "default network." This area of the brain seems to be involved in internal activities such as self-monitoring, reflection, and daydreaming. It's called the default network because it's the part of the brain that becomes active when you're not focusing on anything in particular in the outside world. If you're paying attention to what's going on around you, an area of the brain called the external network is more active.

Normally when the default network is active, the external network is inactive, and vice versa. So how does this work in practice? Rafael Malach, at the Weizmann Institute of Science, in Israel, discovered that when people are watching the exciting parts of action movies, the external network is what's active.[20] Moreover, it's active in the same way for everyone viewing the film. However, in the quieter parts of the movie, each viewer has his or her own particular pattern of brain activity. Now that the gripping action is over, each individual is engaged in the inner activities of daydreaming, or comparing the movie to his or her own experiences, or wondering what's going to happen next, or wishing he or she had asked for extra butter on the popcorn. And it's the default network that's active during these times, but in very specific ways in each individual.

Now, when experienced meditators are engaged in "non-dual" meditation practice—where we cease to discriminate between self and other, inner and outer—the default network and the external network do *not* alternate their activities, but are active simultaneously. These contemplatives are paying attention equally to all sensations, inner and outer, without discrimination. This unusual pattern of brain activity seems to accompany the experience of harmony between the awareness of internal and external space. In the experience of those meditating in this way, there is simply a field of awareness that embraces all sensations, without regard to their origins. Again, what's being achieved in meditation is arguably a more accurate perception of our experience—one in which we do not cling to the idea that some perceptions are happening "out there" and that some are happening "in here." When all sensations are treated equally, rather than being compartmentalized into internal and external, there is no internal space or external, but simply space.

This is very different, incidentally, from the kind of delusion that takes place in the minds of people with mental illnesses such as schizophrenia, where inner thoughts are taken to be emanating from someone or somewhere else "out there." In non-dual meditation there is no question of one's own thoughts being mistaken for transmissions from CIA satellites or any such thing. Meditators (healthy ones, anyway) are well aware that their thoughts are their thoughts. The experience of non-dual meditators is also very different from another class of person whose default and external networks are simultaneously active: the Alzheimer's patient. Severe Alzheimer's patients likewise have the default network and the external network functioning simultaneously, but this leads to confusion and disorientation. Jessica Andrews-Hanna, of Harvard University, who studied the default networks of aging people, speculates, "In the meditators' case, maybe it's all cognitive; maybe they have the ability to say, 'Now I want to control these two [networks] together.' If you can turn the brain regions on and off when you want, that's great."[21] Alzheimer's patients do not have that choice.

On Having No Head

It's possible to have something approaching these experiences of non-duality without spending months on retreat or cloistering yourself away as a nun. Susan Blackmore, a consciousness researcher and practitioner of Zen Buddhism, wrote very effectively of being led through an exercise drawn from Douglas Harding's 1961 book, *On Having No Head: Zen and the Rediscovery of the Obvious*. She explains how she was hiking with a bunch of Buddhists in the English countryside, when one of her companions asked her to point her finger to a distant hill and to concentrate on what she could see there. Blackmore duly complied. She was then asked to repeat the exercise, but this time pointing at a spot that was a little closer, then at her feet . . . her chest . . . so far so good. Then she was asked to point her finger at the space between her eyes and to concentrate on what she saw. She found to her astonishment that her head had vanished. (Try the exercise for yourself. It worked for me.) Here's how Blackmore described the experience:

> "I had no head. There was my body all right, with its visible feet, legs, tummy, chest, and then what? Of course I know I have a head. I can touch it and see it in the mirror, but I'd never noticed that I can't see it myself, directly; that my whole life I've been walking around without a visible head. I laughed happily. *On top of this headless body seemed to be the whole world of friends, and grass, and trees, and hills. I'd lost my head and gained the world"*[22] [emphasis added].

Blackmore's experience is one that can be easily replicated, and it is very startling. It produces a sense that the boundary between the outer world and inner world has partially dissolved, and that what we see as the outer world is somehow within us, or that we somehow are co-extensive with it. Again, it seems that our sense of self-identification can be manipulated rather easily. The problem is that we simply never question the arbitrariness of the distinction between inner and outer. Having at some point in our lives come to the conclusion that experience is divided into that which takes place in an interior space and that which takes place in an exterior space, we cease to think about the matter.

What Is Space Anyway?

In all this talk (roundabout as it may sometimes appear) on the Space Element, and on how we come to distinguish between internal and external space, there's one small problem we haven't even touched on: "What is space anyway?" This question challenges us because our common-sense notions of what space is simply don't accord with reality. We tend to have ingrained ideas of space as an invisible, absolute, and unchanging background within which matter—occupying space but separate from it—exists and moves. As it happens, however, we know that none of this is true. Experiments show that space is warped, compressed, and stretched. Matter creates "dimples" in space; much as a bowling ball placed on a trampoline will create a deformation in its fabric, so too does matter create distortions in the fabric of space. A rotating body, like a planet or star, will not only "dent" the space around it, but space itself will be dragged along in its wake, in much the same way that a rotating spoon will cause a vortex in a cup of tea.[23]

As an object moves through space, space itself becomes compressed in the direction of the object's travel. Space is capable of expansion, and in fact the universe has been expanding ever since the Big Bang, between 13.5 and 14 billion years ago. The very question of what space is expanding into, if not more space, boggles the mind and reflects the difficulty we have of conceiving the true nature of our universe.

To make things even more puzzling, empty space is not empty. Space vibrates with energy, and even the most barren of vacuums is seething with activity. Within a vacuum, pairs of particles and antiparticles are forever popping into existence and then annihilating themselves, because particles and their antimatter counterparts cancel each other out.[24] Given the sheer weirdness of all this, it's hard to conceive of what space actually could be.

The question "What is space anyway?" raises some interesting questions about the notion of our being independent selves with bodies that are separate from the rest of the world. A recent theory with the name of Loop Quantum Gravity (LQG) holds some promise for uniting the seemingly irreconcilable models of quantum mechanics (good for describing things that happen at tiny scales, and yet useless at the scale of planets and stars) and relativity (good for describing things at large scales and yet inapplicable at the subatomic scale).

LQG, the brainchild of Lee Smolin, a researcher at the Perimeter Institute for Theoretical Physics and an adjunct professor of physics at the University of Waterloo, Ontario, suggests that the fabric of spacetime is, like, well, a fabric. In this theory, space is not smooth and continuous, but instead granular. We're familiar with the concept of matter being discontinuous—a piece of "solid" matter is mostly "empty" space. In fact matter is a good analogy. It used to be thought that matter was continuous, but we now know it's made from atoms and molecules. It no longer seems peculiar to us to consider that there is no water between water molecules. Similarly, LQG suggests that space is made of indivisible chunks about 10 to 35 meters in diameter. And just as there is no water between molecules of water, there is no space between these volumes of space. The meeting points of these chunks of space form nodes, which connect to form an unbroken network that includes the whole universe.

The entire universe, then, is one "thing."[25] According to LQG, what we see as individual particles are no more than tangles in the fabric of the cosmos. If you imagine a net and then imagine picking up one part of the net and twisting it to create a "particle," you can get an idea of what LQG predicts. The theory has a long way to go before it gains general acceptance (if it ever does), though it has already made some predictions that have been verified.

If LQG, or something like it, turns out to be true, then we are all quite literally joined together, woven of the same fabric. Each of us is a part of the warp and weft of the universe, connected by a web of spacetime to every other thing. As Hans Christian von Baeyer, Chancellor Professor of Physics at the College of William & Mary, wrote, "By intuition and reason Democritus penetrated to the very heart of nature when he saw that reality is to be found in atoms and the void; by intuition and reason Aristotle realized that no space could be absolutely empty. But neither man could have foreseen what we are learning today: *that stars and atoms and the vacuum are all part of a single, seamless whole.*"[26]

Moreover, some interpretations of Loop Quantum Gravity do away with the notion of time and space altogether. If space and time prove to be unnecessary for the understanding of the physical nature of the universe, then is it possible that they are artifacts—products of perception—rather than entities that really exist? Space and time could be no more real than the sensation "red," which we see when particular wavelengths of light strike photoreceptors in our eyes. The fact that our perceptions of space and time can be manipulated through meditative technique may suggest that they are just perceptions. It may be that space and time as we understand them in our day-to-day lives are convenient fictions that come about as a result of the nature of our senses, and of the brain and consciousness that organize and seek to understand the information presented by those senses.

The biologist Robert Lanza and Bob Berman, the American astronomer and science author, have a radical theory based on such considerations. They argue that life creates the universe. In essence this audacious theory (called "biocentrism" and outlined in a book of the same name[27]) states that everything we experience exists "only in us." Despite the name "biocentrism," it's not life itself but consciousness that, according to Lanza, creates the universe of experience we inhabit.

Of course it could be argued that the universe is apparently somewhere between 13.5 and 14 billion years old, and that life (at least in our small corner of the cosmos) has been around for only about 4 billion of those years, and that therefore the universe must pre-date life and can get along perfectly well without it, thank you very much. But this misses the point that whatever exists outside of consciousness is inherently unknowable. We're trapped in the assumption that the way we experience things is how things are. We imagine, for example, a red sun setting over a lifeless Earth 4.5 billion years ago. We imagine the sulfur stench of the volcanically generated atmosphere. We imagine the crackle of lightning forking from our planet's alien sky. But wait! None of these things could have happened. Outside of a consciousness equipped with our particular senses, the sun over early Earth had no color, the sulfur had no smell, and thunderstorms produced only vibrations in the atmosphere, not sound. If we try to extract color, form, sound, and other sensory information from our image of early Earth, what do we have? The answer is nothing, a voidness.[28] We can have nothing more than a distant intimation of the nature of the "reality" of the world "out there." The world mediated by our senses is the only one we can know. Like Plato's subterranean prisoners, we can see the shadows on the wall before us, but chained by our fleshly senses and by our limited consciousness, we can never turn around to see what casts them.

In Lanza and Berman's understanding, time and space are yet again simply constructs of consciousness—perceptions that arise from the particular kinds of sense organs and the particular kind of consciousness with which we are equipped. But if this bold dismissal of our assumptions of the external reality of time and space were true, wouldn't we see some kind of evidence of that? In fact we would. And we do, as the authors point out.

Consider quantum entanglement. It's possible for two particles (say two photons—particles of light) to become entangled so that if you affect one of them by measuring its properties, the other will be affected also. This effect is independent of distance, so that in theory you could measure, say, the polarization of an entangled photon on Earth, while simultaneously, on the other side of the universe, the photon's entangled partner will assume the opposite polarization. The two photons, despite their apparent separation in time and space, appear in effect to be one. Could it be that the billions of light-years we perceive as holding the two photons apart don't in fact exist outside our perceptions? The particles certainly behave as if there is no space between them. And moreover, since the effect on the distant photon arises instantaneously, the particles defy our normal conception of time. No effect, according to both our common sense and our tried-and-tested relativistic notions of space and time, should be able to propagate itself across any distance without the lapse of some amount of time. But time simply seems not to apply to entangled particles. Quantum entanglement is not a mere theory; it's been successfully tested over and over again, and is even being used in defense applications to produce unbreakable cryptography. Also, though the effect has not yet been tested over galactic distances, it's been shown to work between laboratories more than a hundred miles apart.

The theory of biocentrism has had its detractors, but also its admirers. Richard Conn Henry, professor of physics and astronomy at Johns Hopkins University, in Baltimore, Maryland, commented:

"[The authors] say 'the animal observer creates reality and not the other way around.' That is the essence of the entire book, and that is factually correct. It is an elementary conclusion from quantum mechanics. So what Lanza says in this book is not new. Then why does Robert have to say it at all? It is because we, the physicists, do NOT say it—or if we do say it, we only whisper it, and in private — furiously blushing as we mouth the words."[29]

When contemplating Space we are dealing, essentially, with a mystery. Certainly, it seems that the brain manufactures a sense of there being an inside and an outside to our experience. It also manufactures a sense of our "owning" a body—even when the body we claim as ours is that of a mannequin or PhD student of the opposite sex. Becoming more aware of the arbitrary nature of these identifications is not a trivial issue. Dr. Ehrsson, who runs the "body-swap" studies, says that his project's goal is "to identify the multisensory mechanisms whereby the central nervous system distinguishes between sensory signals from one's body and from the environment." He sees practical applications of this in improving our understanding of why people experience phantom limbs after amputation, and he also envisages the emergence of "a new direction in man-machine interfacing, neuroprosthetics, and computer science."

Leaving aside issues of therapy and of science-fiction-style brain/machine interfaces, we all suffer as a result of our identification, or over-identification, with our bodies. Our social situation is such that specific shapes and sizes of bodies go in and out of fashion, and meet with approval or disapproval. To the extent that we see our bodies as ourselves, we will suffer as we experience changes in our bodies or in others' perceptions of our bodies. When supermodels' stick-thin physiques are "in," most women become painfully conscious that they are "out," to take just one example. And more profoundly, our existential situation is such that our bodies are programmed to falter, decay, and ultimately fail. The more that we are able to be free from identifying our selves with our bodies, the more we will be able to bear this inevitable decline with dignity and equanimity.

And so, returning to the formal meditative reflection on the Space Element, we practice observing the physical form we inhabit and remind ourselves, "This is not me; this is not mine; I am not this." Having previously let go of the Earth, Water, Fire, and Air elements that constitute this form, the experience of letting go in this way can be profound. We can find ourselves more at peace with our bodies and more at peace with impermanence. We can find ourselves ready for the next challenge—that of letting go of the Consciousness Element.

CHAPTER THIRTEEN

The Consciousness Element

"Instead of being so bound up with everyone, be everyone."
—Jalāl al-Dīn Rūmī[1]

I'm driving along the long, winding, and rather monotonous U.S. Route 4 in New Hampshire, on my way to teach a class at the men's prison in Concord. It's easy to space out, and as usual I'm trying to turn the act of driving into a mindfulness practice. The radio is switched off. I'm not listening to any podcasts. I'm not eating or drinking. I'm trying not to multitask in any way. I simply pay attention to what's going on as I drive. I notice the physical sensations in my body. When another driver comes too close or makes a risky maneuver, I notice the emotions that arise and let go of them as best I can, while wishing both of us well. I pay attention (of course) to what I'm seeing in front of me and in my car's mirrors.

Noticing how my gaze can often fixate on a narrow area in front of me, I become aware of the entirety of my visual field, allowing into awareness everything from the center of my visual field to the periphery. It's like moving from a kind of "dial-up" connection between the world and my brain to a "broadband" one. Doing this generally has a very calming effect on my inner chatter, as if the sheer volume of incoming data I'm paying attention to leaves no bandwidth available for my inner dramas. So as I expand my awareness of my visual field I notice a marked decrease in my inner monologues. A sense of spaciousness arises in my experience. I become distracted less frequently, and it's easier to keep my awareness in the present moment.

Driving mindfully like this, I'm simultaneously aware of the curve of the road, of the vehicles ahead of me, and of the never-ending trees, buildings, signs, and utility poles that flow past me. My mind is quiet and yet full of sensory impressions. Then I notice a curious thing. I can see my hands on the steering wheel, at the ten o'clock and two o'clock positions. I can see the steering wheel turning clockwise and counterclockwise, with my hands upon it. I can feel my hands and arms moving. And yet I have no sense that "I" am making these movements. I'm not aware of giving my hands and arms any conscious or explicit directions. They seem to move of their own volition. They seem to have minds of their own. And yet, they're making precisely the movements needed to keep the car in its lane. There is an intelligence at work here, and yet it is not under conscious direction. The realization is fascinating, and it's so hilarious that for the next few miles I keep bursting into laughter.

So who is driving the car? It's certainly not my conscious self, because my conscious self has only just noticed that my hands are moving. My conscious self has been too absorbed with being mindful of my driving to bother about such trivial details as the physical movements involved in, well, the act of driving. But now I'm captivated by those movements, observing in the periphery of my visual field these two hands skillfully moving the steering wheel to the left and to the right, without my intervention, as if the hands belong to someone else. Who is this stranger with whom I am sharing a driver's seat, sharing a body? With deft finesse he coordinates the movements of my feet on the pedals and my right hand on the gear stick. It's clearly *my* body that is involved in the act of driving, but my conscious mind—which I often identify with as being my "self"—doesn't seem to be doing anything but observing.

It's rather spooky, this sense that "I" am not driving the car. It's as though my conscious awareness is sharing a body with a zombie or robot who does most of the grunt work. It's as if I'm simultaneously awake and sleepwalking. It's like a kind of spirit-possession. I feel almost that I'm in the presence of another. Someone else is moving the steering wheel. Someone else is pressing the gas, brake, and clutch pedals. Someone else reaches down at the appropriate moment and slides the gear stick forward from fourth gear to third. The only reassuring thing about all this is that he seems to be a good driver.

"Consciousness, Purified and Bright"

In the traditional description of the Six Element Practice, we've let go of the other elements, and we're left with consciousness which is, according to the Discourse, "purified and bright." Consciousness is purified because we have ceased clinging to the elements of Earth, Water, Fire, Air, and Space. We no longer see these elements—we no longer see the body—as constituting the self. The mind, relaxing its attempt to grasp the ungraspable flow of the elements, becomes more open and expansive. There's a greater sense of contentment.

Paradoxically, realizing that nothing is stable or reliable, the mind becomes more secure.

Or at least that's what's supposed to happen. Meditating is, however, akin to an artistic performance where the outcome is unpredictable and rarely perfect. Moreover, we don't simply reflect on the elements once and then sit back and experience liberation from clinging. Loosening our identifications completely can take many years of reflection and practice. What's being described in the Discourse is what happens in the ideal meditation. But although the full attainment of that ideal may only come after years of practice, it's common, as we enter the reflection on consciousness, for us to experience at least some degree of freedom and lightness of mind, and to experience a sense of expansiveness and openness. There may possibly be a feeling of connectedness, an appreciation of ourselves as something dynamic and flowing, or a sense of having expanded, attenuated, or otherwise altered our sense of self.

But we have yet to let go of the identification we have with our minds. We haven't explored the assumption that the mind is the essential self, that it is something separate and static, something that constitutes an essence—that which defines who and what we are. In reflecting on the Consciousness Element we cultivate the realization not only that there's nothing to grasp onto, but that there's "no thing" to do any grasping in the first place. The mind needs to stop clinging to itself, and to stop seeing itself as "the self." To paraphrase the comedian Emo Phillips, "I used to think that the mind was the most essential part of myself. Then I realized who was telling me this."

In this chapter we will, as with the earlier elements, question whether our consciousness is truly separate from what we regard as "other." We'll also question whether consciousness is a static "thing" that can validly be clung to and identified with as self.

The Non-Dual Nature of Consciousness

Before delving into the topic of the non-separateness of consciousness, we need to explore what the term consciousness means. This is no easy task, not least because there is no universally accepted definition. What follows is my understanding of consciousness as it is explained in the earliest Buddhist teachings.

We've already touched on one aspect of the non-separateness of consciousness in discussing the Space Element and how all experience takes place ultimately in the mind. When we look at the setting sun or eat a peach, the colors and flavors we experience are not inherent to the objects we perceive. The sun has no color, and a peach has no flavor. Color, flavor, and all the other sense modalities are forms of perception that have arisen in the mind. And yet we experience colors, sounds, textures, etc., as being "out there." Although these qualities exist only in the mind, we experience them "projected" onto an external reality. So too in our consciousness is some sense "out there," in the sense that certain qualities are "painted" onto an underlying physical substrate we can never directly experience. When I see a sunset I see, in a way, myself. Consciousness, then, is not something that is totally internal. And the so-called outside world is not something that is entirely external. Perhaps the best way I can put it is that external perceptions are both self and other, and that the external, objective pole and the internal, subjective pole of these perceptions are inseparable.

The Buddha called the sum total of our sensory experience "the all" and pointed out that we can know nothing beyond that experience.

He didn't deny that there was an underlying reality that was reinterpreted into an internal experience, but he did point out that we can't directly know anything of that reality. He also made comments like "The whole world is to be found in this fathom-long body," suggesting that all we can know is our experience of the world, rather than the world itself.

It's important to understand that the Buddha dismissed the idea of consciousness as something separate from what is perceived. Now, we tend to assume that there's this "thing" called consciousness sitting inside us (usually inside our heads). We generally imagine consciousness as existing separate from the things it perceives. And we assume that this "thing" can be aware of other "things," which may be internal, such as thoughts and emotions, or which may be external, such as objects in the world around us. But to the Buddha, consciousness was an *activity* and not a thing. Consciousness is the activity of being aware of something. There can, by definition, be no consciousness separate from the things of which it is aware, since one cannot have the activity of being aware of something without there being some *thing* that is the object of awareness.

This perspective takes a bit of getting used to, because we are so used to thinking of consciousness as "us" or as "the self." If there is no consciousness separate from the thing cognized, then where does this leave the self? The kind of self the Buddha talks about cannot exist without things that are non-self. Self, being contingent upon non-self, therefore has no separate existence. By way of an analogy, if the self is a river, then it exists in dependence upon the non-self of the riverbank. Without the non-river phenomenon that we call the "riverbank," the river cannot be. River and bank are in effect not separate things; they co-arise and are both parts of a larger phenomenon called the landscape.[2] Consciousness and what it perceives depend on each other and arise together. Both consciousness and the things perceived are part of the landscape of reality.

It's important to point out that the Buddha wasn't saying that the external world doesn't exist—that it's all some kind of fantasy or illusion arising in the mind. As I sat in meditation this morning I could hear my wife and children playing upstairs, could smell the woody scent of incense, and could feel the chill of the early autumn air on my skin. I did not invent my children, my wife, the incense, or the air. They are not fantasies. There are "things" out there that have an objective existence. But I do contribute to my experience of all those things. Leaving aside any emotional connection with my family, the vibrations in the air generated by my daughter calling for her mother are one thing, and (as we've already seen) the experience I have of those as a "sound" are another. If I had different sensory equipment I would experience those vibrations in a completely different way. What we call "the world" is a collaborative venture. But we can never know objective things separate from our sense-impressions, which are interpretations rather than reality.

This picture has a parallel in the world of science and philosophy, where our inner experiences of color, sound, smell, etc., are termed *qualia,* a Latin word related to the English word "qualities." How *qualia* arise in response to external stimuli is a profound mystery that may never be solved. On the one hand we have photons and vibrations in the air that, in ways that are well understood, lead to electrical and chemical activity in the brain. But then on the other we have the experience of a red sunset and the sound of children playing. There is simply no understanding at present of how electrical and chemical activity in the brain translates into actual experience. Yes, we can understand how the stimulation of certain receptors gives rise to electrical and chemical activity in the brain, but chemical and electrical events in the brain are not experiences. Some scientists try to ignore inner experience altogether and to reduce consciousness to electrical activity in the brain, but for most of us this strategy is sorely lacking. We experience! And we know we experience. Something so fundamental cannot easily be ignored, or dismissed simply as the oozing of neurotransmitters or currents of electrons flowing between neurons.

As far as defining consciousness goes, we're even worse off than when it comes to defining life. At least with defining life, we have lists of widely accepted qualities, even if those lists are never entirely free of loopholes and anomalies. But with consciousness there's nothing close to a widely accepted definition. It seems every philosopher or scientist (and those are not always separate categories) has his or her own definition—if he or she even tries to formulate one.

Although I haven't seen him explicitly comparing the difficulty of defining both life and consciousness, the philosopher and neuroscientist Alva Noë, in his book *Out of Our Heads,* links the two fields. "Mind," he writes, "is life." Even a bacterium, he notes, has wants and needs and is an agent in relation to the world. It will move toward food sources and will move away from noxious substances. Its agency is "primitive" and its mindfulness "incipient," but, he points out, "The problem of consciousness . . . is none other than the problem of life." Noë posits that the "mind" of the bacterium is not some property of its internal organization, but rather pertains to "the way it actively meshes with its environment and gears into it." There is both an internal and an external dimension to this meshing:

there are internal experiences and their corresponding neural events, but conscious beings, he suggests, " . . . have worlds precisely in the sense that the world shows up for them as laden with value."[3] The values of a simple organism amount to things like food, poison, light, sex, and kin.

Our world, to extend Noë's argument, is simply that of the bacterium writ large. As well as attributing to the world *qualia* such as color, sound, smell, etc., we add further layers of *value*—likes and dislikes, the concept of "existence," "separateness," "meaning," "status," "right and wrong," etc. Noë's view—like the Buddha's—is essentially non-dualistic. There is in "the all" (to use the Buddha's term) no separate self or other. There can be no consciousness without something to be conscious of. Consciousness cannot exist in an experiential vacuum. But there can also be nothing to experience without the act of consciousness taking place. These two things— the perceiving consciousness and the thing perceived—are in essence one, and are what we call "experience." There's no possibility of there being an external world separate from consciousness in any meaningful sense; imagine subtracting all of your *qualia* (color, sound, touch, taste, smell) from the world around you. What is left? Obviously nothing that we can describe. At the same time, there can be no consciousness separate from the thing to be experienced.

Consciousness, like life, is its own thing and irreducible. Life depends upon chemistry and physics, yet it's something more than these two things. Life is indefinable. If consciousness has co-arisen with life, and is an inseparable part of life, then we're likely to find that consciousness too is indefinable. Just as life cannot be reduced to mere chemistry, consciousness cannot be reduced to mere biochemistry.

Consciousness is its own thing. To be conscious is to experience. To experience is to be conscious. What does it mean to be conscious or to experience? That is something only a conscious entity can understand, and so explanations in terms of chemical and electrical brain activity will always come up short.

The very indefinability of consciousness is another reminder of the ultimate inadequacy of the definitions to which the grasping mind tries to cling. The mind, in order to understand the world in which it operates, has of course to employ definitions. But taking our definitions literally, and assuming that the things we define must correspond in some tidy way to our terms and concepts, leads to oversimplification, confusion, or conflict. This is why to some extent I think that, from the point of view of living a meaningful life, exploring in depth the science and philosophy of consciousness can be counterproductive. It's useful to become aware of certain limitations in the ways we currently think about consciousness—to realize, for example, that consciousness cannot exist without an object—because this can help us change the way we relate to our experience. But a full understanding of what consciousness is may not be necessary, even if such a thing were attainable. Just as we manage to advance medical science, cure disease, and extend life without being able to precisely define what life is, so perhaps can we relieve mental suffering and find meaningful approaches to life without being able to fully define consciousness. We find ourselves once again in the unfortunate position of having been shot with a poisoned arrow. We need enough understanding of the situation to understand its gravity, the need for action, and the best way in which to withdraw the deadly dart. But in seeking to understand every last detail of the danger we're in, and how it came to be, we make an unfortunate position even worse.

The Traditional Practice

In the traditional reflection on the Consciousness Element, as outlined in the Discourse, the emphasis is on recognizing the impermanence of our experiences, which is the same thing, in effect, as recognizing that consciousness is impermanent and interconnected, and that it is not a unitary and static thing. In recognizing these facts, we come to see that not even consciousness forms the kind of separate and static self that we assume we have.

We are encouraged, in the reflection on the Consciousness Element, to observe the coming into being and the passing out of existence of individual moments of perception (or "sense-contacts") and their accompanying feeling-tone. (The formal description in the Discourse is long and involved, and I won't quote it here.) A perception is simply a raw experience of color, sound, smell, taste, or touch, whether externally, in the outside world, or internally, in the mind's eye. According to Buddhist phenomenology (or study of experience), each moment of perception arises in the mind as a "consciousness." This consciousness is tinged with a feeling-tone (*vedana*) that may be pleasant, unpleasant, or neutral. These feelings are not the same as emotions, which are more developed responses such as love, desire, curiosity, jealousy, fear, surprise, etc. The vedanas are more like gut feelings that give us a rough-and-ready sense of whether something we're experiencing is something we want to move toward or away from. You can try this right now. Put down this book and let your eyes roam your immediate environment. Some things you see will attract you and produce a warm glow of pleasure—perhaps a photograph of someone you love, or a treasured possession. Some things you perceive will evoke a response of displeasure—perhaps a stack of unpaid bills or a dangling cobweb that reminds you that you need to do some cleaning. And some things you see, you'll feel relatively neutral toward—perhaps a blank area of wall space or carpet, for example.

Perceptions and their accompanying feelings are constantly rising and falling like ripples in the mind. And in the reflective practice we observe these ripples. The point of observing perceptions giving rise to feelings is that it's in response to these feelings that we start to construct our stories about the world and about ourselves. It's in response to feelings that clinging and aversion arise. We do not simply perceive the world around us in purely sensory terms. As a matter of evolutionary survival, we've learned to project values upon the things we perceive. Generally, when a perception leads to a pleasant feeling, we see the thing perceived as "good" and "desirable." When a perception gives rise to an unpleasant feeling, we see the thing we're perceiving as "bad" and to be avoided, blamed, and possibly even destroyed. Neutral feelings leave us unmoved, uninterested, bored, or restless. Each of these acts of interpretation is technically known as a *sañña*—a word variously translated as "apperception," "recognition," or "cognition."

Now, human beings are animals who tell stories, and in a process that's technically called *papañca,* or proliferation, we generate stories about our experience that are higher-level responses, and not just a hedonic classification into the categories "desirable," "to be avoided," and "uninteresting." We make interpretations that involve categories such as permanence and separateness. We perceive an eddy, to return to that example, and imagine that it is in some way separate from the river and that it is in some way permanent. We experience ourselves, and likewise assume that there is an unchanging core, even if there's much evidence to undermine that conclusion. We see change, and think of it as something fearful and threatening, because we think change *shouldn't* happen to us.

What's the alternative? Instead of meeting our experience (sensation plus feeling) with sañña (interpretation, leading to storytelling), we meet it with pañña (or insight). Insight is something we commonly think of as a kind of knowledge, and in a sense pañña is a kind of knowledge. But insight is a direct and unflinching recognition of the reality of impermanence and non-self. It's a perspective that allows us to respond to our experience with equanimity, fearlessness, and non-grasping. It's a state of emotional non-reactivity that allows spontaneous joy and compassion to emerge.

Now, it is no easy task to watch the mind closely, to observe our perceptions giving rise to feelings, and to mindfully bear with those feelings, aware of their impermanent nature. It can take a great deal of mental training to bring the mind to the point where it can undistractedly observe our experience in this way. Consequently, the mind has to be trained to pay focused attention, usually by cultivating a mindful awareness of the breath. We find that distraction arises when we're paying attention to the breath, because the mind is busy reacting to feelings by proliferating stories. And so over and over again we have to catch the mind daydreaming, to let go of those proliferating thoughts, to bring our awareness back to the physical sensations of the breath. This training makes it easier for us to observe the rising and falling ripples of sensations and feelings, as described in the traditional reflection on the Consciousness Element.

Through observing our consciousness in this way, we come to appreciate more and more that there is nothing stable within the mind. There is no permanent core. And we begin to recognize too that none of these experiences is inherent to the mind. Perceptions, feelings, thoughts, and emotions are simply flowing through us, but are not us; and as we watch them pass we can repeat, "This is not me; this is not mine; I am not this."

The mind, metaphorically, is a kind of stream—a river composed of overlapping waves and currents of experience. There is no self that exists independently of those waves. We also appreciate the non-dualistic perspective that we discussed earlier: the fact that consciousness and the things consciousness is aware of co-arise and are inseparable. It's an interesting experiment just to become aware of what we're sensing, and to see if we can let go, even to a small extent, of the assumption that what we're experiencing is "not-us." If instead we try to consciously adopt the attitude that all we perceive is ourselves, a sense of intimacy and closeness can arise, as the barrier between self and other begins to dissolve.

Consciousness is an activity. It's there when it happens. And sometimes consciousness isn't there, which means that sometimes the self (if we see the self as identified with consciousness) isn't there either. Do you have a self when you're deeply asleep, or when you're anesthetized?

Culture as a River of Consciousness

The traditional reflection considers the interconnected, non-dual nature of consciousness, in terms of how the whole process of cognizing is inseparable from an awareness of the world. But there are other ways to look at the interconnectedness of our minds, so we can come to realize that "our" consciousness is not really ours at all. When I consider my own mind, it quickly becomes clear that my mind depends heavily upon the minds of other beings. In fact my most basic tools for understanding the world have come from other people. For example, I can communicate with you and you with me because we have both learned to use and understand a language. And we have both learned language, of course, from other people. Without the internalization of language from others, our selves would be very different from what they are. It's impossible to imagine extricating language from our very perception of the world. Try this: look at the page in front of you, and try to see the words and letters as mere marks on the paper, lacking in meaning. If you're anything like me, you'll find it's impossible.

In an attempt to discover whether language was innate, the Emperor Frederick II found that language-deprived children did not do well. He bade foster mothers and nurses,

> ". . . to suckle and bathe and wash the children, but in no wise to prattle or speak with them; for he would have learnt whether they would speak the Hebrew language (which had been the first), or Greek, or Latin, or Arabic, or perchance the tongue of their parents of whom they had been born. But he labored in vain, for the children could not live without clappings of the hands, and gestures, and gladness of countenance, and blandishments."[4]

King James IV of my native Scotland reportedly discovered that two children cared for by a mute nurse in an isolated dwelling grew up speaking good Hebrew. But we can safely assume that this was a fabrication designed to inspire the faithful, for when children have been brought up from an early age without exposure to language, they are generally uninterested in human ways and are unable to learn to speak more than a word or two. There have been many cases of children supposedly brought up in the wild by animals, but most of these appear to be as fictional as Rudyard Kipling's character Mowgli, and often have been scams aiming to raise money through exploiting a developmentally disabled child. More credible are the sad tales of isolation that arises from abuse, such as the case of a Russian girl who was locked in a room full of cats and dogs for the first five years of her life. When she was found by police, she was unable to talk and would make noises like those of her animal companions. She was also unable to use a spoon and preferred to lap from a dish. Perhaps saddest of all—and very telling in considering our need for connection with others—she had the body of a two-year-old.[5]

Even once we have learned language, our acculturation goes deep. We learn practical skills, ways of thinking, and patterns of emotion from those around us. The child of religious fundamentalists in a Utah compound will internalize a completely different set of assumptions about the world than, say, the child of two Harvard philosophy professors or the child of two factory workers. We carry around internalized expectations of what is right, good, normal, desirable, and to be feared based on the particular culture we were brought up in or have become used to. We pick up what have been called "memes"— cultural ideas, symbols, or practices transmitted from one mind to another via speech, writing, gestures, social rituals, direct instruction, etc. Without these memes, flowing from one consciousness to another, none of us amounts to very much. Without the transmission of the contents of consciousness, we would not exactly be blank slates, but we wouldn't be fully human either. Like the pitiful little Russian girl who spent five years living with cats and dogs, without the flow of the Consciousness Element we would be little more than wild animals in human form. Our identity depends on the internalization of the consciousness of others. Consciousness, like all the other elements, is therefore something that extends beyond the individual and that, in some sense, flows through us like a river.

The Noösphere: A Field of Consciousness

If each of us is an individual current in a river of consciousness, the sum total of what flows within our collective mind can be regarded as something akin to the hydrosphere or atmosphere. And in fact, in 1926 Vladimir Vernadsky coined the term "noösphere" to denote the "realm of human thought"—a kind of field of awareness in which we all participate. Vernadsky was one of the first to realize that the earth's atmosphere and other systems were produced or conditioned by the biosphere. He saw the noösphere as being an evolutionary advance arising from the inanimate geosphere and the living systems it supported. Mere physics and chemistry give birth to life, and life in turn gives birth to consciousness. And just as life affects the physical world by, for example, producing an atmosphere, so too does the noösphere shape the environment. Pierre Teilhard de Chardin, the Jesuit priest and scientist, worked the concept of the noösphere into a somewhat more scientific, and yet still spiritual, explanation of human origins and purpose.

One of de Chardin's notions was that within the noösphere, individuals' minds were heading in the direction of greater harmony and cooperation with each other. This hypothesis he'd no doubt extrapolated from the very human ability to learn from one another. While other animals show capacity for learning, no other known life-form has the ability to learn as much as we do. And this learning is largely a social endeavor arising from imitation and in fact is a vital part of the flow of consciousness that takes place within the noösphere. The fact that this flow can happen so readily is of considerable interest. If human beings have such a well-developed capacity for learning, surely there must be mechanisms that have allowed this to evolve? While you might think that it's simply our large brains that allow for learning, size, as they say, isn't everything.

Mirrors in the Mind

Our brains contain mirror neurons, which have been called "cells that read minds." First discovered in monkeys, mirror neurons form systems that allow us to understand the actions of others, so that when a child sees an adult perform an action, he or she is able to internally synthesize the same action. My three-year-old daughter is able to imitate my actions extremely quickly. For example, the first time she saw me using a screwdriver, she picked up a pen and mimicked my actions perfectly, down to the little grunts of effort I was making. As soon as she saw me turning my screwdriver, she "felt" herself making the same actions. Not only do mirror neurons allow us to understand and copy the physical actions of others, they allow us also to understand their intentions and feelings too. Humans have evolved to be social creatures, and mirror neurons are the brain's tool for imitative learning and for social understanding. We are wired to be interconnected.

"When you see me perform an action—such as picking up a baseball—you automatically simulate the action in your own brain," said Dr. Marco Iacoboni, who studies mirror neurons at the University of California, Los Angeles, UCLA, in a *New York Times* article.[6] While inhibitory circuits in the brain generally prevent us from acting out these simulations, we understand what the person drawing his hand back is doing and—crucially—what he is *intending* to do. Mirror neurons don't quite allow us to read minds, but they do allow us to place ourselves in another person's shoes so that we can come up with an approximation of his intentions, thoughts, and mental state. These mirror neuron-driven hunches can be remarkably accurate. In a 2005 paper, Dr. Iacoboni and his colleagues showed that mirror neurons could accurately detect whether a person who was picking up a cup from a table intended to drink from it or clear it away.[7] When I see another person in distress, weeping and choking up, and with a facial expression indicating sadness, my mirror neurons create my own personal simulation of those actions, and I am able to feel what the other person is feeling. Studies of mirror neurons are uncovering the biology of empathy.

While other animals, such as chimpanzees, monkeys, and probably dogs, have mirror-neuron systems, those in humans seem to be far more complex. And it's because of our complex mirror-neuron systems that we are able to learn language and other complex behaviors. The human mind is designed to network with other minds, allowing information to flow from one consciousness to another. We have evolved to have minds that are not separate from one another, but are inherently linked. Our minds are nodes in the noösphere.

As if confirming this, a study by Dr. Mirella Dapretto, a developmental neuroscientist also at UCLA, suggested that broken mirror neurons may be involved in autism. People with autism can recognize signs of emotion in others, but they do not empathetically feel those emotions.[8] People with autism are cut off from one of the most important channels of the flow of consciousness from one individual to another—the flow of emotion. Many people with autism experience not just social isolation and an inability to make eye contact, but difficulty in imitating other people's actions and a limited language capacity. They often exist "in a world of their own," obsessed with what other people would regard as trivia and engaged in repetitive movements like rocking.[9] The example of autism gives us a contrast that highlights the extraordinary networking ability of the non-autistic mind. The ability to learn socially and to empathize with others' emotions points to the lack of separateness of our minds, and what an important (although often overlooked) component this is in our sense of self.

The Self, Unplugged

A less drastic, but still powerful, measure of our interdependence is the physical and mental harm caused by isolation, and the corresponding health benefits of social contact. Loneliness increases people's risk of heart disease, stroke, cancer, and lung and gastrointestinal ailments.[10] Isolation pushes systolic blood pressure by up to 30 mmHg by age sixty-five.[11] Mice genetically predisposed to developing mammary cancer will develop more and larger mammary-gland tumors when kept in isolation.[12] The effects of loneliness on health are so powerful that isolation is as bad for you as smoking cigarettes.

Isolation even affects the expression of genes. Steve Cole, of UCLA, led a study there showing that gene expression in at least 209 sites on the genome is affected by loneliness. These changes are related to the elevated levels of inflammation and immune activation, and the reduced ability to fight infection seen in lonely people. One of the study's authors, John T. Cacioppo, a psychologist at the University of

Chicago, points out that feeling bad about being isolated is a mechanism for bringing us back into contact with others: "This very process of feeling bad because of disconnection contributes to what it means to be human . . . It makes us care for other people and want to reconnect when we're disconnected."[13]

Even just thinking about isolation has psychological and physiological effects. Chen-Bo Zhong and Geoffrey Leonardelli of the Rotman School of Management, University of Toronto, Canada, told students—who were engaged in unrelated experiments—that the central heating was malfunctioning and then asked the students to estimate the room temperature. If the participants had been prompted to think about social exclusion before being asked to guess the ambient temperature, they estimated temperatures to be 3°C (5°F) cooler than did students who had been primed with thoughts of social inclusion. In another experiment, students who had been excluded from a game indicated a preference for warmer foods than students who had been included—suggesting the excluded students felt cold. A sense of connection with others is necessary for something as basic as feeling physically comfortable.[14]

On the other hand, just as isolation harms, connectedness helps maintain our health. Bernadette Boden-Albala, professor of sociomedical sciences and neurology at Columbia University, reported that socially connected stroke patients had half the risk of having a second stroke within five years as their isolated counterparts. And even though socially active people are exposed to more viral infections than stay-at-homes, they are half as likely to catch colds. And researchers at the Harvard School of Public Health, tracking more than sixteen thousand elderly Americans for a period of six years, found that those who were socially active had much lower rates of memory loss.[15]

The conclusion can only be that the normal, healthy self is one that is connected to others in a rich tapestry of social networks. The self, in isolation, cannot function normally. Unplugged from the network of human relations, it withers. The self, in effect, is a phenomenon that exists interdependently.

The Self as a Community

The Buddha did not seem to believe that consciousness was a unitary phenomenon. We tend to assume that we each contain one consciousness, and that that consciousness is us, or is part of us. Or that there's one consciousness inside us, and it's aware of many things. The Buddha's view was that this is a false assumption. Instead each event of cognizing is "a consciousness." Since perceptions come and go, so too will consciousness come and go. Each response to a perception is another consciousness. These too come and go. There is no enduring consciousness, no permanent watcher at the helm of our being, observing everything that happens and making decisions. There are just these multiple overlapping waves of consciousness, rising and falling, rising and falling.

A good parallel might be to think of an ecosystem. An ecosystem is dependent upon energy entering from an outside source, usually the sun. That energy is processed by multiple living systems, which end up—through the activities of growing, reproducing, and consuming one another—establishing a system. That system is self-regulating. And it is lacking in a self. There is no central intelligence directing operations, saying, "The insect population is high this year; let's breed more finches to keep the insects in check." An ecosystem is a self-regulating mechanism that is devoid of a self. Similarly, a mind can be seen as a self-regulating system of perceptions and responses to those perceptions. And like an ecosystem, a mind lacks any central control system.

This lack of a central control system is mirrored in the modern hypothesis that we each have multiple selves. Paul Bloom, a professor of psychology at Yale University and the author of *Descartes' Baby: How the Science of Child Development Explains What Makes Us Human,* has written about the multiplicity of selves he's observed in his work and in his personal experience: "Many researchers now believe, to varying degrees, that each of us is a community of competing selves, with the happiness of one often causing the misery of another," he wrote in an article in *The Atlantic.*[16]

Bloom's view, he says, is "conservative" in that "it accepts that brains give rise to selves that last over time, plan for the future, and so on." But his view is also radical in that "it gives up the idea that there is just one self per head. The idea is that instead, within each brain, different selves are continually popping in and out of existence. They have different desires, and they fight for control—bargaining with, deceiving, and plotting against one another."

The experience of competing selves can be seen in the everyday experience in which one self wants to lose weight and the other wants to enjoy pizza. But we can also experience multiple selves when we find ourselves arguing with another person inside our head. Who is arguing with whom? Who wins in such a debate? Who suffers from the insults that are bandied about? In a more amicable tone, children often have conversations with imaginary friends. But who is talking to whom? Bloom recounts that the writer Adam Gopnik's young daughter had an imaginary companion, Charlie Ravioli—a hip New Yorker whose central characteristic was that he was always too busy to play with her.

In the multiple-selves model, *the* self is just a temporary hijacking of executive control by one particular constellation of priorities. Consciousness in this view is not an enduring "thing" but a series of events popping into and out of existence. Of course we still have a *sense* of having a permanent self, but this doesn't seem to correspond to anything that exists in reality. This theory of multiple consciousnesses, each doing its own thing and in competition with other consciousnesses, has as far as I know no explicit parallel in Buddhist teachings (although the teaching of the five hindrances suggests five emotional centers around which multiple selves can constellate). And yet the notion that there is an absence of a unified self is very much a part of traditional Buddhist thinking. The observations of Buddhist meditators clearly suggest that there is nothing corresponding to a unitary self, although there will almost inevitably be a belief in such a self. This belief is near-universal and compelling. But it simply does not correspond with what we see, either on the basis of sustained introspection or in terms of what we know about how the brain works.

The Watcher and the Decider

Sometimes we identify the self with our *awareness* (our ability to notice our experience) or our *agency* (our ability to make decisions). It feels as if we exist in the midst of our experience, receiving sensory information from the outside world and from our internal states, which together form a kind of movie in the brain. We observe and experience these sensory inputs. The self, we assume, is what watches the movie. In response to our evaluations of these sensory inputs, we decide on some course of action, and then we act. It's as if, within us, there is an observer/experiencer/decider.

The problem is, no structures in the brain and no measurable activity taking place in the brain correspond to these assumptions. There is no central area of the brain that observes, experiences, and makes decisions. And much of what happens in the brain happens outside of consciousness.

Susan Blackmore in her book *Ten Zen Questions* highlights the discrepancy between what we assume goes on when we perceive, evaluate, and decide, and what actually happens in the brain. She does so by considering a simple scenario: someone throws a ball toward us, and we reach up and catch it easily.[17] We assume, she points out, that we *consciously* notice the ball coming toward us, that we *consciously* make evaluations about its speed and trajectory, and that we *consciously* coordinate the movements of the body so that we snatch the ball from the air mid-flight. What is so unreasonable about that, you might ask?

First, the visual system, Blackmore points out, consists of multiple pathways snaking through the brain. Among these are two main paths: a dorsal stream that controls fast actions, and a slower ventral stream that perceives and recognizes objects. You may have had the experience, while playing a fast-paced game such as squash or badminton, of surprising yourself by managing not only to get your racquet in position to intercept a fast-moving projectile hurtling toward you from mere feet away, but also to send the projectile flying back toward the only unguarded part of the court. These are moments of sudden grace that we sometimes dismiss as luck, but that on good days happen so frequently we realize we are seeing an inner intelligence at work. Such decisions—and actions—are taken within timescales so short that we do not even have time to register consciously what is going on. We have responded to the input flowing through the faster dorsal stream, even though that information is processed outside of conscious awareness.

Blackmore does not mention a related and very interesting fact: that some people who have experienced brain damage that prevents them from consciously seeing anything—that is, they are profoundly blind—can perform actions such as catching balls, weaving their way unerringly around obstacles in their path, and cleanly picking up objects. This phenomenon has been termed "blindsight," and it produces deeply paradoxical situations. Beatrice de Gelder—of Harvard Medical School and Tilburg University in the Netherlands—has a video of a blind man, "TN," successfully navigating a corridor littered with obstacles. TN is profoundly blind as the result of two strokes that destroyed his visual cortex. His eyes work, but his brain simply cannot process the visual information it receives—or at least TN cannot become conscious of such visual information. And yet, in the video, we see him deftly threading his way past trash cans, a shredder, a camera tripod, and cartons of letter-sized paper. He moves exactly as a sighted person would—although a little more slowly—neatly avoiding every obstacle. And yet he cannot consciously see a single one of them.[18]

Another patient, a woman called "DF," became blindsighted after carbon-monoxide poisoning from a broken water heater damaged her visual cortex. Like TN, she cannot consciously perceive shapes or objects. And yet she opens her fingers to the appropriate width when picking up an object, and she can twist her hand to the correct angle when asked to put it through a slot. She acts as if she can see, and yet she can't.[19]

Blindsighted individuals process visual information and respond to it, but "seeing" in this case is taking place in visual pathways that operate outside of conscious awareness. Blindsighted individuals clearly act, and yet there is no conscious perception, nor are decisions to act being made with the involvement of conscious awareness. TN does not know he is avoiding obstacles when maneuvering through a cluttered corridor, and DF is unaware of how she "knows" to adjust her grip to pick up a cup one moment and a pencil the next.

The implication of these cases frankly sends a shiver down my spine. We are so used to thinking of our conscious self as having the functions of observing and deciding on actions, that it's a shock to realize the extent to which observing and acting can take place with no conscious involvement. We're back to the inner zombie—the stranger within me who takes care of the driving while I'm busy being mindful. We think "we" are in control, but presumably the mechanisms that allow TN to maneuver through a cluttered corridor or DF to accurately grasp an object she cannot see operate in the rest of us too. We too respond to visual information being processed in channels of the brain not accessible to conscious awareness. We just don't notice that this is going on. We're caught up in the grip of the delusion that the conscious mind is in fact running the show.

Fully sighted individuals have in fact been shown to act without conscious perception taking place, and without decisions being made consciously. Mel Goodale, of the University of Western Ontario, in London, Ontario, employs a perceptual trick that makes circular blocks of identical size look as if they're different sizes. Subjects will invariably report after visual inspection that one block is larger than the other, and yet videotape shows that whichever block they reach to pick up, they open their hands to the same width. The conscious self is fooled by the optical illusion, but the body still responds appropriately. The conscious self may think it is acting in such cases, but it clearly isn't. Where is the "self" in all this?[20]

Although Susan Blackmore's book doesn't, as I mentioned, make reference to the oddities of blindsight, she does point to the famous and very revealing experiments carried out in the 1970s by the neuroscientist Ben Libet. Libet asked volunteers to perform the simple physical task of flexing their wrist at random times of their own choosing. By monitoring their brain activity, he was able to establish that the motor areas of the brain became active a good half second before the volunteers judged that they had made the conscious decision to act. It is now well-established that our decision-making is a *post-hoc* conscious labeling of activities that begin outside of awareness. In other words, we make decisions before we're consciously aware of having done so, and once we become conscious of the decision having been made we then consider that we've decided. If the conscious "me" doesn't even know I've made a decision to flex my wrist, in what way have "I" decided to act?

Libet's findings proved to be controversial, as you might expect. Some critics claimed that his equipment was not sensitive enough and that he was simply picking up on static in the readings. But John-Dylan Haynes, at the Bernstein Center for Computational Neuroscience in Berlin, Germany, confirmed Libet's findings when he led a study using fMRI to look at the brains of people asked to tap one of two buttons randomly, using a finger of either the left or right hand.[21] Haynes saw part of the prefrontal cortex, where decisions are made, light up a full *seven seconds* before an action was taken. What's more, he was able to correctly predict, 60 percent of the time, which button a volunteer would press. Quite literally his fMRI machine can know, seven seconds before you do, when you will make a random movement. Haynes reckons that what Libet was detecting was only the last stage of the unconscious decision-making process. Sometimes the workings of consciousness seem akin to a building whose heating systems click on in response to changes in the ambient temperature—purely automatic systems functioning without a central decider.

Nevertheless, we feel like we're in control, right? Well, we may *feel* we are. Another perspective comes from split-brain studies. Split-brain surgery is a radical procedure used to treat severe epilepsy. It involves severing a narrow band of tissue—called the corpus callosum—that connects the two hemispheres of the brain and allows them to communicate. When someone has had his or her brain split this way, the two hemispheres are unable to exchange information—they're forced to work independently. This has some unfortunate side effects, but it does limit the severity of epileptic seizures. Because the brain's left and right sides have somewhat different functions, split-brain patients make ideal test subjects for studying these specializations, and for studying the relationship between the left and right brains.

In one intriguing experiment, split-brain subjects were presented with two cognitive tests simultaneously—one to each side of the brain.[22] (This is possible because of the way in which the left and right visual fields are wired up, respectively, to the right and left hemispheres of the brain.) The subjects were presented with a picture and asked to point to an object that went with that picture. Both sides of the brain performed perfectly. When the left hemisphere was shown a chicken foot, the right hand would point to a chicken. When the right hemisphere—simultaneously—was shown a picture of snow, the left hand would point to a shovel. But now the subject had to explain why he made his choice. And he had to do this using only his left hemisphere—the side of the brain that deals with language. But the left hemisphere had only seen one of the pairs of images! The responses—typically something like, "I saw a claw and I picked the chicken, and you have to clean out the chicken shed with a shovel"—made no sense at all. These "explanations" were in fact fictions—*post hoc* rationalizations—because there was in fact no causal connection whatsoever between the actions of the left and right brains, which were acting in an uncoordinated way.

In other experiments, the word "laugh" was shown to the left field of vision (connected to the right cerebral hemisphere). The subject would laugh. When asked to explain why he had laughed, the subject would say something like, "Oh, you guys are just really funny!" The right brain initiates laughter because it has seen the word "laugh." The left brain has not seen that word, but knows that the subject has in fact laughed. And so the left brain is forced to invent a plausible-sounding reason for why the laughter occurred.

So, when someone has a split brain—two hemispheres acting independently, with no communication between them—how many "selves" does that person have? One? If so, how does this self maintain its integrity when the two halves of the brain cannot communicate? The post-hoc rationalizations for actions that we see in split-brain patients are strikingly similar to those we saw in Libet's experiments. In both cases, decisions are made and then the conscious mind has to retrospectively assign an explanation. At no point does the individual—split-brain or otherwise—feel an absence of control. The sense of there being a "self" making the decision is present, even though that's clearly not what's going on.

These findings from science suggest that the conscious mind is good at claiming responsibility for actions, but often seems not to be involved in them. The conscious self is often utterly out of the loop.

When the Self Goes AWOL

Anyone who has paid attention to the activities of the mind will have noticed that conscious awareness comes and goes. If conscious perception is the self, then it is a self that is highly unstable, unruly, and discontinuous. Where is the self when conscious awareness is absent?

Even when we are making a determined effort to remain mindfully aware of our experience—as in meditation—there's a rather humbling tendency for the mind to go AWOL. In meditation, we begin by setting our attention onto some object such as the breathing. After some time, we realize that we have been in a state of distraction. For how long? It's hard to say. Maybe it was thirty seconds. Maybe it was five minutes. What were we thinking about? That's hard to say as well. Just as the memory of our dreams begins to slip away the moment we awaken, so, often, are we unable to recall the mind's exact object of obsession from only a few moments earlier.

We sleep. Where is the inner observer when we are asleep? We spend only a small amount of our sleeping time in dreams; the rest is spent in a state of deep sleep. The two hours or so of REM sleep that we typically get each night—in which dreaming is experienced—arguably involve some kind of conscious awareness But in deep sleep, it would be hard to argue that we are conscious in any way at all. An individual in deep sleep can be prodded, poked, and yelled at without showing the slightest signs of responding. Nor is there much going on inside. When awoken from deep sleep, we're typically groggy, disoriented, and unable to describe what, if anything, we were experiencing only moments before. This lack of responsiveness corresponds to the neurons in areas deep inside the brain having taken a break from their normal activities. In deep sleep, the brain in fact appears to be in something of a "powered-down" state in which essential maintenance subroutines are operating, probably involved in tasks such as consolidating memories.[23]

Our Fickle Memories

Despite all the evidence suggesting that we have multiple selves, and that conscious awareness isn't good for much other than taking the credit for decisions that are actually made unconsciously, we still have that persistent sense of having a self. People often have the sense in fact that some unchanging thread of consciousness runs through their lives. Many people will point to their memories as constituting such a "core" to their being. "I know I'm me, and I know that I'm the same me I was last week and last year and decades ago. I have my memories," we think. And yet memory is not as permanent as we like to think it is.

I first began to notice the peculiarity of memory when I reflected on some of my earliest recollections. In one of these, I'm two years old and have just locked my mother out of the house. She's outside, explaining how to turn the knob on the dead bolt. I'm feeling panicky because I think I'm going to get into trouble, and I'm running back and forth between the front door and the living-room window. My earliest memories seem to begin at an unusually early age, but otherwise this is a very ordinary recollection. But, what's this? As I recall this incident in my mind's eye, I can actually see my two-year-old self running back and forth—*from the outside!* Now of course, at the time I locked my mother out of the house I was not actually outside my own body observing events unfold. Clearly this memory is not a *recording* of what I actually saw that day, but some kind of *reconstruction*—a reimagined version of the event. And studies have shown that our memories are in fact not fixed recordings like those on a DVD disc but are more like a Word document on a computer's hard drive—a file that is opened, edited, and re-saved, the contents changing over time.

In 2007, the neuroscientist Joseph LeDoux and his colleagues at New York University—in an experiment reminiscent of the popular film *Eternal Sunshine of the Spotless Mind*—pulled off the remarkable feat of erasing specific memories from rats' brains. LeDoux and his team had conditioned rats to associate a beep with a painful electric shock. They would begin by playing the sound to the rats, who would immediately pay attention given that this was a new and unusual stimulus. A few seconds later the rats would receive an electric shock. The memory of this was so profoundly etched into the rats' brains that the very next time they heard the beep, they would adopt a hunched, defensive posture. A single pairing of the beep and the shock was enough to lay down a deep-rooted memory leading to an automatic tensing of the body.

However, when the researchers later replayed the sound—causing the rats to retrieve the memorized association between the sound and pain—and simultaneously administered an enzyme inhibitor, the rats would lose that specific memory. The next time the beep was played they had to learn, as if for the first time, that the sound was followed by a shock. By conditioning the rats to fear two distinct sounds, but only administering the drug while they were hearing one of them, the researchers showed that this was not a case of general memory loss, but the effacement of one specific memory.[24]

The enzyme inhibitor was preventing the formation of new proteins. What appears to happen is that in remembering the association between the beep and the painful stimulus, that memory becomes vulnerable. Every time a memory is retrieved, the proteins found in the synapses between the neurons are disassembled. Calling a memory into conscious awareness in effect destroys the original copy. The memory is now like a file that exists only in your computer's Random Access Memory, the original having been deleted from the hard drive. The memory that has been retrieved in your mind is now vulnerable, just like, say, a Word file you're working on if it hasn't been saved to your computer's hard drive. Normally, the memory would be "saved" back into the brain in the form of new synapses. But the administered enzyme inhibitor prevented the rats from saving the memory, and so it was lost.

Of course rats are unable to tell us about their experience, and so there's no way of knowing whether they had totally lost the memory in question, or whether they merely lost their emotional connection to it. The latter may well be the case, since similar experimental treatments tried on human posttraumatic stress disorder sufferers, by Alain Brunet of McGill University, have left patients able to remember traumatic events in their lives, but in a more emotionally detached way. However, the drugs used in treating PTSD patients are different from the highly toxic compounds used in the rat trials, and they work in a different way. The possibility remains that we are able to erase specific memories in rats, even though the drugs used are too dangerous to be given to humans.[25]

The astonishing thing about the enzyme-inhibitor experiments is that they confirm that memories are not etched permanently in the brain. Instead, every time a memory is retrieved, it is destroyed and then re-created, and it becomes a memory of a memory. Any current memories we have are copies of copies of copies . . . many times over depending on how many times we have recalled that particular experience. Because of this process of creating, destroying, and re-creating memories, our recollections are unstable and subject to alteration. Each time we recall an event from our lives, the memory of the event can change. If my mother were, for example, to insist (falsely) that my baby sister had been locked in the house with me and was crying in her crib the entire time I was running back and forth between the front door and the living-room window, there's a good chance I would incorporate that fiction into my future recollections. In fact, simply by imagining that scenario, I may have altered my memory of that event. Indeed we'll often notice—especially with other people—that their retelling of an anecdote drawn from real life evolves over time, and it seems quite possible that the "new and improved" version of the tale is taken to be a genuine memory. Our recollections, it appears, are highly vulnerable to the power of suggestion, both hypnotic and otherwise.

Thanks for the Memories

Imagine you've just witnessed a hit-and-run accident, but you had only a quick glance of the vehicle involved. It all happened so quickly, and you're traumatized by what you've just seen. Adding to the confusion, police cars and ambulances have rushed into the scene, with lights strobing and people in uniforms bustling around. Everyone seems to know what they're doing but you. A policeman comes to take your statement. You're pretty sure there was only one person in the vehicle, but things happened so quickly . . . The policeman, perhaps having particular suspects in mind, asks if possibly there was also a passenger in the car. Once this question is asked, there's a chance that you might very well imagine the car you saw—but this time with a passenger. And the mind, especially under conditions of stress, may be unable to distinguish this imagined image from a genuine memory. Further questions come—is it possible that one of the people in the car had a beard? Was the driver black? Could the passenger have been wearing a hat? Could leading questions like these—"Is it possible . . . ?"—cause you to construct an elaborate and false memory? It seems they can. Sometimes, as a result of questioning, people even become convinced that they themselves have committed crimes of which they are innocent.

In one important study, Elizabeth F. Loftus,—distinguished professor at the University of California, Irvine, and one of the foremost researchers in the area of repressed memories—and colleague Jacqueline E. Pickrell presented twenty-four participants with four stories based on events from when they were between four and six years old. Three of the stories were true, and one was false. The true stories came from accounts by the participants' relatives and had been chosen because they were memorable and not particularly dramatic. The relatives also provided the background setting for another event that could have happened, but which in fact did not—an incident in which the participant as a child had become lost in a shopping mall. The relatives confirmed that no such incident had taken place, but supplied details—such as the name of a specific shopping mall—in order to make the account convincing.[26]

The participants were told that they were involved in the study to determine their ability to recall the details of memories from childhood. Each was given a written account of the four events—the three real ones and the fake account. They were asked to write down which events they remembered and to add any further details they could recall. Subsequently, the participants were interviewed twice about the four memories and again asked to supply any details they could remember; they were also asked to rate the clarity of their recollections. It was then revealed that one of the memories had been made up, and the participants were asked to guess which one it was. Five of the twenty-four participants falsely believed that the story of being lost in the mall was a real memory. Considering that no hypnosis was used and that the study was carried out under conditions that were not particularly stressful (no policemen scribbling down your every word, for example), a "success rate" of more than 20 percent in persuading people that a fictitious event had in fact happened is fairly significant. Similar results have been seen in other studies at Western Washington University, where none of the participants recalled the false event during the first interview, but 20 percent subsequently said they remembered something about the false event when interviewed again.[27]

But does this have any relevance for us outside of traffic accidents and laboratory studies? Apparently it does. A study of the July 2005 bombings in London found that people were able to convince themselves they had seen things that had not in fact happened. Some 84 percent of people interviewed in the United Kingdom reported that they had seen closed-circuit-television footage of the bus bombing in London's Tavistock Square. No such footage exists. Despite that, people were able to give graphic details of what they had "witnessed" on the video. One detailed response said, "The bus had just stopped to let two people off when two women got on, and a man. He placed the bag by his side, the woman sat down and doors closed. As the bus left there was an explosion and then everyone started to scream."[28] Former president George W. Bush recounted several times the shock he experienced on 9/11 as he watched on television the footage of the first plane hitting the World Trade Center, but the first film of that event wasn't broadcast until the following day. Imagination can easily become memory.

Another intriguing experiment by Elizabeth F. Loftus suggests that memories can actually "jump" from one person to another. Loftus and her colleagues asked volunteers to imagine another person pushing his or her hand through glass. On later questioning, some of the volunteers who had imagined this became convinced that it happened to them. Loftus commented that these results may explain why some patients in group therapy complain that other patients "steal" their stories and symptoms. Simply hearing somebody else tell a story, it seems, can implant a false memory in our minds—if we mentally picture the incident.[29]

To add one more resonance of *Eternal Sunshine of the Spotless Mind,* scientists—as well as being able to erase specific memories, or to at least (in humans) mitigate their emotional impact—have been able to directly implant a memory into the brain, using laser beams. This highly improbable-sounding feat, performed by Gero Miesenböck, of the University of Oxford, was carried out on the humble fruit-fly brain, not that of a human.[30] Fruit flies, like humans or lab mice, learn by trial and error. If they encounter something unpleasant—a bad smell or a painful electric shock, for example—they quickly learn to avoid that stimulus in the future. Miesenböck and his colleagues used some educated guesswork to identify which part of the fly's brain is involved in this type of learning. A fly's brain is so simple that it turns out a mere twelve neurons are involved in creating these memories. Miesenböck used laser beams to activate those neurons while the flies were exposed to a certain chemical, and he found that the flies had learned to avoid that chemical in the future.[31]

This technique is highly unlikely ever to be used in humans, Miesenböck points out. Apart from everything else, the fruit flies had to be specially prepared by having a virus injected that would carry a light-sensitive chemical to the appropriate neurons in the brain. Immense ethical hurdles would proscribe using such methods in humans. But the possibility exists that a totalitarian government could eliminate unwanted behaviors, such as a tendency toward dissent, by directly manipulating the brain to make dissent seem like a painful thing to do.

Memory is not the video-like recording of events we tend to assume it is. We never have a full recollection of anything that's happened to us, and our memories are constructed from hints, scraps, and traces found within the mind. Rather than being permanent, our memories are volatile and malleable. A memory is created afresh each time it is accessed. A "permanent" memory is not a static record within the brain, but something more akin to communication by means of Chinese whispers—where with each retelling comes the danger that the story will be altered. Corroboration of an event by another person can alter our memories, as can simply imagining that something happened.

The "Perpetual Flux" of Self

Even if our memories are liable to change, most people will point to the sense of continuity they have with younger versions of themselves as a confirmation of the existence of a permanent self. The idea holds that there is a sameness or identity to the person we are now and the person we were at age ten or twenty, and the person we will be at seventy-seven. David Hume tackled this notion by means of an introspective examination of the process of change. "We are," he pointed out, "never intimately conscious of anything but a particular perception; man is a bundle or collection of different perceptions that succeed one another with an inconceivable rapidity and are in perpetual flux and movement."[32]

Buddhism argues along essentially identical lines—that there may be similarity and continuity within a person's consciousness over time—without there being any identity or sameness. Our old friend, the vortex in the river, can illustrate this. When we watch a vortex that has formed in a certain part of a river, we see something that looks substantially the same from moment to moment. But the substance is quite literally changing as we observe it. The pattern is what remains similar, but even that of course is not identical. The vortex stays in *approximately* the same position. It's of *approximately* the same shape and size from one moment to another. It's this that leads us to think there has been no essential change, even though the contents within the form—and the form itself—have changed.

In terms of the human mind, personality traits can be relatively stable. I, for example, have been introverted over the course of my life. I like to spend time alone, and being with other people for a prolonged period generates a form of mental exhaustion only rectified by solitude. But there have also been times in my life when I have been quite the party animal, delighting in the company of others. The quality of introversion, though it's accompanied me throughout my life, is not one that is fixed. Instead, like the size and shape of the vortex, it has wobbled around a mean level of introversion. And that mean level does not seem to be one that is permanent, either. The personality inventories that I've taken from time to time have shown that the qualities of introversion and extroversion have become more balanced as I have matured. I'm more confident and relaxed around other people than ever.

If you can stand a little more biography, I used to be afflicted with the character traits of irritability and hypercriticism, and I would spend a lot of time being angry. If you had known me in my mid-twenties you probably would have described my personality as that of an angry person. But again, as a result of practicing mindfulness (stopping my mind from indulging in critical or angry thoughts) and of practicing lovingkindness meditation (cultivating a more appreciative attitude toward myself and other people), I'm no longer prone to anger to the same degree. People who get to know me now are often very surprised to hear what I used to be like. The elements of what make up a personality can be very malleable.

Although there seems to be little or nothing that's unchanging in us, there is a persistent sense of continuity. Is this a problem for the Buddhist way of looking at the self, or at the illusion of the self? Actually, it's part of the way that Buddhist teachings view the self. A traditional image is to think of a rope. A rope is not a single thing but a composite of innumerable smaller strands of fiber. No single strand runs the entire length of the rope; in fact an individual strand may cover only a few inches of the rope's entire length. And so the rope has no "essence." Similarly, what we call a "self" has no essence, but instead is formed of innumerable physical and mental events that overlap and provide continuity. The rope, or the self, does indeed have continuity, but it lacks "identity." That is, one end of the rope is composed of entirely different stuff from the other end of the rope. This then is the underlying principle of selfhood in Buddhism—that there's continuity but no identity.

Buddhist teachings completely accept the notion of continuity, so there's no question of a perceived sense of continuity of "ourselves" in any way undermining the Buddhist view. In fact, even our sense of continuity is an impermanent and ever-changing phenomenon. The sense of continuity that we have at age twenty is very different from the sense of continuity that we have at age fifty or seventy. Additionally, there are clear interruptions to our sense of continuity. When you woke up this morning you probably very quickly forgot any dreams you'd been having. The waking self and the dreaming self are in a way different selves. What's more, there were periods of time during the night—when you were in a state of deep sleep—when you had no sense of self whatsoever, when you had no experience. There was no sensing going on and thus no one there to have a sense of continuity! Our sense of continuity is itself discontinuous.

It seems to me that having predicated a permanent and unchanging self, we simply assume that our sense of continuity is more perfect than it actually is. But in fact the experiments in change blindness outlined in Chapter One suggest that our consciousness is essentially discontinuous. Virtually every time we blink, a new "self" comes into existence and an old "self" dies. So, in the Harvard change blindness experiment, when the person behind the desk is replaced by someone else, we simply don't notice. After all, the "you" that talked to the first library worker no longer exists and has been replaced by a new "you."

Where Does This Leave Us?

Where does this leave us? Or should I say "us"? The body does not constitute a separate and unchanging self. Neither does consciousness constitute a separate and unchanging self. Consciousness is not a thing that exists inside us, separate from the world. Instead consciousness is an activity inseparable from the perception of the world. Consciousness is not a static thing, but a constant flow of multiple experiences, each of which is impermanent. Consciousness does not exist in isolation but is part of a greater whole—the noösphere—in which information flows from mind to mind, thanks in part to "mind-reading cells" called mirror neurons. Perception can happen without consciousness, and responses to each perception most certainly happen without conscious intervention. We think we make decisions consciously, when in fact consciousness is a kind of plagiarist, taking responsibility for actions that are initiated outside of conscious awareness. Sometimes consciousness ceases, as when we're profoundly asleep. Our very memories—our record of who we are—are unstable and can change from moment to moment. Consciousness is not an unchanging thing, but is discontinuous. Personality traits can change, with new ones coming into existence and old ones passing away. Realizing all these things can help us recognize that consciousness cannot constitute, alone or in conjunction with the body, a permanent and unchanging self. Exploring these findings through the lens of science can bring about the same unweaving of the self that the traditional Consciousness Element reflection is meant to achieve, as we observe experiences rise and fall like waves, and note, "This is not me; this is not mine; I am not this."

In the traditional Six Element Practice, what happens when we have let go of consciousness? Sometimes at the end of the practice I feel serenely calm and at peace. I'm liberated from identifying with my experience. My body doesn't define me. I'm not my thoughts or emotions. There's nothing to fear, nothing to resist, nothing that I need to change. But what am I? I sometimes have a sense that I am a field of awareness in which all my experiences arise. But that too is me identifying something as the self, and that identification is just one more thing to be let go of. The ultimate goal is a complete absence of clinging to identifications, or to anything whatsoever. The goal is to be comfortable with a profound sense of letting go, a letting go that leads to freedom and peace. It's a peace that arises from a complete sense of security. Recognizing that there is nothing unchanging, we abandon the fruitless effort to find security by trying to hold back change. Instead we accept change fully, and find security through non-grasping. We fear letting go, but once we do, we find there is nothing to fear.

So far we've explored one particular reflective practice that helps us loosen our sense of self. We may at times have found ourselves hanging onto our selves, not wanting to change. We may have found our sense of self challenged and experienced unease at contemplating our own impermanence. We may have experienced a sense of existential confusion. We may have felt an expanded sense of the self and a feeling of connectedness. We may have experienced a sense of openness and wonder. These are all valid and even useful responses, if we are prepared to examine and learn from them—and to let go of them.

But we don't spend our entire lives reflecting on the elements. We have lives to live. How do we move toward challenging our sense of fixed and separate selfhood in the context of work and family? How can we bring about a greater sense of freedom and fearlessness in our day-to-day lives? How can we bring more compassion into our lives? How can we live as rivers, flowing without holding on? What would it be like if we did? These are questions for the final two chapters.

CHAPTER FOURTEEN

Stepping into the Stream

"Men may dam it and say that they have made a lake,
but it will still be a river. It will keep its nature and bide its
time, like a caged animal alert for the slightest opening.
In time, it will have its way; the dam, like the ancient cliffs,
will be carried away piecemeal in the currents."
— WENDELL BERRY[1]

We began by examining our existential fear of impermanence: a fear that permeates our entire lives in one form or another. We saw how this fear, even when it's hidden from conscious awareness, leads us to cling to things we hope will offer a sense of security. We also saw that, as a strategy, clinging is counterproductive because, like bad medicine, it actually causes us further pain; anything we cling to in search of security is subject to change, so that our supposed sources of security end up failing us. The Buddha's insight into this thorny existential tangle was that any form of clinging was a cause of suffering, that the most damaging form of clinging was clinging to the idea that we ourselves are permanent and separate, and that true security came from fully accepting the reality of impermanence. And so the Buddha's path is one of accepting the inevitability of change, and of progressively abandoning clinging.

The Six Element Practice is a means of letting go of the core delusion of an unchanging self and its separateness. It's a way, in other words, to face reality full on, fearlessly accepting the reality of change.

Traditionally, it's said that when we break the three fetters (mentioned in Chapter One, "The Self I Don't Believe In"), we "enter the stream." Entering the stream is the technical term for having let go of the belief in an unchanging and separate self; a person who has done this is called a "stream entrant." Sometimes the image of entering the stream is taken to mean that we're crossing from this shore, where we suffer, to the far shore of spiritual awakening, where the suffering caused by fear no longer exists. The implication is that in plunging into the river, we have abandoned our attempts to cling and have had the courage to face impermanence. We've left behind the familiar and are heading into the unknown. It's a good image. But the image of stream entry is also explicitly used in the early teachings to suggest that we *ourselves* become the stream. Bhikkhu Thanissaro, a contemporary teacher and translator, explains, "The term 'stream' in 'stream-entry' refers to the point where all eight factors of the noble eightfold path[2] come together," and goes on to quote a passage from the early scriptures:

> "Sariputta, 'The stream, the stream': thus it is said. And what, Sariputta, is the stream?"

> "This noble eightfold path, lord, is the stream: right view, right resolve, right speech, right action, right livelihood, right effort, right mindfulness, right concentration."[3]

The Eightfold Path is a way of breaking down our life into manageable areas of practice. Thus, saying that the eightfold path is the stream is the same as saying that our life is the stream. Instead of our fear creating a countercurrent or dam of fear that holds us back, we confidently embrace impermanence, and plunge into a process of self-transformation. Using language that echoes this interpretation, the modern master Hsuan Hua described the stream entrant as "One Who Has Entered the Flow."

We can think of "entering the stream" as involving the *recognition* that everything that constitutes us is in motion. Through the Six Element Reflection we observe the elements flow by in much the same way we would if we were sitting on a riverbank. We no longer make the fruitless effort to hold back the flow of the elements. The physical elements, energy, space, and even experience are flowing unstoppably through us. In fact there is no "us" apart from the flow. When we finally realize this, we see ourselves as a river. We have entered the stream.

The key to entering the stream is changing the way we see ourselves and our world. The stream entrant is said to have opened his eyes to the reality of impermanence. One passage says that opening our eyes to reality means recognizing that "Whatever is subject to origination is all subject to cessation."[4] Stream entry involves a permanent insight; once you've directly seen the reality of impermanence, you can't "unsee" it. It's considered to be a very significant step on the path of spiritual development. It's not full enlightenment, as Buddhism understands it, but is what I sometimes like to call "entry-level enlightenment," and it's an irreversible step on the way to attaining full awakening. Entering the stream is not only an irreversible insight and an important step on the spiritual path, it's said to be readily attainable in this very life. You don't need to think in terms of giving up your family and job, or even of spending years on retreat. In the Buddha's day many thousands of householders were said to have entered the stream.

The Six Element Reflection we've been engaging with is a way of helping us to see our lives differently. We learn to see ourselves, our bodies, our minds, the world, and our relation to other beings in a new way. But seeing is only half the story. Because of this seeing there's a radical letting go. The seeing is not just seeing, but *seeing through* a delusion so that we're no longer fooled by it.

As we saw in Chapter One, the three fetters we must break in order to enter the stream are:

The fetter of fixed self-view.
The fetter of doubt.
The fetter of dependence upon rules and observances.

The fetters are impediments because they prevent us from cultivating more mindfulness and wisdom, love and compassion. I'd like to offer an outline of how we can use the teaching of the three fetters to help us enter the stream. I'll outline each fetter, explain how it holds us back, and (most importantly) suggest how to break free of its hold. I have three different slogans to summarize how we work with each fetter. These slogans are "Live in the Gap," "If You Want to Climb a Mountain, Start at the Top," and "Steer for the Deep."

1. Live in the Gap:
Breaking the Fetter of Fixed Self-View

The first fetter, fixed self-view, handicaps us right from the start because we believe at some level that change just isn't possible.

There are actually two forms of this view. The first, and most commonly recognized, is the conviction that the self is something fixed and unchanging. We assume that because we have a certain personality trait, it's something we're just stuck with. It's as if we've been handed a personality and we just have to make do with it. And so do other people: "Love me, love my faults." We often end up using personality traits as self-descriptions, and then we end up turning our self-descriptions—for example, "I'm the nervous type"—into self-fulfilling prophecies. We become attached to the way we see ourselves, and seeing ourselves as "the nervous type," we avoid taking the kinds of risks that would actually allow us to grow in confidence. We may also, in defining ourselves as "the nervous type," fail to recognize times when we actually are confident and courageous. We very commonly filter out any perceptions that contradict our preferred view of ourselves. Our self-view becomes a trap. And because we have the view that we are essentially fixed, we don't make any effort to change.

The other form of fixed self-view is the one in which we believe that the self is something purely conditioned by factors outside our control. We may accept the possibility of change, but we never do any actual changing because we think that the self is merely a product of our environment. We think that other people "make us mad," for example, or, "If only such-and-such would change, *then* I'd be happy." We'd be happy if only our job were more fulfilling. We'd be less grumpy if other people were more cooperative and sensitive toward us. We'd be less anxious if only the world was less uncertain. Happiness is always seen as depending on something external and out of our control. We see ourselves as victims rather than as capable of determining our own fates. We believe that in order for change to come about in us, the world has to change first.

These are opposite views—the self is fixed and unchanging, versus the self is conditioned by externalities—but both amount to the same thing: we're not in control of our own lives. And both versions of the fetter can afflict one person at different moments.

There's another way of relating to the self, however. We can accept that we've to some extent been handed a personality for which we have to take responsibility. Some of what we are is due perhaps to our genes, and some perhaps to our past conditioning. And we can also accept that outside factors have an effect; we're not immune to the influence of things and people around us. But there's another important influence on who we are and how we experience life. And that's ourselves. We are self-conditioning beings. We shape our own lives through the choices we make.

In a passage that recurs repeatedly throughout the earliest Buddhist teachings, we're reminded of five reflections that everyone is encouraged to keep in mind daily:

> I am subject to aging.
> I am subject to illness.
> I am subject to death.
> I will be separated from all that is dear to me.
> I am the owner of my actions, heir to my actions, born of
> my actions, related through my actions, and have my actions
> as my arbiter. Whatever I do, for good or for evil, to that
> will I fall heir.[5]

This echoes the advice, given by many thinkers over the millennia, that the most meaningful life arises when we bear impermanence in mind. Life is short so let's make it meaningful, is the message. We can choose how to live. We can choose our actions. We can shape our own lives.

The first important question we must ask ourselves is, *Am I aware that I am making choices in every moment?* Whether we realize it or not, we choose courses of action all the time. In every moment, we are making decisions. We are already creating our lives, but we are likely doing this without any awareness that we are doing so. We act blindly, and in doing so we often create lives with which we're unhappy. We make poor choices that lead to frustration and suffering, choices that prevent us from experiencing life as fulfilling and joyful.

We cannot choose what happens to us in life, but there is a "gap" between stimulus and response, and within that gap is the freedom to choose. We are able, if we pay attention, to notice a moment of openness in which we can choose our actions. In practicing mindfulness we're attempting to live in the gap, staying in a position of maximum freedom from habit. Now, these "actions" I'm talking about are not necessarily external ones. In fact for the most part they are not. The mind moves much more rapidly than the body, and for every external action we take there are perhaps hundreds of actions of mind. It's largely our thoughts, and the emotional qualities associated with them, that create our experience.

The second important question we need to ask ourselves is, *What choices should I make?* In short, we have to choose between fear and love. In every moment of perception, we are able to choose between these two courses. Fear is marked by clinging, aggression, doubt, anxiety, and denial. Love is marked by letting go, being flexible, compassionate regard, confidence, and an intelligent curiosity. We have these choices in every moment of our lives.

The choices we have to make—which are essentially ethical ones to do with how best to live our lives and what we value—apply even in the most trivial-seeming situations. For example, we are hurrying somewhere and someone in front of us is dithering, blocking our way. How do we respond? If we are not watching the mind's operations and are on automatic pilot, we'll likely become irritable and impatient. We act as if we were the center of the world. How dare this person not be aware of us and not put our needs above his! Can't he tell we have places to be?

If, however, we are observing our responses, we may notice an initial gut response of frustration because of our route being blocked, but we then can choose to respond with patience toward the other person and with compassion toward ourselves. We don't repress our gut feeling of frustration, but neither do we turn it into a drama in which we see the other person as pitting himself against us.

I mentioned earlier that there's a gap between stimulus and response, and that it's in that gap where we have the freedom to choose *how* to respond. I'd like to pinpoint the gap a little more closely, since it's where we're attempting to live. In any given situation, there is an act of sensing (for example, seeing the person dithering in front of us when we're in a hurry). The sensing is simply raw data that is visual, auditory, etc. Whenever we sense something, however, we contribute a "feeling-tone" to it. This is a purely automatic process over which we don't have any immediate control. That's why, generally, when you're in a hurry and someone's in front of you, you'll feel an unpleasant sensation in the pit of your stomach. We talked about these feelings (which are distinct from emotions) in Chapter Thirteen ("The Consciousness Element").

Feelings can be pleasant, unpleasant, or neutral in tone. We don't choose the feelings that follow upon our sensations, but what we can choose is how we respond to those feelings. What we tend to do, habitually and unreflectively, is generate aversion in response to unpleasant feelings (like the person blocking our way). We'll tend to latch onto perceptions that have pleasant feelings associated with them. And we'll probably just ignore perceptions connected to neutral feelings. So it's after the arising of feelings that the gap can be found. What we mostly need to be concerned with is how we respond to the feelings that arise in life. We can choose to hold on or to let go, to be hostile or loving, dogmatic or curious, closed or open. These choices in fact are the essence of the practice of ethics we outlined in Chapter Three ("Self Is a Verb").

Living in the gap between stimulus and response is something we can aim to do in every moment. Although most of the situations we face in life are trivial in terms of their content, like the example above, the cumulative effect of our responses is not at all trivial. The cumulative effect of our responses is what we call our experience. The overwhelming majority of our suffering comes from making reactive responses to life's small challenges. This is why two people in an identical situation may end up having totally different experiences, with one person becoming stressed and miserable, and the other serene and confident.

In order to take charge of our lives we use the faculty of mindfulness, so that we can observe the meeting of the mind with the world and can choose our actions wisely. When we choose our actions we also choose the quality of the experience we create for ourselves. The kind of ethical choices we're talking about have long-term effects on the mind. By repeatedly making choices based on confidence, loving-kindness, patience, etc., we turn those responses into ingrained habits. Eventually we reach the point where we no longer have to think consciously about how to respond; we simply find ourselves acting more ethically, and find our minds more balanced, equanimous, and peaceful. By refraining from responding with irritation, fear, and so forth, we find that these habits become weaker and less prevalent.

Bringing awareness to the mind and encouraging it to respond with love rather than fear is the basis of Buddhist ethical practice, and also of Buddhist meditation, which is essentially the practice of ethics in relation to the contents of the mind. In ethics we have to choose how to respond to external events. In meditation we have to choose how to respond to internal events such as perceptions, thoughts, and emotions. While meditating, although we have withdrawn to some extent from external activities—perhaps sitting in a quiet room with our eyes closed—we find that the mind produces a constant stream of inner chatter and vivid imagery. We plan, we go over past grievances, we fantasize about things we'd like to be doing, we worry, and we tell undermining and limiting stories about ourselves.

A thought presents itself to us while we are meditating, and we can respond in different ways. We may find ourselves, for example, imagining an argument. We dig up some bone of contention and gnaw at it relentlessly, coming up with clever putdowns and withering comebacks. And we work ourselves into a state of anger—in effect rehearsing and perfecting a future conflict. This is the kind of thing that goes on in the mind when we're not really paying attention. In some sense we've chosen this course of action, even though the choices are being made habitually and unconsciously. But in meditation we are trying to be mindful and not to let the mind simply take a thought and run with it. Instead we decide whether or not a particular thought-stream is one we want to strengthen or abandon.

In meditation we're making the effort to be more conscious, or mindful, by paying attention to what is going on in the mind, and by noticing whether or not it's what we want. So we notice that the inner argument is bringing about a state of conflict and tension, and we realize that we have a choice. Do we want to encourage this way of being or not? Do we want to keep causing ourselves suffering? Do we really want to generate more conflict? What we are attempting to do in many forms of meditation is simply to let go of unhelpful trains of thought. Typically we will notice the train of thought, let go of it as best we can, and return to paying attention to some neutral experience such as the breath. In the short term, the mind becomes calmer as we repeatedly let go of disturbing thoughts. We find that our emotions are more peaceful because we're no longer stirring them up. In the longer term, we find that we change our character. There's less craving and more contentment, less frenzy and more calmness, less ill will and more compassion.

In some forms of meditation, however, we go beyond simply letting go of unhelpful thoughts and instead consciously cultivate thoughts that help unravel our tight knot of self. In lovingkindness meditation, for example, we drop into the mind such thoughts as, "May all beings be well; may all beings be happy; may all beings be free from suffering." As with all our other, more spontaneously generated thoughts, these have an effect upon how we feel. Over time our emotions begin to feel more expansive and loving, and we find that we have more patience, even when calling to mind people with whom we typically experience conflict.

In meditation, therefore, we begin to appreciate the constructed nature of the self. As the psychologist John Dewey pointed out, "The self is not something ready-made, but something in continuous formation through choice of action."[6] Every time we make a choice, we play a part in forming a new version of the self, and we also remind ourselves of the self's unfixed nature. We begin to see more and more clearly that our present experience is produced by largely unconscious patterns of thought. And we begin to see how mindfulness and lovingkindness can give rise to a different kind of self. The self is therefore seen less and less as something static and outside our control. We begin to increasingly realize that we are able to take responsibility for ourselves, not just for our actions in the world but for our thoughts and emotions as well.

This then is how we break the fetter of self-view: we take responsibility for ourselves, we cultivate mindfulness, and—living in the gap—we choose how we are going to respond to what life throws at us. Later, we take this practice further by developing an awareness of the impermanence of the self, and we abandon clinging to anything that we might have imagined as defining the self.

2. If You Want to Climb a Mountain, Start at the Top: Breaking the Fetter of Doubt

We need to clarify exactly which kind of doubt acts as a fetter. Doubt in the sense of intellectual honestly, in the sense of a questioning approach to our experience, is the opposite of a fetter. On the contrary, it's something liberating. The kind of doubt that acts as a fetter is fundamentally an unwillingness or inability to see reality. It's a fearful avoidance of recognizing impermanence. It's an unwillingness to reflect. It's denial. It's a refusal to be clear and to commit oneself. Doubt is sometimes compared to water in which mud has been stirred up. When the mind is stirred up with doubt, we're not able to see clearly. And, like muddy water, the mind afflicted with doubt is incapable of reflecting.

Let's say we've decided to take responsibility for ourselves. We may be aware of some habit we have that holds us back; let's say it's the tendency to blame others instead of taking responsibility for ourselves. So some situation arises in which we've become angered, but instead of considering that it's we who have become angry in *response* to something another person has said or done, we remain fixated on the claim that the other person "made" us angry. We've abdicated responsibility for ourselves. Even when it's pointed out to us that we're doing this, we still remain focused on blaming the other person. We know what we should be doing, but we just don't do it. We know what we shouldn't be doing, but we do it anyway. What's going on?

Fundamentally, there's fear involved. We're afraid of taking responsibility. All our lives, perhaps, we've blamed other people. *And that's what we feel comfortable doing.* To stop doing what we're familiar with involves a step into the unknown, and the unknown is fearful. We have to let go of the safe and the familiar. In order to break the fetter of doubt we need to develop the courage to face reality. We need to cultivate an understanding of the impermanent nature of the world and of the self. We need to come back over and over again to reminding ourselves of how things really are. We need also to keep reflecting on our experience: How does suffering arise? How does it feel when we step into the unknown? How does it feel to free ourselves from constricting habits?

We need also to develop an understanding of ourselves as a process rather than as static. Doubt, the second fetter, grows out of fixed self view, the first fetter. We believe that we can't change, and that our habits, faults, and personalities are fixed. This leads to doubt and fear. Perhaps it's not really possible for us to change, we might wonder. Or perhaps we don't have what it takes? Or perhaps we're inherently flawed and defective? When we see ourselves as process, as *becoming*, we can feel more confidence in ourselves. We don't see ourselves as stuck, but as being "in process." We don't just relate to the present configuration of our selves, but we see the present in relation to our past and our future. We can see how we've changed in the past, and we can imagine that change continuing into the future.

One practice I've found invaluable over the years is to develop what in personal-development circles they call a "personal vision statement" or "personal mission statement." This is a written document that contains a clear outline of what's important to me. The terms "personal vision statement" and "personal mission statement" I frankly find unappealing, and you too may wish to come up with your own: a "personal constitution," or "personal road map," or the like. Whatever term you use, this document embodies our values and our ideals.

I developed mine by spending some time in reflection. I imagined it was ten years in the future, and I had gone home only to find my house full of friends, relations, and colleagues. I'd arrived at a surprise party—to celebrate me! One by one, people came forward and talked about what they most appreciated in me: my character, my achievements, and what they had learned from knowing me. I then wrote down what I'd heard while it was fresh in my mind. What this exercise does is create a direct link between your deepest values and your conscious mind, so that you can more clearly see what's of greatest importance to you. In itself this is a powerful tool for combatting doubt, because we cut through the surface clutter of the mind and its often rather trivial day-to-day concerns and uncover a level of ourselves that's more authentic and wise.

After editing, I found I had a document a few paragraphs long to which I could turn each day as a source of guidance and inspiration. This is what I call "borrowing confidence from your future self." Referring to your personal vision statement becomes a way of seeing yourself not as stuck as you are, but as a dynamic process moving on a trajectory into the future. You identify less with yourself as you are, and come to see yourself in terms of your unfolding potential.

In traditional practice, we connect with our potential through practices that are traditionally known as "friendship with the wise" and "noble conversation." These are both ways of reinforcing a sense of our potential so that we identify less with our current limited self. Through witnessing others approaching life's problems in a mature way, we can learn to emulate the skills they have developed. Through focused and purposeful discussions about life, we can tap into our own inner wisdom and guidance.

The Zen saying "If you want to climb a mountain, start at the top" is a way of summing up how we break the fetter of doubt. Doubt is unclarity and an unwillingness to commit. It's fear and confusion. Doubt is allayed by our developing a clearer vision of where we're headed in life. When we're going anywhere, we have to start with a sense of where we're headed. First we start at the top of the mountain, keeping our goals in mind, and then we begin the journey. We of course have to fully accept that we're also starting from where we are, but we also have to accept that where we are is not a place. We are all arrows in mid-flight; where we are is a moment on a trajectory, not a position at rest.

Having goals is potentially fraught with difficulties, to the extent that some people suggest it's better not to have them. But the issue really comes down to how we relate to our goals. Joseph Goldstein neatly points out that we can relate to our goals as aspirations or as expectations. When we cling to the idea of attaining our goals—where we have expectation—we suffer. We are in effect constantly asking, "Are we there yet?" We blame ourselves for not yet being at the goal and cause ourselves unnecessary suffering. When goals are merely aspirations, they are lightly held in mind, and we see them as navigational beacons giving us a sense of direction. We don't grasp after them. We even change them when necessary—not on a whim, but when accumulated experience has revealed a deeper understanding of our life's mission.

3. Steer for the Deep: Breaking the Fetter of Dependence on Observances

So we may have decided to take responsibility for our lives, recognizing that our life is our own creation and overcoming a tendency to see ourselves as fixed and unchanging. We may have developed a clear sense of the direction in which we want that life to move, helping dispel doubt. But in life it's easy to become distracted. The complexity of living overwhelms us and we lose sight of our wider goals. The trees prevent us from seeing the forest. In the fetter of dependence on rules and observances, our practice dies because we've lost sight of why we're doing it. We may be doing the right things, but we're doing them for the wrong reasons. We're following the letter rather than the spirit.

I see this a lot when people are working on living more ethically. Instead of keeping the focus on their own minds, making the wisest choices they're capable of in any given moment, they become overly concerned with judging other people. They've lost sight of the point of ethical practice. One of the most ironic things I can remember from the early days of my own practice was how annoyed I used to get at disturbances to my meditation. I'd be sitting in my bedroom cultivating lovingkindness, and outside on the street there would be a lot of noise. In particular there was a newspaper vendor who used to yell at the top of his voice, *"Mail, Post, Standard! Mail, Post, Standard!"* Every Sunday morning while I was meditating, he'd be yelling his mantra. And I *hated* him. I used to have violent fantasies about what I'd like to do to the guy. And this was while I was trying to cultivate *lovingkindness!* Obviously there was a disconnect. I thought I was trying to cultivate love and compassion, but what I was actually cultivating was anger and hatred. I'd lost sight of the purpose of my practice, in a big way!

I was struck also by the German teacher Ayya Khema talking about how the phrase "Everything's impermanent" becomes repeated so often that we don't even think of its meaning. We forget to look at our experience and recognize change taking place. Instead we stay in the realm of words, simply *telling ourselves a story* about how everything changes. When I realized that I didn't have a self, one of the things that struck me was how obvious it was. How could I not have noticed before? One of the reasons, perhaps, why I didn't notice that everything constituting me is forever changing is that I was too busy thinking about impermanence to notice it directly in my own experience.

So our task is to be in the present moment, but to keep that moment oriented toward our ideals. For this I borrow a phrase from Walt Whitman: "Steer for the deep waters only." Whitman meant this as a statement of almost reckless courage, but I take the words as a reminder to stay oriented toward the depths of ourselves. Fundamentally, we have to keep asking ourselves the question, *Is what I'm doing taking me in the direction I ultimately want to go in?* We need to keep questioning ourselves in this way.

So these three points—*Live in the Gap; If You Want to Climb a Mountain, Start at the Top;* and *Steer for the Deep*—become practices for breaking the fetters. As we practice these, we need to constantly work on developing mindfulness and lovingkindness. We need to move from fear to love in our daily lives. But above all, we need to keep observing change in our own experience, noting how every sensation, thought, and emotion is impermanent. As we notice this repeatedly, it eventually sinks in that *this is it*. Reality has been here all along—it's just that we haven't been prepared to accept it. We eventually come to recognize that the self is nothing but change. This brings with it a surge of confidence as our doubts vanish. And as our understanding of impermanence reaches new depths, we find that everything we do becomes a support for deeper insights yet. The fetters have broken, and we have not just entered the stream, not just realized that we are the stream; we have come to realize that we were always the stream. We come to realize that we never had a self to lose.

CHAPTER FIFTEEN

The Self Beyond Measure

"The only man who behaved sensibly was my tailor;
he took my measure anew every time he saw me."
—GEORGE BERNARD SHAW[1]

I was putting my daughter to bed one night when I realized I did not have a self. It was an odd and delightful moment: odd because I hadn't fully realized until then that I even had a belief in a self, and delightful because it was an experience that was joyous and liberating. In hundreds of discussions and in dozens of lectures, I had explained to others the Buddhist view that there is no fixed self (and when I say I have no self, I mean of course that I don't have one that's unchanging). Very often the explanations I gave would be met with some puzzlement and even some resistance. This was not, I presume, because my account was unclear, but because the teaching itself clashes with deeply held assumptions and even convictions we hold about the nature of the self. It seems we really are convinced that there is something separate and permanent about ourselves even if, when challenged, we find it difficult to point to where exactly the separateness and permanence reside. Nevertheless, intellectually I was convinced of the arguments that I put forward. It was something I'd reflected upon a great deal, and I could give numerous examples from my own experience of the malleability of the self. But on some level, evidently, I had maintained the belief that my self in fact was something fixed.

Now, gazing at my two-year-old daughter as she rolled over to face the wall and began drifting into sleep, I could see with utter clarity that I had never had a self. My belief in a self had vanished. I wasn't, however, merely swapping one belief for another. I wasn't abandoning the belief in a fixed self while adopting a belief in another kind of self. My former belief was gone, but what had taken its place was not another intellectual conviction but a direct *experience* of impermanence. As I gazed into my own mind, I saw not a thing but a process. I saw no substance, but merely activity. I saw no being, only becoming. As various perceptions, thoughts, and feelings came and went, I saw them as being something like twinkling stars in the night sky. Except, of course, that stars appear in fixed positions. This was more like a night sky where the glittering lights were not fixed objects but merely the sky itself scintillating randomly. I'd never seen anything so beautiful.

More precisely, the image that had occurred to me in my daughter's bedroom was one of a kaleidoscope. I realized that until that moment I had been under the grip of something like "change blindness." You'll recall that change blindness describes our inability to recognize change. In mid-conversation, due to some trickery, the person we are talking to is replaced by another. We simply do not notice. Two photographic slides are presented to us one after another, with a blank slide in between. The two images are almost the same, but some major feature—a building, a fence, a person—has been added or subtracted from one of them. We flick back and forth between the two photographs, knowing that there is a difference but unable to see it, until on the seventh or eighth or ninth comparison we notice the difference. I've argued that change blindness applies to our experience of ourselves; from moment to moment, our experience of ourselves changes, and yet somehow we're convinced that nothing has in fact altered. One thought is replaced by another. One emotion disappears and another takes its place. In a sense, one self disappears and another takes its place. But somehow we're convinced that no real change has occurred.

The mind's tendency to overlook *becoming* and to create the illusion of being plays into this experience of change blindness. Just as "the guy behind the desk" remains "the guy behind the desk" even when his clothes, hair, face, and height have all changed, so "my self" remains "my self" even though the experiences I'm labeling with that term have largely or entirely altered. Just as the concept "the guy behind the desk" is a static placeholder, preventing us from appreciating that one self has been replaced by another, so the notion of "myself" is a static label that prevents us noticing that one version of our self is continually being replaced by another. Our blind faith in our labels causes us to ignore the vast amount of change that is actually going on, moment by moment within our own experience. The labels "I," "me," "mine," "myself" do not change, and so we tend to ignore the fact that what they label does change.

But now, for me, sitting in my daughter's bedroom, a story-book open on my lap, the illusion of permanence was gone. Just as my daughter was dozing off, I felt like I was waking up. It was as if up until that moment I had been in the grip of an illusion, convinced that there was some kind of fixed and unchanging picture to be seen. As she rolled over to face the wall, I turned my attention to face my own experience. Now, gazing at the kaleidoscope of that experience, I was exquisitely aware of the continuous change that was taking place. There was no "picture" (in the sense of a static image) to be seen, but a continually changing mosaic of impressions. And I had no sense that there was anything lurking behind those impressions. This was it. This was all there was. And it was enough.

For the next few days I found myself wondering, "Do I *really* not have a self? Could it be true?" There was a sense of disbelief and even doubt; I would scrutinize my experience and for a moment feel uncertainty. At first glance it would seem as if there were some "thing" there, some kind of self, some kind of entity—but only for a moment. The kaleidoscope would continue turning, and the "self" that I thought I had glimpsed would vanish, to be replaced by a new constellation of experiences. It seemed at times that I had an endless succession of momentary selves. Every time I looked closely at my experience there would be that initial sense that there was some "thing" there, some static picture at the far end of the kaleidoscope. But the rotation would continue and the elements of my experience would slide into a new configuration. Every time I looked, there was that same sense—a momentary illusion of "something" being there, followed by a perception of flow and change. Eventually those lingering doubts passed.

As I mentioned in Chapter One, I was reminded of times when I have glanced at a watch or clock—the old-fashioned analog kind with a second hand that ticks. At first I have the impression that the second hand is not moving. For what seems like an age it just sits there. "Has this thing stopped?" I find myself thinking. But then the hand jumps forward and the illusion breaks. The same illusion would seem to take place when I glance at my mind: for the long moment of the first glance I see my mind as static rather than in movement. In reality, of course, the change taking place in my mind is continuous. There is no succession of fleetingly short selves, but instead a never-ending process of change. Each time this realization happened, on those first days, I'd feel like laughing out loud.

But what, you may wonder, about my experience of the body? It's simply not possible to be directly aware of the physical turnover of molecules within my cells or the ongoing replacement of cells within my tissues. That's true. What I do notice as I bring my attention to the body is a continuously changing pattern of sensation. From within, we do not experience something called "the body," but shifting patterns of sensation. There are sensations such as pressure, temperature, and a tingling sense of aliveness, and these sensations, just like my experience of the mind, form an ever-changing kaleidoscope of perception.

The point of the reflections in the Six Element Practice, I came to realize, was not to bring about an *ongoing* awareness of how we are physically connected to the universe, but simply to undermine any basis we might have for believing in a self by training ourselves to see things in terms of process and change. Or at least that's *ultimately* the point of the reflections. Those of us who have grown up in an industrialized culture are often woefully disconnected from the cycles of nature. We're not aware of where we come from. We're not aware of where we're going. We think of ourselves as being one thing and nature being another. We act without considering how we affect the rest of nature. We're blind to the observation of the Scottish naturalist, John Muir, who wrote, "When we try to pick out anything by itself, we find it hitched to everything else in the universe." Part of our growth as individuals has to involve healing the psychic fractures we have created between humankind and nature—and thus contemplating how our bodies are tied in to the great cycles of the elements is a necessary development. But in the end, what we're doing is pulling the rug out from under our belief in a separate self. Developing a more ecological sensibility is just a step on the way—perhaps a necessary one, but perhaps also not a sufficient one.

In day-to-day life it's profoundly healthy to contemplate the connectedness of the body. But it's necessary to take another step and to let go of the concept of the body. We don't really have bodies. What we have are ever-changing experiences that we "fix" by applying the static label "body" and by clinging to that label as if it represented something static. In reality, our experience—of the body and mind—changes moment by moment, and like John Tanner's tailor in Shaw's *Man and Superman,* we must forever take our measure anew. But each moment we do so, the self moves on, water slipping through our fingers. There is no measuring of the self.

Signs of Progress

I don't, as I have mentioned earlier, expect that you will entirely lose your sense of self as a result of reading this book (although I don't entirely rule out the possibility.) Our sense of a fixed self is hard like a rock, and it is not broken by one strike of the hammer, but by many. In my case, the realization that I had no fixed self was precipitated by the demands and stresses of parenthood, but those challenges were merely the latest in a series of hammer blows against the monolith of self-belief. The innumerable blows that had gone before—the sum total of all the reflection and practice I have done in my life—also had an effect, even though no single act had proven decisive.

Reflecting on the Six Elements while reading this book may have constituted a series of strikes against your own notion of having a fixed itself. It may be that deep within, fissures have begun to appear, even though on the surface they are undetectable. "Sudden" awakenings are not unheard-of, although the suddenness is more apparent than real—the rock has to be ready to split. I'd be surprised, however, if your sense of self had not undergone at least some temporary change as you engaged with the material we've been exploring together. I hope that's something you've noticed. Reflecting on impermanence, as we have done, can change how we perceive ourselves in a number of ways. Contemplating the ways that we are connected to the world can help us to experience states of mind that are enriching: states such as gratitude, appreciation, and wonder. These emotional states suggest we are beginning to transcend a sense of fixity and separation. They are emotional states of connectedness. There may be a sense of mystery, or even just of confusion, as our settled assumptions are challenged.

Sometimes fear may be evoked, and although fear may not be a pleasant emotional experience, it is more real than denial; fear arises when our sources of security are called into question. As we've seen, we keep an awareness of our own mortality at bay by clinging in many ways, and the fact that fear has been experienced is a sign that we are beginning to let go of our defensive strategies and are beginning to reveal our underlying vulnerability. Having been exposed, this vulnerability is something we can begin to work with creatively rather than defensively, by learning to become comfortable with change. When fear arises we need to walk toward and not away from it. On the other hand, another sign of progress is the sense of liberation that arises as we abandon the shackles of restricting views. We find that we become more confident in ourselves, experience less fear, and take charge of our lives.

Our sense of what we are can be loosened up by reflecting on the Six Elements, so that we come to see ourselves not as "stuck" but as having the potential for change. At first, this sense of our potential for change can be mainly intellectual, but it can quickly percolate into our emotional life as we gain a sense of faith in our potential and an emerging sense of confidence in our ability to break free of old and limiting habits. Eventually, we can lose any sense that we have a "self" that is in any way fixed or unchanging. At this point we enter the stream. But what next?

Whither Flows the Stream?

At the source—living streams.
In my veins ripples air like sap of birch,
Rippling around me and above—the
Midsummer sun, the buzzing of honeybees.

At the source are living streams. . .
I don't ask where they flow.
I melt into the floating shadows of trees,
Wrap myself in the trembling song of birds.

At the source, at the very source, is a glow. . .
I don't ask whither flows the stream.

At the deepest source is a glow.
Through me ripple sod and sky,
Birches and the midsummer sun.
What am I in this eternal flow?

—From "Intermezzo," by Janina Degutytė[2]

Perhaps, as the Lithuanian poet Degutytė suggests, we should or need not ask where the stream flows. In a sense we never can know, because we are stepping into the unknown. But although we may never know exactly where our steps will lead us, we need some sense of the direction in which we should walk, or we might end up frozen in place. As Francis Greenwood Peabody pointed out in a sermon published in 1911, it's natural that each of us should ask, "Whither flows the stream on which I desire to embark, and whither whirl the eddies which may detain my course?"[3]

Although I see losing my sense of self as a significant step, I also recognize that there remains plenty of work to be done. I still act in ways that cause me and others suffering. I sometimes snap at people, get lost in an anxious train of thought, or cause myself pain by craving things I can't have. There are deeper levels of clinging and identification to be exposed and relinquished. There are habitual patterns of craving, defensiveness, aggression, and denial to be abandoned. To me, these appear as semi-autonomous programs running in the background of my mind. I may have lost my self, but I still very much have an ego. These ego functions have evolved with specific purposes in mind (to protect me from suffering) but are neither well-designed nor suited to the kind of life I lead. They are caveman-level mental programs running in a technological, and largely peaceful, world. They certainly aren't congruent with the values by which I aspire to live. So there's more letting go that I have to do—deeper and more subtle levels of clinging to be abandoned—in order to become freer and happier. The Six Element Reflection is, I'm sure, a vital part of my future path as I seek to identify and abandon deeper and subtler levels of clinging. I may have overcome the delusion of having a fixed self, but the habit of identifying something as myself goes on, and until all vestiges of clinging are abandoned I will find myself repeatedly in a state of emotional conflict, without contentment and equanimity.

Having lost my sense of a fixed self, the question arises: how do I proceed? I've sat with this question for some time now, and the answer that has arisen time and again has been the need to dwell on the non-duality of subject and object. This is a topic I brought up in both the Space Element (Chapter Twelve) and Consciousness Element (Chapter Thirteen), where I talked about the fact that we can know nothing about the outside world beyond the filters of our perceptions. We have this thing called experience, and we assume that part of our experience is about "the outside world." All our experience, however, ultimately takes place in the mind. The *qualia* that we experience—color, sound, smell, taste, textures—are all sensory modalities that arise in the mind. The setting sun is not really red; red is an experience that arises in the mind. The ineffable "peachy" flavor of a peach is again something that arises in the mind.

There are two mistakes that we can make in approaching non-duality. One mistake is what I would call "naive realism." This is the assumption we all generally fall into: that there's a world of objects "out there" and that my consciousness "in here" perceives them. Naïve realism sees an absolute and fundamental distinction between self and other. This assumption is of course entirely natural. But it also involves a subtle level of clinging. We create a polarization in our experience between what we call a subject (ourselves) and an object (whatever we perceive), and the mind tends to cling to this distinction. Having created a definition, the mind assumes that there's some absolute reality supporting that definition.

The other mistake in approaching non-duality is in retreating into solipsism: the theory that we can never know anything but ourselves, a theory that in some cases takes the form of believing that the entire universe is an illusion created by our own minds. Spiritual or metaphysical solipsism—a goal chosen by some mystical traditions—is an attempt to overcome naive realism, but it's a goal fraught with inconsistencies. After all, the world does surprise me. The neighbors' cat that pushes its nose curiously against the glass of my office window is not something that I invented. I cannot control him by wishing him gone. I'm quite confident that he still exists when he wanders home for food; when he next appears he will be, to all intents and purposes, the same cat. He has the stability of a "real world" object, rather than the instability of a cat I might meet in my dreams. Spiritual solipsism is still fundamentally based on a *view* of the self—specifically the view that everything is the self—and if there's a view then there is some kind of clinging involved.

In the spiritual tradition I follow, the aim is simply to accept one's experience without labeling it as self or other. We don't decide that self and other are absolutely real, or that the self is real and the other is unreal, or any other variation on this theme. We simply let go of identifying any part of our experience as the self. Since we don't cling to anything as being the self, we also don't think of anything as being other than the self. What happens when we let go of clinging to the distinction between subject and object? That is what I'm currently working with. Especially in my meditation practice, I approach my experience with the assumption that there is simply experience, with no absolute distinction between subject and object. There is no idea "I am perceiving." There's no idea that there's a separate world being perceived. There's just experience. Adopting this viewpoint isn't hard, incidentally, although maintaining it is. Over and over again I find myself slipping from a non-dual perspective to one of duality, usually when my mind has become distracted by some thought that has arisen. But during the times when non-dual awareness has arisen, it's deeply refreshing and restful. Dualistic awareness is not only compulsive but tiring. It's compulsive in that the mind turns to it over and over again even though we know very well that it doesn't bring any satisfaction. It's tiring in that a constant effort is being made in order to reinforce a delusion.

Bringing a sense of non-dual awareness into ordinary activities gives rise—in my experience at least, and on those rare occasions I can manage to pull it off—to a sense of fascination which almost amounts to being in love with life. While I can maintain that mode of awareness, I find that the slightest thing is absolutely fascinating. Nothing, not even a tired and irritable child, seems in any way threatening or challenging to my equanimity. Instead, challenges simply become an opportunity for creativity. Creative responses to difficult circumstances arise naturally and as a kind of playfulness, although I still find an unfortunate tendency to slip into a more dualistic way of perceiving that's more prone to conflict and stress.

"Nothing's Personal"

I said that I lost my self while I was putting my daughter to bed, and I think it's no accident that it happened when I was with her.

I've experienced many stressful situations in my life. But nothing has tested me as much as being a parent. The combination of sleep deprivation, financial stress, and the seemingly never-ending stream of demands parenthood has placed upon me, has often tested me to my limits and beyond. As my daughter reached that stage of development known as the "terrible twos," complete with willfulness, full-blown meltdowns, and temper tantrums, I sometimes found myself resorting to yelling in order to get her to do what I wanted. It was greatly distressing to see this irruption of violent energies into my mind. I found myself speaking in ways that were not congruent with my ideals. I couldn't help but think that in expressing my anger I was teaching my child that might is right and that anger is how you get what you want. One time, in the midst of a bedtime that had gone on for close to two hours and in which my daughter had been thrashing around violently in an effort to avoid sleep, she pinched me, and in an instinctual move that bypassed my conscious mind altogether, I pinched her back. I was shocked at this lapse, and by the way this reflex action managed to dodge past my ethical sensibilities. I was deeply ashamed and disappointed with myself, and I felt the urgent need to learn to be kinder and more creative.

As all this was going on, I was at the same time reflecting deeply about the Six Elements and about the nature of the self. By some kind of inner alchemy, the reflections I was engaged in began to have a transforming effect on the way I saw my daughter. I found myself beginning to appreciate more and more that she did not have a fixed self. As I saw her going into a tantrum because she could not get what she wanted, I began to have a keen appreciation that she was a "work in progress."

I had watched her develop over the course of two years. When she was a small baby, happiness seemed to be her default state of mind, and her simple joy at being alive seemed only to be temporarily obscured when hunger or physical pain intervened. I watched her delight in the simplest things. She seemed to have no self. Until she was almost a year old she demonstrated no craving whatsoever, beyond the simple desire for food and affection. If she had hold of something I did not want her to have, I could simply remove it from her gently and she would not protest. She was still, at this point, largely free from what I think of as "ego." Then at about one year of age, craving, grasping, and anger arose; she would protest if something was taken from her or if she could not get something that she wanted. The ego had arrived.

It's rather humbling to consider what it must be like to experience new emotions like these. I can't think of any equivalent from my experience of adulthood. As my daughter passed the two-year milestone, she would swing rapidly from wanting to be protected, cherished, and cared for, to wanting to be independent. And many of her greatest frustrations seemed to arise from that area, because she was simply not allowed to do the things she wanted to do. Again, it's humbling to imagine what it must be like to make the transition from complete dependence to burgeoning independence, while your parents act as benevolent jailers, preventing you from doing much of what you want to do.

With all this in mind, as a tantrum would begin to take possession of my daughter, I would find myself seeing her not as a "self" that was doing something inconvenient to my "self," but as an ever-changing vortex of causes and conditions, struggling to make sense of itself and of the world into which it had been thrust. In a sense, there was nothing personal going on, and therefore nothing to be taken personally. Because I no longer saw her tantrum as one side in a battle of wills, I found myself able simply to appreciate the painful situation in which my daughter found herself. I was able to look at this defiant, foot-stomping little girl, and often feel no frustration—only compassion. I realized, in some of her most provocative moments, that she needed my loving support as she dealt with the inevitable changes that come with growing up just as much as she needed the boundaries that her mother and I were laying out for her.

We very frequently take things to be personal when they're not. We sometimes act as if the weather is conspiring against us, or we sometimes feel like heavy traffic has been sent specifically to make us late, and when anything bad happens to us, we can often be heard asking "Why me?" as if we've been personally singled out for misfortune. The new perspective on my daughter that was beginning to emerge allowed me to recognize that her tantrums, her insistence on doing things herself even though it would make us late, her destruction of cherished household objects, that none of these things was personal. In a sense, there was no "person" there doing all those things, and there was no "person" on my end that was their victim. There were simply causes and conditions unfolding in the world.

While all this was going on, I was beginning to have the experiences I described in the Consciousness Element chapter, where while driving I'd realize that it wasn't my conscious self that was steering the car. I soon started to notice the same phenomenon while walking, cooking—in almost every activity. I look back, for example, at this book and have a pervasive sense that "I" did not write it.

It was these developments—the need to find a radical new approach to dealing with the difficulties of parenthood, and reflecting on impermanence and not-self—that seemed to be the immediate precursors to my losing my sense of having a fixed self. Of course losing my sense of self in the context of parenthood would not have happened were it not for many years of fumbling with the business of spiritual practice. Had I not prepared the ground by working at developing mindfulness, cultivating lovingkindness, and reflecting, the fruit of not-self would not have ripened in my mind.

But amongst all these conditions, it was my reflections on the Six Elements that I feel were the most potent. The Six Element Practice is a powerful method for undercutting our false faith in a fixed and separate self. It relentlessly strips away our clinging and lets us see that ultimately there is nothing to fear by living without a self. For me the benefit of living like a river is the benefit of living compassionately, without imposing limitations on myself or upon other people.

Relating to someone as a "self"—on the basis of how we see them right now—is like seeing a video reduced to a single frame, or seeing a ball hurtling through the air caught in a photograph. It's life-denying. It's a static way of seeing things. In taking a snapshot of a thing, we lose its sense of trajectory, the sense that it's headed some-where. We're disconnected from the reality of change and process. But imagine if we could consistently see a person not as a thing but as a process—if we could, at least in our imagination—see that person evolving toward wisdom and compassion. How might that change both them and us? That's the challenge for us all.

I work with this challenge in the work I do in prisons, where I take meditation and other practices from the Buddhist tradition behind bars. I work, often, with people who are murderers and sex-offenders. Many of them have committed crimes against children. How to relate to these people and their crimes? As people, most of the men I work with are intelligent, seemingly compassionate, interesting, and inquisitive. I can judge them as they seem to be in the moments I'm working with them. Or I can judge them by the worst thing that each has done in his life. In a way, neither of these approaches seems adequate. A human being is a trajectory, not a fixed point in time and space, and any definition I impose on another person limits both them and me. At times I carry around in my mind the mantra, "All beings are, from the very beginning, Buddhas," as a reminder to relate to others on the basis of their potential. When I manage to relate to another person as a changing, evolving being who has the capacity for wisdom and compassion, I'm more likely to act toward them in a way that helps them grow into their potential. And I think it helps me grow into my own potential as well.

One of the paradoxes found in Buddhist teachings is the idea that we cannot be truly compassionate toward other beings unless we abandon the idea that they have selves. Defining others is the cruelest thing we can do to them, because it denies their true nature, which is change. In a sense, we become others' jailers when we imprison them in our fixed views of them. It's only when we see selves as inherently *becoming* that we are able to respond to others without judgment and with a compassionate response that encourages the emergence of their own Buddha-like qualities of insight and compassion. It's only when we recognize that selves are rivers, flowing onwards in a never-ending process of becoming, that we are able to be fully compassionate.

I'd like to leave you with an image from the poem, "St. Francis and the Sow," by Galway Kinnell, which evokes this sense of calling forth another being's potential by reminding it of its own beauty:

The bud
stands for all things,
even those things that don't flower,
for everything flowers, from within, of self-blessing;
though sometimes it is necessary
to reteach a thing its loveliness,
to put a hand on its brow
of the flower
and retell it in words and in touch
it is lovely
until it flowers again from within, of self-blessing.[4]

Notes

Introduction: Fear and Clinging in the River of Life

1. P. G. Wodehouse, *My Man Jeeves*. (Charleston, South Carolina: BiblioLife, 2008), 118.

2. Eric D. Miller, "Imagining loss and mortality salience: Consequences for romantic-relationship satisfaction," *Social Behavior and Personality Journal* 31, no. 2 (2003): 167–180.

3. Terror Management Theory was first developed in the late 1980s by Skidmore College psychology professor Sheldon Solomon, University of Arizona psychology professor Jeff Greenberg, and Colorado University psychology professor Tom Pyszczynski. It is inspired by the theories of Ernest Becker (author of the Pulitzer Prize-winning book *The Denial of Death*), Sigmund Freud, and Freud's long-term colleague, Otto Rank.

4. Eva Jonas, Immo Fritscheb, and Jeff Greenberg, "Currencies as cultural symbols—an existential psychological perspective on reactions of Germans toward the Euro," *Journal of Economic Psychology* 26, no. 1 (2005): 129–146.

5. Abram Rosenblatt, et al., "Evidence for Terror Management Theory I. The Effects of Mortality Salience on Reactions to Those Who Violate or Uphold Cultural Values," *Journal of Personality and Social Psychology* 57, no. 4 (1989): 681–690.

6. "Evidence for Terror Management Theory I," 681–690.

). Jay Dixit, "The Ideological Animal," *Psychology Today*, January 2007.

8. Tom Pyszczynski, Jeff Greenberg, and Sheldon Solomon, "A Dual-Process Model of Defense Against Conscious and Unconscious Death-Related Thoughts. An Extension of Terror Management Theory," *Psychological Review* 106, no. 4 (1999): 835–845.

9. B. Rutjens, et al., "Things Will Get Better: The Anxiety-Buffering Qualities of Progressive Hope," *Personality and Social Psychology Bulletin* 35, no. 5 (2009):535–43.

10. Jeff Greenberg, et al., "Terror Management and Tolerance: Does Mortality Salience Always Intensify Negative Reactions to Others Who Threaten One's Worldview?" *Journal of Personality and Social Psychology* 63, no. 2 (1992): 212–220.

11. John R. Hibbing, et al., "Political Attitudes Vary with Physiological Traits," *Science* 321, no. 5896 (2008): 1667–1670.

Chapter One: The Self I Don't Believe In

1. Quoted in Amartya Sen, "Other People," in *2000 Lectures and Memoirs: Volume 111 of Proceedings of the British Academy*, (Oxford: Oxford University Press, 2001), 319.

2. Joseph Heller, *Catch 22.* (New York: Simon and Schuster, 1996), 190.

3. This experiment was featured in "The Mind's Eye," the third episode of a BBC television miniseries called *Brain Story,* which first aired in 2000.

4. D. J. Simons and D. T. Levin, "Failure to detect changes to people in a real-world interaction," *Psychonomic Bulletin and Review* 5, no. 4 (1998): 644–649.

5. As mentioned, many websites offer such experiments. Searching the Internet for "change blindness demonstration" will bring up a selection.

6. Daniel J. Simons and Christopher F. Chabris, "Gorillas in our midst: sustained inattentional blindness for dynamic events." *Perception* 28, no. 9 (1999): 1059–1074.

7. Jesse Bering, "Never Say Die: Why We Can't Imagine Death," *Scientific American Mind*, October 2008.

8. Rainer Maria Rilke, *Letters to a Young Poet,* trans. Joan M. Burnham (Novato, CA: New World Library, 2000), 35.

9. See Thomas W. Clark, "Death, Nothingness, and Subjectivity," in Daniel Kolak and R. Martin (eds.), *The Experience of Philosophy*. (Belmont, CA: Wadsworth Publishing, 2002), 556.

10. Jesse M. Bering, "Intuitive Conceptions of Dead Agents' Minds: The Natural Foundations of Afterlife Beliefs as Phenomenological Boundary," *Journal of Cognition and Culture* 2, no. 4 (2002): 263–308.

Chapter Two: An Encounter in the Workshop

1. Charles Cotton (tr.), *The Essays of Michel Eyquem de Montaigne* (Chicago: Encyclopaedia Britannica, 1952), 317.

2. The story of the encounter between Gautama (the philosopher) and Pukkusati is from Bhikkhu Nanamoli and Bhikkhu Bodhi, *The Middle Length Discourses of the Buddha*, 2nd edition (Somerville, MA: Wisdom Publications, 2001), 1087–1096.

3. For a very readable introduction to the historical background of the time of the Buddha, I'd suggest Michael Carrithers, *The Buddha* (Oxford: Oxford University Press, 1983).

Chapter Three: Self Is a Verb

1. Barbara Sher and Barbara Smith, *I Could Do Anything If I Only Knew What It Was* (New York: Random House, 1995), 99.

2. Robert Thurman, *The Holy Teaching of Vimalakirti* (University Park, PA: Pennsylvania State University Press, 1976), 15.

3. Edward Conze, *Thirty Years of Buddhist Studies: Selected Essays* (Columbia, SC: University of South Carolina Press, 1968), 127.

4. Hammalawa Saddhatissa (tr.), *The Sutta Nipata* (Abingdon, UK: Curzon Press, 1994), 106.

5. Saddhatissa, *Sutta Nipata*, 16.

6. Bertrand Russell, *A History of Western Philosophy* (London: Routledge, 2004), 251.

7. Marcus Aurelius, *Meditations* II:7.

8. Ibid., V:23.

9. Milinda's Greek name was Menander I. He was a descendant of the Greeks who had settled in India in the wake of Alexander's epic journey of exploration and conquest.

10. The discussions are found in a text called "The Questions of King Milinda." See, for example, Henry Clark Warren, *Buddhism In Translation* (Whitefish, MT: Kessinger Publishing, 2003), 113.

11. Bhikkhu Bodhi, *The Connected Discourses of the Buddha: A New Translation of the Samyutta Nikaya, Volume 1* (Somerville, MA: Wisdom Publications, 2000), 1254.

12. This particular analogy uses the fivefold analysis of the *skandhas* (form, feeling, perception, habitual predispositions, and consciousness), rather than the six elements.

13. Alva Noë, *Out of Our Heads: Why You Are Not Your Brain, and Other Lessons from the Biology of Consciousness* (New York: Hill and Wang, 2009).

14. Noë, 5.

15. Noë, 48.

16. Noë, 10.

Chapter Four: On Reflection

1. "The Question," *The Matrix*, DVD, directed by Andy Wachowski and Lana Wachowski (1999; Burbank, CA: Warner Home Video, 2001).

2. S. N. Goenka and Patrick Given-Wilson, *Satipatthana Sutta Discourses: Vipassana Meditation and the Buddha's Teachings* (Onalaska, WA: Pariyatti, 1998), 24.

3. Wolfgang Köhler, *The Mentality of Apes* (New York: Harcourt, Brace & Company, Inc., 1926), 271.

4. Martin Goldstein, *How We Know: An Exploration of the Scientific Process* (Boulder, CO: Westview Press, 1981), 194.

5. Arnold H. Modell, *Imagination and the Meaningful Brain* (Cambridge, MA: MIT Press, 2003), 29.

6. Denis Brian, *Einstein: A Life* (Hoboken, NJ: John Wiley and Sons, 1996), 159.

7. Rainer Maria Rilke, *Letters to a Young Poet,* trans. Stephen Mitchell (New York: Vintage Books, 1986), 9.

Chapter Five: The Body as Mirage

1. Lynn Picknett, *Mary Magdalene* (New York: Carroll & Graf Publishers, 2003), 88.

2. There's a good account of Rodgers's flight, "The *Vin Fiz*: The First U. S. Transcontinental Flight" at the U.S. Centennial of Flight Commission website: centennialofflight.gov/essay/Explorers_Record_Setters_and_Daredevils/Vin_Fiz/EX6.htm. See also Eileen F. Lebow, *Cal Rodgers and the Vin Fiz: The First Transcontinental Flight* (Washington, D.C.: Smithsonian Institution Press, 1989).

3. William Molesworth (ed.), "De Corpore," *The English Works of Thomas Hobbes* (Evanston, IL: Adler's Foreign Books Inc., 1966), 136.

4. Jerry Garrett, "Boyd Coddington, Hot Rod Hero, Dies at 63," *New York Times*, February 27, 2008.

5. Hannah Devlin, "Third of transplant patients believe they take on donor's traits," *The Times*, June 5, 2009.

6. "Donor organ 'personality' worry," *BBC News*, June 5, 2009, news.bbc.co.uk/2/hi/8084936.stm.

7. Geoffrey Stephen Kirk, John Earle Raven, and Malcolm Schofield, *The Presocratic Philosophers: A Critical History with a Selection of Texts* (Cambridge, UK: Cambridge University Press, 1983), 290.

8. Bhikkhu Nanamoli and Bhikkhu Bodhi, *The Middle Length Discourses of the Buddha* (Somerville, MA: Wisdom Publications, 1995), 533–536.

9. Strictly speaking, this is true, but the Buddha's discussions suggest that he was well versed in the scientific theories of his day. It seems to me quite likely that in his youth the Buddha had studied such subjects, although I doubt he ever saw himself as being a scientist.

10. *The Middle Length Discourses of the Buddha*, 281.

11. Nicholas Wade, "Your Body Is Younger Than You Think," *New York Times*, August 2, 2005.

Chapter Six: Trapped in the Elements

1. Byron, "The Bride of Abydos," line 381.

2. Janine Willis and Alexander Todorov, "First Impressions: Making Up Your Mind After a 100-Ms Exposure to a Face," *Psychological Science* 17 (2006): 592–598.

3. Charles C. Ballew II and Alexander Todorov, "Predicting political elections from rapid and unreflective face judgments," *Proceedings of the National Academy of Sciences* 104 (2007): 17948–17953.

Chapter Seven: The Communal Self

1. Antoine de Saint Exupéry, *Flight to Arras* (Alcester, UK: Read Books, 2007), 74.

2. This account of Karen's story comes from the following sources: Claire Ainsworth, "The Stranger Within," *New Scientist*, no. 2421 (15 November, 2003): 38, where she is anonymized as "Jane" and "(So-Called) Life" (radio broadcast), *Radio Lab*, WNYC, March 14, 2008.

3. Neng Yu, et al., "Disputed maternity leading to identification of tetragametic chimerism," *New England Journal of Medicine* 346, no. 20 (2002): 1545–52.

4. *Extraordinary People:* "The Twin Inside Me" (London: Cicada Films, 2006).

5. Claire Ainsworth, "The Stranger Within."

6. *Radio Lab*, "(So-Called) Life."

7. Kathy A. Svitil, "We Are All Chimeras," *Discover*, May 2007.

8. C. E. Boklage, "The frequency and survivability of natural twin conceptions," in Louis G. Keith, Emile Papiernik, Donald M. Keith, et al., *Multiple Pregnancy: Epidemiology, Gestation and Perinatal Outcome*. (New York: Taylor & Francis Group, 1995), 41–2, 49.

9. Claire Ainsworth, "The Stranger Within."

Chapter Eight: The Earth Element

1. Deborah Gillan Straub, *Native North American Voices* (Detroit, MI: UXL, 1997), 181.

2. Louis Mayeul Chaudon, *Historical and critical memoirs of the life and writings of M. de Voltaire* (London: G. G. J. and J. Robinson, 1786), 290.

3. Bhikkhu Nanamoli and Bhikkhu Bodhi, *Middle Length Discourses of the Buddha* (Somerville, MA: Wisdom Publications, 1995), 1089.

4. Neil deGrasse Tyson, "The Cosmic Perspective," *Beyond Belief: Science, Reason, Religion & Survival* (San Diego, California: Salk Institute for Biological Studies, 2006), haydenplanetarium.org/tyson/watch/beyondbelief.

Chapter Nine: The Water Element

1. Emma Gilby, *Sublime Worlds: Early Modern French Literature* (London: Modern Humanities Research Association, 2006), 95.

2. Hugh G. Evelyn-White (tr.), *Hesiod: Works and Days* (Charleston, SC: Forgotten Books, 2007), 25.

3. Homer, *The Iliad*, 73.

4. Bhikkhu Bodhi and Nyanaponika Thera, *Numerical Discourses of the Buddha: An Anthology of Suttas from the Anguttara Nikaya* (Walnut Creek, CA: Rowman Altamira, 1999), 193–4.

5. Stephen Henry Schneider (ed.), *Encyclopedia of Climate and Weather, Volume 2* (New York: Oxford University Press, 1996), 817–823.

6. Adam Nieman, "Global Water and Air Volume," *Science Photo Library*, E055/330, sciencephoto.com/images/imagePopUpDetails.html?id=690550330.

7. Campbell Robertson, "Iraq Suffers as the Euphrates River Dwindles," *New York Times*, July 13, 2009.

8. Elisabeth Rosenthal, "An Amazon Culture Withers as Food Dries Up," *New York Times*, July 24, 2009.

Chapter Ten: The Fire Element

1. John Sutton Tuckey (ed.), "Three Thousand Years Among the Microbes," in *Mark Twain's "Which Was the Dream?" and Other Symbolic Writings of the Later Years* (Berkeley, CA: University of California Press, 1967), 447.

2. Bhikkhu Nanamoli and Bhikkhu Bodhi, *The Middle Length Discourses of the Buddha* (Somerville, MA: Wisdom Publications, 1995), 1090.

3. Bhikkhu Thanissaro, *The Mind Like Fire Unbound* (Barre, MA: Dhamma Dana Publications, 1993), 17.

4. Ibid., 18.

5. Ibid., 17.

6. Stephanie Pain, "The Intraterrestrials," *New Scientist*, March 7, 1998, 28.

7. Anne Casselman, "Life Forms 'Resurrected' After Millennia in Ice," *National Geographic News*, August 6, 2007.

8. William J. Broad, "Scientists Find Smallest Form of Life, If It Lives," *New York Times*, January 18, 2000, F1.

9. Luis P Villarreal, "Are Viruses Alive?" *Scientific American*, December 2004, 100.

10. Josie Glausiusz, "Your Body Is a Planet," *Discover*, June 2007, 44.

11. Ibid.

12. Steven R. Gill et al., "Metagenomic Analysis of the Human Distal Gut Microbiome," *Science* 312, no. 5778 (2006): 1355–1359.

13. Jeffrey I. Gordon, "The gut microbiota as an environmental factor that regulates fat storage," *Proceedings of the National Academy of Sciences* 101, no. 44 (2004): 15718–15723.

14. T. Matsuzaki et al., "Antidiabetic effects of an oral administration of *Lactobacillus casei* in a non-insulin-dependent diabetes mellitus (NIDDM) model using KK-Ay mice," *Endocrine Journal* 44, no. 3 (1997): 357–65.

15. Glausiusz, "Your Body Is a Planet," 45.

16. Josie Glausiusz, "Function of Appendix Explained," *Discover*, January 2008, 69.

17. Royston Goodacre, "Metabolomics of a Superorganism," *The Journal of Nutrition* 137 (2007): 259S–266S.

18. Gwen Ericson, "Gut Microbes Can Increase Body Fat," *Washington University in St. Louis Record*, November 17, 2004, record.wustl.edu/news/page/normal/4745.html.

19. Lois Baker "UB scientist publishes first human microbiome analysis," *SUNY at Buffalo Press Release*, June 1, 2006, eurekalert.org/pub_releases/2006-06/uab-usp053106.php.

20. Jeffrey I. Gordon et al., "Host-bacterial mutualism in the human intestine," *Ending the War Metaphor: The Changing Agenda for Unraveling the Host-Microbe Relationship*, (Washington, D.C.: National Academies Press, 2006), 41.

21. Garry Hamilton, "Viruses: The Unsung Heroes of Evolution," *New Scientist*, August 27, 2008, 38–41.

22. University of Georgia, "Retroviruses Show That Human-Specific Variety Developed When Humans, Chimps Diverged," *Science Daily*, August 2, 2002, sciencedaily.com/releases/2002/08/020802075138.htm.

23. Tae-Min Kim, Seung-Jin Hong, and Mun-Gan Rhyu, "Periodic Explosive Expansion of Human Retroelements Associate with the Evolution of the Hominoid Primate," *Journal of Korean Medical Science* 19, (2004): 177–85.

24. Miranda M. Lim et al., "Enhanced Partner Preference in a Promiscuous Species by Manipulating the Expression of a Single Gene," *Nature* 429, (2004): 754–757.

25. Luis P. Villarreal, "Can Viruses Make Us Human?" *Proceedings of the American Philosophical Society* 148, no. 3 (2004): 315.

26. Douglas Fox, "Why We Don't Lay Eggs," *New Scientist*, June 12, 1999, 26.

Chapter Eleven: The Air Element

1. Coleman Barks (tr.), *We Are Three: New Rumi Poems* (Athens, GA: Maypop Books, 1987), 6.

2. S. H. Hooke, *Middle Eastern Mythology* (Mineola, NY: Dover, 2004), 24–26.

3. Raymond L. Lee and Alistair B. Fraser, *The Rainbow Bridge: Rainbows in Art, Myth, and Science* (University Park, PA: Penn State Press, 2001), 6.

4. Friedrich Max Müller (tr.), *The Sacred Books of the East, Volume 15: The Upanishads, Part 2* (New York: Elibron Classics, 2000), 203.

5. Christopher Hitchens, "Believe Me, It's Torture," *Vanity Fair*, August 2008.

6. Müller, *The Sacred Books of the East, Volume 15*, 133.

7. Bhikkhu Nanamoli and Bhikkhu Bodhi, *The Middle Length Discourses of the Buddha* (Somerville, MA: Wisdom Publications, 1995), 1090.

8. James Randall Miller, *Thoughts From Earth* (Bloomington, IN: Trafford Publishing, 2004), 65.

9. Jack Hassard and Julie Weisberg, *Environmental Science on the Net: The Global Thinking Project* (Tucson, AZ: Good Year Books, 1999), 40.

10. Ibid.

11. Donald R. Prothero and Frederic L. Schwab, *Sedimentary Geology: An Introduction to Sedimentary Rocks and Stratigraphy* (New York: Macmillan, 2004), 214.

12. Malcolm Dole, "The Natural History of Oxygen," *The Journal of General Physiology* 49 (1965): 9.

13. "The Last Word," *New Scientist*, May 18, 1996.

14. J. E. Lovelock, and J. P. Lodge, "Oxygen in the Contemporary Atmosphere," *Atmospheric Environment*, 6 (1972): 575–578.

15. Antoine de Saint Exupéry, *The Little Prince* (Ware, UK: Wordsworth, 1995), 82.

16. "The SeaWiFS instrument looks at the world's oceans and land to observe the plant life and phytoplankton. In this flat projection view, you can see the whole world pulse with life." Available at svs. gsfc.nasa.gov/vis/a000000/a002000/a002076/index.html.

17. *Dhammapada,* v. 46.

18. Ibid., vv. 168–174.

19. Edward Conze, *Buddha's Law Among the Birds* (Delhi: Motilal Banarsidass, 1974), 35.

20. Joseph Goldstein, "Self and Selflessness," MP3 audio file (Barre, MA: Dharma Seed, 2008), dharmaseed.org/teacher/96/talk/4110/.

21. *Meteorologica III,* 2. 371–372.

22. Douglas Allchin, "Newton's Colors" (Minneapolis, MN: SHiPS Resource Center), http://www1.umn.edu/ships/updates/newton1.htm.

Chapter Twelve: The Space Element

1. This account is based on a *National Geographic* video located at http://news.nationalgeographic.com/news/2008/12/081203-swapping-video-ap.html, and on Karl Ritter, "Body-Swap Illusion Tricks Mind in New Study," *ABC News*, abcnews.go.com/Technology/wireStory?id=6373782.

2. Valeria I. Petkova, H. Henrik Ehrsson, "If I Were You: Perceptual Illusion of Body Swapping," *PLoS ONE* 3, no.12 (2008): e3832. doi:10.1371/journal.pone.0003832.

3. Josie Glausiusz, "When the Brain Loses the Body," *Discover*, December 2007, 23.

4. Ibid.

5. Alessandro Farnè et al., "Tool-use induces morphological updating of the body schema," *Current Biology* 19, no. 13 (2009): 1157.

6. Alison Motluk, "Body Talk," *New Scientist*, November 14, 1998, 11.

7. *BBC News*, "Out-of-body experience recreated," August 24, 2007, news.bbc.co.uk/2/hi/6960612.stm.

8. Bigna Lenggenhager et al., "Video ergo sum: manipulating bodily self-consciousness," *Science* 317 (2007): 1096-1099.

9. Bhikkhu Nanamoli and Bhikkhu Bodhi, *Middle Length Discourses of the Buddha* (Somerville, MA: Wisdom Publications, 1995), 1091.

10. Bhikkhu Nanamoli (tr.), *The Path of Purification: By Bhadantacariya Buddhaghosa* (Singapore: Singapore Buddhist Meditation Centre, 1997), 500.

11. Nanamoli and Bodhi, *Middle Length Discourses of the Buddha*, 283.

12. Nicholas Epley and Erin Whitchurch, "Mirror, Mirror on the Wall: Enhancement in Self-Recognition," *Personality and Social Psychology Bulletin* 34, no. 9 (2008): 1159–1170.

13. Jesse Bering, "Think you're good-looking? Think again," *Scientific American*, February 18, 2009, scientificamerican.com/article. cfm?id=think-youre-good-looking.

14. Andrew Fraknoi, "How Fast Are You Moving When You Are Sitting Still?" *The Universe in the Classroom* (2007), astrosociety.org/ education/publications/tnl/71/howfast.html.

15. William J. Szlemko et al., "Territorial Markings as a Predictor of Driver Aggression and Road Rage," *Journal of Applied Social Psychology* 38, no. 6 (2008): 1664–1688.

16. David J. Pollay, "Change Your Seat, Change Your Life," *Happy News*, September 21, 2007, happynews.com/columns/david-j-pol- lay/952007/change-seat-change-life.htm.

17. John Suler, "The Dynamics of Sitting," www-usr.rider.edu/~suler/ sitdynamics.html.

18. Sandra Blakeslee, "Flesh Made Soul," *Science and Spirit Magazine*, March 21, 2008, science-spirit.org/newdirections. php?article_id=740.

19. Andrew Newberg, "The Effect of Meditation on the Brain Activity in Tibetan Meditators: Frontal Lobes," andrewnewberg.com/pet1b.asp.

20. Carina Storrs, "Contemplating Oneness: The Neuroscience of Meditation," *ScienceLine*, August 13, 2009, scienceline. org/2009/08/13/storrs-neuroscience-meditation-fmri-brain/.

21. Ibid., scienceline.org/2009/08/13/storrs-neuroscience meditation-fmri-brain/2/.

22. Susan Blackmore, *Ten Zen Questions* (Oxford, UK: Oneworld Publications, 2009), 64.

23. One experiment confirming Einstein's predictions about space being "dragged" along by the rotation of matter, involving NASA's Gravity Probe B Relativity Mission, is reported in: Stephen Ornes, "Einstein Was Right," *Discover*, July 2007, 13.

24. See, for example: Tim Folger, "What Fills the Emptiness," *Discover*, August 2008, 24–28.

25. Smolin explains Loop Quantum Gravity in: Lee Smolin, "Atoms of Space and Time," *Scientific American*, January 2004, 66–75.

26. Hans Christian von Baeyer, "Vacuum Matters," *Discover*, March 1992, discovermagazine.com/1992/mar/vacuummatters9/.

27. Robert Lanza and Bob Berman, *Biocentrism: How Life and Consciousness Are the Keys to Understanding the True Nature of the Universe* (Dallas, TX: BenBella, 2009).

28. Robert Lanza and Bob Berman, "Biocentrism; How Life Creates The Universe" (book extract), *MSNBC.com*, June 16, 2009, msnbc.msn.com/id/31393080/.

29. Richard Conn Henry, review of *Biocentrism: How Life and Consciousness Are the Keys to Understanding the True Nature of the Universe,* by Robert Lanza and Bob Berman, henry.pha.jhu.edu/biocentrism.pdf (2009).

Chapter Thirteen: The Consciousness Element

1. Coleman Barks (tr.), *Rumi: The Book of Love: Poems of Ecstasy and Longing* (New York: HarperCollins, 2005), 67.

2. I'm indebted for this analogy to Wyman H. Herendeen: "What is a river?... Is it the water between its banks, or the banks which embrace that protean element?... If the banks, created by the furrowing water, is it not also the meadows, fields, and forests

which are no less the product of their movement . . . " Wyman H. Herendeen, *From Landscape to Literature: The River and the Myth of Geography* (Pittsburgh, PA: Duquesne University Press, 1986), 4.

3. Alva Noë, *Out of Our Heads: Why You Are Not Your Brain, and Other Lessons from the Biology of Consciousness* (New York: Hill and Wang, 2009), 41–42.

4. G. G. Coulton, *St. Francis to Dante* (London: David Nutt, 1906), 242.

5. Tony Halpin and Jenny Booth, "Feral Girl in Siberian City of Chita Was Brought Up by Cats and Dogs," *Times Online*, May 27, 2009, timesonline.co.uk/tol/news/world/europe/article6373089.ece.

6. Sandra Blakeslee, "Cells That Read Minds," *New York Times*, January 10, 2006, F1, nytimes.com/2006/01/10/science/10mirr.html.

7. Marco Iacoboni et al., "Grasping the Intentions of Others with One's Own Mirror Neuron System," *PLoS Biology* 3, no. 3 (2005): e79. doi:10.1371/journal.pbio.0030079.

8. Blakeslee, "Cells That Read Minds."

9. Vilayanur S. Ramachandran and Lindsay M. Oberman, "Broken Mirrors," *Scientific American*, November 2006, 63–69.

10. Josie Glausiusz, review of *Loneliness: Human Nature and the Need for Social Connection*, by John Cacioppo and William Patrick, *Discover*, August 2008, 73.

11. Stu Hutson, "Absence makes the heart grow weaker," *New Scientist*, March 28, 2006, newscientist.com/article/dn8908-absence-makes-the-heart-grow-weaker.html.

12. *BBC News*, "Social isolation 'worsens cancer,'" September 29, 2009, news.bbc.co.uk/2/hi/health/8279425.stm.

13. Samir S. Patel, "Why Loneliness Is Bad For You," *Discover*, January 2008, 63.

14. Matt Kaplan, "An icy stare really does make you feel cold," *New Scientist*, September 19, 2008, newscientist.com/article/dn14766-an-icy-stare-really-does-make-you-feel-cold.html.

15. Jolanda Jetten, Catherine Halsam, and Nyla R. Branscombe, "The Social Cure," *Scientific American Mind*, September/October, 2009, 26.

16. Paul Bloom, "First Person Plural," *The Atlantic*, November 2008, http://www.theatlantic.com/doc/200811/multiple-personalities.

17. Susan Blackmore, *Ten Zen Questions* (Oxford, UK: Oneworld Publications, 2009), 36–37.

18. *New Scientist*, "Blind man 'sees' his way past obstacles - video," December 22, 2008, newscientist.com/articlevideo/dn16324/5551273001-blind-man-sees-his-way-past-obstacles.html.

19. Bob Holmes, "Irresistable Illusions," *New Scientist*, September, 05 1998, 32.

20. Ibid.

21. "Machine detects our decisions before we know them," *New Scientist*, 19 April, 2008, newscientist.com/article/mg19826525.600-machine-detects-our-decisions-before-we-know-them.html.

22. This experiment was carried out by Michael Gazzaniga. See: David G. Duemler, *Bringing Life to the Stars* (Lanham, MD: University Press of America, 1993), 65.

23. Stephen Ornes, "For Kids: Brain Cells Take a Break," *Science News*, May 27, 2009, sciencenews.org/view/generic/id/44207/title/FOR_KIDS_Brain_cells_take_a_break.

24. Susan Kruglinski, "How to Erase a Single Memory," *Discover*, January 2008, discovermagazine.com/2008/jan/how-to-erase-a-single-memory; Jessica Ruvinsky, "Is It Possible to Erase a Single Memory?" *Discover*, July 2007, http://discovermagazine.com/2007/jul/eternal-sunshine; and WNYC, "Memory and Forgetting" (radio broadcast), *Radio Lab*, June 8, 2007, wnyc.org/shows/radiolab/episodes/2007/06/08.

25. Kathleen McGowan, "How Much of Your Memory Is True?" *Discover*, July-August Special Issue, 2009, discovermagazine.com/2009/jul-aug/03-how-much-of-your-memory-is-true.

26. Elizabeth F. Loftus and Jacqueline E. Pickrell, "The formation of false memories," *Psychiatric Annals* 25, (1995): 720-725.

27. Elizabeth F. Loftus, "Creating False Memories," *Scientific American*, September 1997, 70–75.

28. Becky McCall, "Memory surprisingly unreliable, study shows," *Cosmos*, September 15, 2008, cosmosmagazine.com/news/2193/study-shows-memory-surprisingly-unreliable.

29. Philip Cohen, "Thanks for the Memories," *New Scientist*, February 22, 1997, 12.

30. Gero Miesenböck et al., "Writing memories with light-addressable reinforcement circuitry," *Cell* 139, no. 2 (2009): 405–15.

31. Ira Flatow, "Making Memories with Fruit Flies" (radio broadcast), *Talk of the Nation*, October 16, 2009, npr.org/templates/story/story.php?storyId=113870272.

32. David Hume, *A Treatise of Human Nature*, I, IV, vi.

Chapter Fourteen: Stepping into the Stream

1. Wendell Berry, *The Unforeseen Wilderness: An Essay on Kentucky's Red River Gorge* (Lexington: University Press of Kentucky, 1971), 54.

2. The Eightfold Path, also known as the Noble Eightfold Path, is one of the principle teachings of the Buddha, and it outlines the way to the cessation of suffering. Since suffering is said to be caused by clinging, the Eightfold Path is therefore a way to abandon clinging and to accept the reality of impermanence. The eight elements of the path should not be seen as being practiced sequentially, but as being practiced concurrently. In other words, the path is "eightfold" in the sense that it is comprised of eight "lanes" that run side by side, not in the sense that there are eight steps to be taken, one by one. Two of the factors of the path—right view and right resolve—relate to the cultivation of wisdom. Right view represents the cultivation of an accurate way of seeing the world,

while cultivating right resolve involves lessening our clinging, and the negative emotional states that arise from clinging. Right speech, right action, and right livelihood comprise the ethical dimension of the path, where we let go of clinging as it expresses itself in our daily actions. Right effort, right mindfulness, and right concentration comprise the path of inner, meditative transformation, through which we progressively purify the mind of clinging and encourage compassion and fearlessness to arise.

3. SN 55.5, quoted at accesstoinsight.org/lib/study/stream2.html.

4. Mv 1.23.5 quoted at accesstoinsight.org/tipitaka/vin/mv/ mv.01.23.01-10.than.html.

5. AN 5.57 quoted at accesstoinsight.org/tipitaka/an/an05/an05.057. than.html.

6. John Dewey, *Democracy and Education* (New York: Macmillan, 1916), 408.

Chapter Fifteen: The Self Beyond Measure

1. George Bernard Shaw, *Man and Superman: A Comedy and a Philosophy* (New York: Brentano's, 1916), 37.

2. Gražina M. Slavėnas (tr.), "In Memoriam Janina Degutytė (1928–1990)," *Lituanus: Lithuanian Quarterly Journal of Arts and Sciences* 38, no. 2 (1992), lituanus.org/1992_4/92_4_01.htm.

3. Francis Greenwood Peabody, *Sunday Evenings in the College Chapel* (Boston: Houghton Mifflin, 1911), 256.

4. Galway Kinnell, "Saint Francis and the Sow," from *Mortal Acts, Mortal Words* (Boston: Houghton Mifflin, 1980), 9.

Reader's Guide

1. Take one simple item of food you're about to eat—some fruit or a piece of breakfast cereal, for example—and visualize where it came from, imagining the water, soil, and air that went into forming it. Then visualize where, in turn, that water, soil, and air came from. Continue this reflection as you eat the food. What effect does this have on you? What do you feel as you imagine the food becoming part of your body?

2. Notice the breath flowing into and out of your body, and inwardly repeat the words, "This is not me; this is not mine; I am not this." What do you feel? What thoughts and images spontaneously come to mind?

3. Consider which aspects of your self you regard as part of your core identity and which are peripheral. How do you decide which are which? Is it possible to draw a clear distinction?

4. Imagine that through some hospital error you'd been taken home as a newborn by a different family, who immediately moved to a different country and who spoke a different language and practiced a religion different from your own. Do you think of the "alternative you" as still being "you," or would the "alternative you" be another person?

5. Think about your very earliest memories. As you consider them, is there a point at which you find it difficult to identify with that early "you" as being you? Where is that point? What's different about the "you" before and the "you" after that point, if it exists? What about the "you" who pre-dates those memories? Most people's first recollections are from around age four. To what extent do you find it even possible to identify with an existence you can't remember?

6. Imagine that through advances in technology, all your body parts (heart, liver, lungs, limbs, etc.) could be replaced one by one with tissues and organs grown in a lab. Would there be a point at which you ceased to be you?

7. Now imagine that parts of your brain could be replaced with computer circuits that had the same functionality as the original neurons. Would you cease to be you when just one part had been replaced, or all of them, or at some point in between? How would you know?

8. We rarely see our bodies and faces as they really are, and some research shows that we tend to hold an idealized image of our faces in mind. Try looking at your face in the mirror, to see if

you can see what you truly look like. Do you have little tricks that "improve" how you look, such as only focusing on what you think are your best features, or putting on a certain expression? Do you find you're critical and unable to accept what you see? Are you able to move toward a greater acceptance of how you really are?

9. If you're sitting in a room, become aware of the space around you, using your senses of vision and hearing and your spatial sense. In a way, your consciousness is filling the space around you. Consider that in some sense everything you are perceiving is part of you, and note how that changes your sense of the self/other split. How does this affect your sense of self?

10. Pay attention to any language you use that may define and limit you. This could include telling yourself or others that you "can't" do certain things, or that you have a certain personality type. Can you notice a tendency to reinforce your sense of identity? What happens to your sense of self when you don't do that?

11. For one week, try to consciously change some of your habits: your route to work, where and what you eat, where you sit, the people you talk to, your sources of news and entertainment. How does this change your sense of self?

12. Fear seems to underlie most, if not all, of our craving and clinging. For a full day, try to notice every mental, physical, and verbal act of craving, or clinging, and see if you can detect any underlying fear. What, from these observations, did you notice you fear

the most? If it helps, when you notice, say, that you're craving something (it could be anything, from recognition to a pair of shoes), ask yourself: what do I fear will happen if I don't get this thing I desire?

Index

terror management theory (TMT), xviii–xxiii, 309n3

Thales of Miletus, 124–25

thinking, 56–60

the three fetters, 22–24, 276–90
   dependence on observances, 288–90
   doubt, 284–88
   fixed self-view, 276–84

Todorov, Alexander, 89–90

Upanishad, 170–71, 182

Vanishing Twin Syndrome, 103
   see also chimeras; Keegan, Karen

Vernadsky, Vladimir, 245

viruses, 150, 160–63

the *Vin Fiz*
   cross-country flight of, 63–65
   as metaphor for the self, 65–68

vipassana, 51–54
   see also insight meditation

vision statements/mission statements, 286

Voltaire, 105

Water Element, xvi, 30, 123–40
   being the river, 127–30
   flowing quality of, 125
   preciousness of water, 136–39
   reflection for, 130–36

Whitman, Walt, 289

About the Author

B odhipaksa was born Graeme Stephen in Scotland in 1961. He developed a strong interest in science at an early age, and studying the physiology of perception led to an interest in Buddhist philosophy and practice. After graduating as a veterinary surgeon from the University of Glasgow in 1984, Bodhipaksa decided that due to conflicts with Buddhist ethics he would not practice as a vet. Instead, he worked first in a Buddhist printing cooperative and then moved into the field of community education, where he worked bringing educational and personal development opportunities to single parents and vulnerable young people in an impoverished town on the outskirts of Glasgow.

After his ordination into the Triratna Buddhist Order in 1993, Bodhipaksa became the director of Dhanakosa, a retreat center in the Scottish Highlands, where he led many meditation retreats. He later became the director of the Edinburgh Buddhist Centre and the Rocky Mountain Buddhist Center in Missoula, Montana. Bodhipaksa completed an interdisciplinary masters' degree at the University of Montana, exploring the overlap between Buddhism and business (traditionally known as "Right Livelihood").

Bodhipaksa went on to found Wildmind (wildmind.org), which is an online meditation resource and publishing company. He now lives in New Hampshire with his wife and two children, whom they have adopted from Ethiopia. He has a strong interest in teaching meditation in prison, and he keeps up contact with several former inmates who were formerly part of the group he helps run for those behind bars.